WOMEN
WARRIORS

TEN COURAGEOUS LIVES OF WOMEN WHO WENT TO WAR

TRACEY-ANN KNIGHT

AMBERLEY

To my husband Paul. Thank you for your love, support and above all patience; we both know that does not come naturally. To my mother Norma and mother-in-law Susan for your excellent beta reading and advice. And to my daughter Taylor for being you. Never lose that enthusiasm for life.

First published 2017

Amberley Publishing
The Hill, Stroud
Gloucestershire, GL5 4EP

www.amberley-books.com

Copyright © Tracey Knight, 2017

The right of Tracey Knight to be identified as the Author of this work has been asserted in accordance with the Copyrights, Designs and Patents Act 1988.

ISBN 978 1 4456 6218 3 (hardback)
ISBN 978 1 4456 6219 0 (ebook)

British Library Cataloguing in Publication Data.
A catalogue record for this book is available from the British Library.

Typesetting and Origination by Amberley Publishing
Printed in the UK.

WOMEN
WARRIORS

CONTENTS

INTRODUCTION

So dreadfully safe! O, damn the shibboleth
Of sex! God knows we've equal personality.
Why should men face the dark while women stay
To live and laugh and meet the sun each day.

These were the words of British poet Nora Bomford expressing her frustration at being denied the right to fight for her country in the First World War and the injustice it was 'that men should suffer war's horrors while women remain the protected ones'.

The concept of the female warrior has fascinated people throughout history but in today's world where same-sex marriage, the rights of the transgender community, and women soldiers on the front lines are hotly debated, these stories seem particularly relevant. Literature, plays and popular ballads, dating as far back as the sixteenth century, have all celebrated the tales and legends of women soldiers, sailors, heroines and goddesses. The Greeks have the Amazons, the Celts their warrior queens and there are the Valkyrie warrior maidens of

Norse mythology; perhaps the most famous of these women is the Christian martyr Joan of Arc. But in reality, war and the military have traditionally been the preserve of men, while women's roles in combat were mainly unofficial and supportive. They would cook, clean, mend, nurse, move bodies and perform other duties necessary for the military to function. Yet despite their valuable service, theirs were not a respected role and these women have been labelled 'petticoats', 'camp followers' and even 'parasites'.

As the role of women became more necessary in the Second World War, their contribution also became better understood and appreciated. But the 'combat taboo' that prevented women from crossing onto the battlefield was still strongly enforced, even in situations when the rule seemed counter-intuitive. One example of this was in the anti-aircraft gun batteries where the 'ack-ack girls' had one of the most exacting and dangerous jobs available to women during the conflict as they protected the British people during the Luftwaffe bombing campaign. Female crew members were given one of three roles; the spotter would identify enemy aircraft, range finders would calculate the distance and trajectory required to hit the target, and predictors would calculate the correct fuse length. While these were all vital roles, women battery members were forbidden to either load or fire the gun. They were even forbidden from wielding a weapon while on duty and instead would carry sticks or brooms as a means of 'protection'. These restrictions were not there to keep female crew members from danger (in fact 369 members of the ATS were killed in just a three-month period by V1 bombs) but were to prevent women from crossing the line from their perceived role as life-giver to life-taker. As female crew members were not considered to be 'in combat' they were not considered soldiers, therefore, when they came under fire, they were also deemed ineligible for the bravery medals issued to their male counterparts, even if they had stood side by side.

More than seventy years after the ack-ack girls were officially denied combat soldier status, the British Military has finally decreed that women's roles should be extended into frontline positions. Previously, women have served in various support arm positions such as medics, engineers and administrative roles but, as of November 2016, they have been permitted to serve in combat roles in the Royal Armoured Corps. By 2018, women will be also allowed to serve in the Infantry, Royal Marines and RAF regiments. These women soldiers will be given equal status with their male counterparts and will be required to reach the same standards of fitness and training currently required to qualify for these roles. Chief of the General Staff Sir Nick Carter stated categorically that 'there will be no lowering of training or qualifying levels for soldiers in ground close-combat roles.'[1] This is a great step forward for a woman's right to serve, but Britain has been far slower than many other places in the world in instituting this step. Norway allowed women into combat roles in 1985 and Canada followed suit in 1989. Much earlier, Lieutenant Marie Baktscharow became leader of the first Russian women's 'battalion of death' in 1917, which led to other all-female combat units such as the 1st Petrograd Women's battalion. The Serbian Army also decided to harness the power of women soldiers in the First World War; British Army Nurse Flora Sandes served in the Serbian 2nd Infantry Regiment and became the only British woman officially to serve as a fighting soldier during the conflict. Evidence of women's desire to fight and defend themselves and their country can be traced even further back. In 1803, the women of the town of Neath petitioned their lord, Henry Addington, First Viscount Sidmouth, for the right to bear arms against a rumoured French invasion, pointing out that 'there are in town about 200 women who have been used to hard labour all the days of their lives such as working in coal-pits, on the high roads, tilling the ground.'[2] The English Civil War saw many great ladies defending their homes and castles from invaders; for example, Lady Arundel fought Parliamentary forces for nine days with an 'army' of twenty-five men to prevent them taking Wardour Castle in May of 1643. These women may have been hailed as heroic and fearless but they were also considered exceptions to the natural female character and therefore ultimately dangerous.

These were the women who fought openly, or were open about their desire to fight, but there are many more tales of hidden women warriors to be found throughout history. They can be found on British naval ships throughout the eighteenth century and in the army, with more than twenty of the cases verified on the battlefields during the War of the Spanish Succession, the battle of Madras and in the armies of both sides during the American Civil War. It is estimated that there were approximately 250 women serving with the Confederate troops and 1,000 with Union armies during this conflict. In the following chapters, we will meet several of these extraordinary women – from the English Civil War's Trooper Jane, sailors such as Hannah Snell and Mary Ann Talbot, to American revolutionary Deborah Sampson Garrett. Across centuries and continents, these women all had one thing in common – they chose to hide their gender in order to fight as men.

Notes

1. www.forces.net/news/tri-service/no-lowering-standards-allow-women-front-line. Monday 04/04/2016 09.42
2. Ziegler, Philip, *Addington: A Life of Henry Addington, First Viscount Sidmouth* (London: Collins, 1965), p. 114

I

KIT CAVENAUGH
AKA PRIVATE CHRISTOPHER WALSH, AKA MOTHER ROSS – 'THE PRETTY DRAGOON'

I heard the cannon play, and the small shot rattle about me[1]

Among the wounded at the Battle of Ramillies 1706, in modern-day Belgium, lay a trooper by the name of Private Christopher Walsh. Known to his comrades as 'the pretty dragoon' due to his soft complexion and youthful good looks, Walsh had survived the battle with French troops for the village of Autreglize unscathed, only to be knocked unconscious by a stray shell on the ride back to camp. This was not the first time his involvement in the War of the Spanish Succession had resulted in injury for Private Walsh. Enlisting at twenty-six years of age in the Duke of Marlborough's infantry, Walsh had his first taste of battle at Landen 1693, when he received an injury to the ankle that kept him off the field for two months. Walsh was injured again in 1702, this time in the ranks of the Second Dragoons Royal

Scots Greys, when a musket ball to the hip proved far more serious, requiring surgery in the field. Battlefield surgery in the 18th century could prove just as gruelling and deadly as the injuries themselves. With little in the way of real medical supplies available, no pain relief beyond a tot of brandy, and appallingly poor hygiene, a soldier would face the removal of shrapnel or even the loss of limbs by rudimentary procedures using razor blades, saws and even kitchen knives as surgical instruments. Infection was rampant owing to patients, instruments and surgeons remaining unwashed between surgeries. For Private Walsh, however, this practice proved his salvation, for had the surgeons stripped his body to prepare for surgery they would have made a startling discovery: Private Walsh was, in fact, a woman.

On this occasion Walsh was able to survive her wounds with her secret undiscovered and continued to fight, sleep, and carouse alongside her fellow soldiers without revealing the truth about her gender for a further four years. At Ramillies, however, it would appear her good luck had come to an end. Unconscious and vulnerable, she was taken to the hospital in Meldre (or Meldret) where, to check for further injuries, she was stripped to the waist. Upon seeing her naked torso for the first time the surgeon exclaimed 'Ye gods! This soldier is a woman – look these nipples have been sucked!'[2] Private Walsh was not only a woman; she was also a mother.

An Independent Woman

Born Christian Cavenaugh in 1667, the daughter of wealthy tenant farmers, Kit (as she was known) was well educated for her station in life. Her parents had ensured she was raised with the manners of their betters. She could read, sew, play the piano and was trained to run the family home and farm. With a healthy dowry from her father's brewery business in Dublin, Kit would have been in the perfect position to one day gain an advantageous marriage. However, Kit was always far more comfortable out in the field with the cowhands than in the parlour. Never one to let propriety get in the way of her fun, she loved to ride, and run through the countryside near Leixlip Castle where she grew up. At seventeen Kit made an indecent deal when she agreed to turn somersaults displaying her naked bottom to a passing nobleman for the price of one crown. She was clearly not the type of girl to follow the straight and narrow – nor one for the primrose path. She would not let society's constraints on her as a woman restrict her life choices. Instead, she would seek her own way of life and identity in a journey that would take her away from her farm and across the seas to the battlefields of Europe. Along the way she would be known by several names, including Kit Walsh, Private Christopher Walsh, Mrs Davies and finally Mother Ross. She would be a daughter, businesswoman, wife, mother and soldier.

The Cavenaugh family became embroiled in the early Jacobite rebellion when Kit's father, despite being Protestant, chose to support and fight for the Catholic James II. The failure of James's attempt to depose the Protestant William and Mary from the throne led to a dramatic reduction in the Cavenaugh family fortunes. As punishment for his treachery, all property and goods owned by the family were seized by the Crown. Kit's mother was able to secure a pardon for her father but he succumbed to a fever caused by his injuries in battle, leaving Kit and her family destitute. It was in this vulnerable position

Kit found herself an object of seduction by a family friend who 'deprived [her] of that inestimable jewell [*sic*] which a maiden ought to preserve'.[3] Fearing herself pregnant, Kit left her home to take refuge with her aunt, who ran a tavern in Dublin called The Pig and Bagpipes. Kit found tavern life very much to her liking and was to stay in that business for the rest of her civilian life. Her parents had instilled in her a natural work ethic. With her education and her gaiety of temper, she was able to fit in well with the rough crowd in the taproom. She could joke with farmers and soldiers while being firm enough to keep them in their place should one get out of hand and expect more from the tavern girl than was on offer. As a result, Kit was very successful in her new life – so much so that upon her aunt's death, she made Kit the sole heiress of all her possessions, including The Pig and Bagpipes. Kit was now in an enviable position for a woman in the latter half of the seventeenth century; as a single woman in control of her own business, she was entirely self-sufficient. Women of this time were usually entirely bound to the men in their life. As children, they were the chattels of their fathers, until one day they would become legally bound to their husbands. This is a concept expressed in the 'giving away' of a bride from father to husband at the altar. If a woman did find herself in possession of money or property, upon marriage this would automatically be transferred to the control of her husband, including any wages she earned after the marriage. This would continue to be the case until the Married Women's Property Act of 1870 and subsequent legislation that began to slowly give women rights over their own money and possessions. In short, there seemed to be no motivation for Kit to marry, but she had not counted on falling in love.

Richard Walsh had been her aunt's servant and, as the new landlady, was now in Kit's employ. It is entirely in keeping with Kit's independent, assertive personality that she would choose, as a husband, a man whose social status was below her own. However, before she would consent to marry him, she proposed an audacious agreement in a similar vein to a modern day prenuptial agreement. She gained a promise from Richard that he would not try to claim her worldly possessions as his own. Instead, in her own words, he declared he would remain her servant and resolved she would remain mistress of her belongings, including her business. Of course, this would not have been at all legally tenable but it was enough to assure Kit that she would maintain her authority as landlady, and clearly she was the authority within the marriage too. Kit seemed to have accomplished the impossible for a woman of her time. She was a happily married mother of two, while maintaining her independence and respectability as a successful businesswoman. This bliss was not to last.

Four years after the marriage, in 1662, Kit was heavily pregnant with their third child when Richard failed to return home from an errand. He had left to pay the suppliers on James Street in Dublin, carrying with him the huge sum of £50; he never returned. His wife began to panic as night fell and she organised a search party made up of friends, neighbours and customers. Many women would start to doubt their spouse, to think perhaps he had absconded with the money leaving behind the responsibilities of husband, father and businessman for a carefree life of debauchery. However, Kit's trust in Richard never wavered. She described Richard in her memoirs as a devoted husband and father 'remarkable for his sobriety'.

Instead, Kit was convinced her husband had been murdered and mourned his loss for over a year before she received an astonishing letter that documented the true circumstances of his disappearance.

Richard had left the tavern that day and had dutifully paid their bills but, on the journey home, he had met an old school friend who was now an ensign in the Royal Navy. After drinking together, at the ensign's expense, Richard was persuaded to go on board ship where he passed out from excess alcohol, a story that contradicts Kit's belief in his sobriety. When he awoke from his drunken stupor, he found the ship had sailed and he was now on the shores of Holland. Lost, broke and with no means of returning home, Richard chose to join one of the many English infantry regiments that were to be found across Flanders. He wrote of his heartbreak to his wife:

Dear Cristian,

This is the twelfth letter I have sent you without any answer to my former, which would both surprise and very much grieve me, did I not flatter myself that your silence proceeds from the miscarriage of my letters. It is from this opinion that I repeat the account of my sudden and unpremeditated departure, and the reason of my having enlisted... It is impossible for me to paint the despair I was in, finding myself thus divided from my dear wife and children, landed on a strange shore, without money or friends to support me. I raved, tore my hair, and curst my drunken folly, which brought upon me this terrible misfortune, which I thought in vain to remedy by getting a ship to carry me back, but there was none to be found... I now am, though much against my inclination, a private sentinel in Lord O——'s regiment of foot, where I fear I must pass the remainder of a wretched life...[4]

It may have been a simple accident as Richard claims, or it is possible he had fallen foul of one of the tricks used by the military to increase their numbers? The practice of impressments, which forced men into military service, dates as far back as Elizabethan times. The impress service, or 'press gang' as it was more commonly called, would seize upon 'undesirables', such as vagrants, and force them into service. Often a shilling would be placed in a man's pocket while he was incapacitated or simply unaware as proof that he had pledged his service to the Crown. Another method used was to trick men into vulnerability using alcohol, as appears to have happened with Richard. Once on board ship the pressed man would be offered a choice. He could either sign up as a volunteer and receive pay or he could remain a pressed man, and receive nothing. This was a far more common practice in the navy but, in times of war, it is not inconceivable the army used the same unscrupulous method to swell its ranks. Was Richard tricked by his friend into serving? In his letter he declared his friend's innocence, however, there are tales of serving soldiers receiving bounties for recruiting during manning shortages. Whether it was intentional, or just an unfortunate turn of events, the result was a man torn from his family with no means of returning.

Kit was in despair at this news. Her husband and the father of her children had come back from the dead but she could forever be separated from him. However, a woman of her fortitude and forbearance was not going to allow her happy home to be ripped apart by war and circumstances apparently beyond her control. Instead, she determined to mount a rescue, follow Richard across Europe and bring him home. But she would not go in the traditional female role as a camp follower, to mend and launder; no, she would fight to bring her husband home, she would be a soldier. Kit immediately began to organise her departure. She left her elder children with family, and her youngest child with a nurse, her middle child had died. Kit then set out to obtain her disguise. She cut her hair and donned her husband's attire; a suit coat and breeches, a frilled white shirt, stockings with frills at the knees and a quilted waistcoat to conceal her breasts. She also purchased extra shirts, a hat, a wig and a silver-hilted sword. She then concealed about her person 50 guineas with which to buy her husband's freedom, and set out to join the local regiment and bring her 'brother' home.

This reaction to a threat to a loved one with decisive action was entirely in keeping with Kit's personality. During her father's absence, the Cavenaugh family were alone in an increasingly turbulent Ireland. As Protestants fighting for the Catholic James II, the Cavenaugh family were in an especially precarious position. This tension came to a head one day when her mother's church was attacked by papists. They surrounded the building, barricading the door, trapping all inside. When Kit heard of her mother's predicament she did not hesitate to come to her defence: 'I snatched up a spit and thus armed came to her assistance ... I thrust my spit through the calf of [the sergeant's] leg, removed the things which blocked the door.'[5]

Kit was arrested for her actions but was lucky enough to escape punishment. Given her obvious predisposition towards violent action, her reaction to her husband's dilemma is perhaps unsurprising. It would not have been in Kit's makeup to accept a situation and stoically wait at home for it to reach its conclusion. Perhaps she had inspiration from watching her father bedecked in his regimentals, galloping off to war, or perhaps she wished to become a legend such as the much-admired French Captain Bordeaux, who had been a companion of Mr Cavenaugh's, a young officer exalted on the field for his gallantry and courage. Apparently he had fought with Kit's father at the Battle of the Boyne. On one occasion Captain Bordeaux was invited to the Cavenaughs' home to regroup, and even shared a bed with Kit before leaving with her father to join the remaining Jacobite troops in Connacht. But it seems the captain had been more than a figurative comrade-in-arms to Mr Cavenaugh; there was a strong suspicion this was actually his mistress. Had Kit discovered Bordeaux's secret or was she shocked when Bordeaux's female gender was revealed after she died at the English siege of Limerick? It is possible that Bordeaux's actions influenced Kit when creating her alter ego.

A Soldier's Life for Me

At the time when Kit was facing her worst personal crisis, the European nations were also facing a crisis of increasing magnitude. France's victory in the Franco-Dutch War had seen the consolidation of its power over Europe. Louis XIV was determined to further extend France's empire across Europe, and to threaten Britain and her North American colonies. A Grand Alliance of European powers, including Spain and the Holy Roman Empire, was determined to halt Louis' assault.

William III's decision to join the war in 1688 meant it was necessary to recruit an increasing number of troops from across England, Scotland and Ireland. Recruitment officers for the military were to be seen in every major city across Britain attempting to persuade any man of fighting age to take the king's shilling. As a result, Kit found that enlisting was in fact the easiest part of her plan.

Kit joined the ranks of Captain Tichborne's Company of Foot in the Duke of Marlborough's infantry under the name Christopher Walsh in 1693. She was immediately accepted and given a guinea enlisting money and a crown to drink the king's health. The need for King William to have boots on the ground meant even a cursory examination by medical officers was deemed unnecessary due to her obvious health and lack of disabilities. She was perceived by the outside world just as she wished to be seen, as a healthy young man in the prime of his life.

Kit was now on her way across the sea towards a bloody war in progress (which would become known as the Nine Years' War), with the aim of finding her beloved husband. She boarded a ship with her fellow recruits and sailed to Williamstadt in the Netherlands, where her training as a British soldier began. She was issued with her regimentals, consisting of white holland shirts, blue leggings and gold-buttoned red tunic topped by a grey coat in a flimsy material known as sleazy. A black tricorne hat, leather shoes with big buckles and thick gloves finished off the look. A buff-coloured belt with a frog was worn to hold her silver sword at the waist (a sword she was later to use defending the honour of a young lady). No doubt Kit would have appeared young and fresh-faced yet distinctly masculine in this attire. Her fellow soldiers gave her the nickname 'the pretty dragoon' due to her youthful good looks and the fact that Kit knew her way around laundering and mending of materials. Kit took this gentle mocking with good humour and settled into service life with relative ease. However, she could never get too close to any of her comrades for fear they would discover her secret.

Bedecked in her regimental colours, Kit was now the image of the troops she had admired so long ago as they had marched through her home town of Leslip. The irony should not be overlooked that these troops, which included her father, were in arms against King William, the very monarch Kit was to fight for and proclaim herself honour-bound to follow. Whatever her allegiance during her youth, Kit was to become a strong supporter of King William and was especially appreciative of his prowess as a soldier and his willingness to lead his troops from the front.

The army Kit had joined was still a disjointed one. The regiments may have been united under one king but they were in no way uniform in their organisation, instead they were a mix of militia and private regiments under the command of local lords. The commanding officer was personally responsible for the equipment, uniforms and the daily subsistence of each member of his regiment. A good commander would ensure his troops were well-equipped and that the sutlers, responsible for provisions, provided good quality food at reasonable prices. Some commanding officers were not so diligent in their duties and could force a soldier to pay for their uniform from their *8d* per day wages, of which *6d* was already allocated towards subsistence. The quality of their daily lives was now entirely in the hands of their commanding officer.

Every minute of Kit's day was now controlled and regimented. Morning parade would begin at 7 am, followed by the mounting of the guard and prayers before the regiment, and an inspection of both quarters and uniform. A breakfast of cold porridge was then served, which would need to sustain them through a morning of drilling. Broth, bread and stew for lunch was followed by afternoon marching practice. Punishments for minor infractions of the rules, such as poaching or leaving camp without permission, would include confinement, drill or extra duty. However, more severe crimes, such as selling ammunition or powder, could result in death by firing squad. The rules and restrictions of her daily life meant Kit was less free as Private 'Christopher' Walsh than she had been as a businesswoman. However, Kit seemed to thrive in the environment; this new way of life brought out her intelligence and flair for innovation. She relished the challenge not only of outwitting her male colleagues and superiors, but also the rigours of the life of a soldier. She was noted for her 'quick wittedness and indomitable courage'[6] by those who served with her. Indeed, she seemed born to follow the drum.

Maintaining the Secret

Army life in the seventeenth century meant crowded tents and cramped quarters, so how did Kit manage her day-to-day life without giving herself away? The journey across the sea to Holland was perhaps Kit's most dangerous time. Hammocks were slung a shoulder width apart, allowing no privacy. There were six privies to serve 100 men so Kit had to be extremely careful not to betray herself on the journey. Once she reached land and her unit, her regimental dress gave Kit a sense of camaraderie with her colleagues as well as a degree of security in maintaining her deception. The real danger for her would be when it was removed. However, as regular washing was not yet customary among battlefield combatants, Kit was able to avoid discovery. Instead of washing, pig's hair was rubbed over the body to remove lice, and perfume was used to disguise the smell; so Kit would never have needed to remove her clothing under normal circumstances. She also found a clever way of concealing her secret when urinating. She fashioned a silver tube with leather straps, which she placed in her breeches; it was a clever device similar to those now sold to female campers. It enabled Kit to urinate standing up alongside the other soldiers without arousing suspicion.

'I Heard the Cannon Play'

Kit's first foray into battle came not long after her arrival, when the allies faced the forces of France at Landen, which lies in the present-day Belgian province of Flemish Brabant. Kit and her comrades had trained hard and were armed with flintlock muskets with bayonets attached. These were weapons that required a cool head and a strong arm to fire in the midst of battle. With her background of hoisting bales on the farm and barrels at the Pig and Bagpipes, Kit had no problem with the physical aspect – but now she would be firing at real troops, not targets, and they would be firing back. She would have to be prepared to kill, and as the bayonet was a prevalent weapon on the battlefield at this time, she must be prepared to do so at very close range. She found her first taste of battle a terrifying experience: 'I heard the cannon play, and the small shot rattled about me, which, at first, threw me into a sort of panic.'[7] However, she soon rallied her spirits and entered into the battle with enthusiasm, until she was wounded by a musket ball to the ankle. It was a slight injury, but one that left her incapable of serving on the frontline for two months. The battle was a great loss for the allies but Kit had managed to come through it and had discharged herself with honour. Her taste for combat and her loyalty to King William were ignited as William had reportedly led the attack from the front and even on foot – an action that endeared him to his troops, and in particular to Kit who saw his actions as heroic.

The following summer Kit found herself in a dangerous situation when she was taken prisoner with a number of Dutch and English soldiers by a patrol of French troops. They were stripped of their uniforms, although probably only their coats and boots, then taken to Saint-Germain-en-Laye where Kit was held captive for nine days before her release. As an English trooper, Kit was treated quite well in comparison to the treatment meted out to the Dutch. Their clothes were returned to them, and they were given clean straw, bread, tobacco and a pint of wine per man. The Dutch troops were not so fortunate, being left in the dark, in their own filth and almost naked. Again, Kit was lucky to escape undiscovered.

English troops were given the option to defect to the French army. The war was such that any increase in numbers on either side could turn the tide of the battle and, therefore, the war's outcome. Kit refused to betray her oath and saw those who did – there were reportedly seven of her company who accepted the offer – as traitors to the king, as indeed they were. She mentions nothing about how changing sides would affect her chances of finding Richard. She also turns down an opportunity to end her imprisonment by betraying her sex to her captors. At this point in her life, Kit is clearly dedicated to her position as a British soldier.

Romance and 'Fathering' a Child

Kit had still had no success in finding Richard, although she continued to question any company of troops she came across about his whereabouts. But rather than being heartbroken, as Kit claims, she seemed to be enjoying herself immensely. To pass the time, she began to court the pretty daughter of a local tradesman. It is unclear if this relationship points to lesbian inclinations on her part; perhaps it signified simply an attack of vanity. She takes a great deal of pride in the fact that she was often complimented on her looks as both a man and as a woman. Did she perhaps feel the loss of flirtation enough to indulge in some herself? Kit is certainly not backward in declaring her own virtues in the biography she later agreed to have written about her. She would have enjoyed compliments and admiration even without any sexual attraction. I do not believe this affair proves her to be anything other than heterosexual. She herself owns that her flirtation was foolish and 'could not go beyond platonic love'. She may have simply missed the company of women. To flirt and be known as a ladies' man is a camouflage technique used by other women posing as men in uniform. Dr James Barry, a woman who posed as a man throughout medical school and her military career, would often keep company with the prettiest young women at a party to deflect any attention from her own girlish appearance, while Hannah Snell, a female marine in disguise, also had a brief encounter with a woman during her service.

The significance of this relationship increased for Kit when the object of her affection was sexually assaulted by a sergeant from another company. Kit always seemed to jump to the defence of those she perceived as being in her care. This time she did so by engaging the sergeant in a duel. Kit claimed victory in the affray but was arrested as the instigator – and more junior – soldier. An appeal from the girl's family resulted in her pardon, but she lost her place in the regiment after this incident and was transferred to Lord John Hayes Regiment of Dragoons. Kit is quick to point out that this was a change for her own safety against reprisals by the sergeant in question and not a dishonourable discharge. Honour was very important to Kit; indeed, she even offered marriage to the girl, knowing she would be rejected due to her lowly position as a mere trooper, in order to prove herself 'an honourable man'. The drama of this 'romance' did not make Kit more cautious in her interactions with the women who were to be found around the camp. In fact, her flirtation cost her dearly when a camp follower, slighted by Kit, claimed she was the father of her child – something that Kit could not disprove without revealing her secret. As incensed as Kit was, she was forced to pay maintenance for the child until its death a month later. In fact, this incident helped to cement Kit's reputation as a young man of spirit and vigour.

Kit was now a proud member of the mounted regiment the Royal Scots Dragoon Guards, commonly known as the Scots Greys. Kit had always had a fascination with the spectacle of the military, especially the grandeur of the mounted troops. In her biography, Kit describes her love of riding bareback on the farm and, indeed, in her description of her father setting out to bear arms for King James she seems far more upset about the loss of her horse than of her father. Describing her horse she says, 'he was so feisty... I would put on his bridle and lead him into a ditch and bestride him bare backed.'[8] While her mother lamented her father's absence and feared him going to war, Kit was unable to understand her mother's feelings. Instead, Kit admires the glorious sound of the martial music and the spectacle the troops made in their gold and silver coats. Now Kit was a part of that spectacle with her new uniform of a red coat with blue facings that proclaimed the regiment's royal standing. She also received a rise in pay to one shilling and two pence per day, plus eight shillings and two pence subsistence, although she was expected to pay for the upkeep of her horse herself. Her skill on horseback held her in good stead and she made a good show for her new officers. She became proficient in the use of her new armaments, a short musket with a bayonet for use on horseback, plus a hatchet and a straight sword, which she was to use to good effect during the Siege of Namur.

The French had taken the strategic position in 1692 and strengthened its fortifications to make it nearly impenetrable. Three years later King William led an allied attack to assault the castle. Kit was among the 3,000 English troops that successfully reclaimed the position for the allies. She became known throughout the regiment as a brave and capable soldier, even before the discovery of her gender made her famous. After the discovery, however, she was described as 'a very coarse woman'.[9]

War of the Spanish Succession

The year 1697 brought the end of the conflict with the signing of the Treaty of Ryswick and with it, an end to Kit's service. The final two years of her service had seen little fighting and very little was resolved by the conflict. She returned to Dublin with no further news of her missing husband. However, this is where Kit's choices become more complex. Christian Walsh was now free to return to her home, her family and her business but Kit was disinclined to let 'Christian' live again. Instead, she visited her family incognito and upon seeing they were not in need of immediate funds, left them where they were. Before leaving for the war she had 'disposed of her children', as she described it, her eldest with her mother and her youngest with a nurse. As previously mentioned, her middle child had died before her departure; an event Kit refers to in only one brief sentence in her memoirs. She never refers to the children by name and although Kit claimed to be unable to pay the nurse who looked after her youngest child, she still had the money she had secreted away to pay for Richard's release. Kit chose to remain in her male disguise for the next four years of civilian life, before returning to the military at the first opportunity. Kit is a woman of strong passions. I am sure when she was a wife and mother she was completely devoted to her family, but her attention was easily diverted and her passion was now completely taken by her 'great inclination' for military life and 'Christopher' Walsh is far more alive to her than her former identity as Christian. When recruitment began again in 1701, 'Christopher' was an early recruit to Lord Hay's regiment of Dragoons. With Richard having been missing for nine years, Kit herself admits she has all but given up on finding him at this point. There seems to be no motive for Kit to re-enlist other than her wish to follow the flag.

At the end of the seventeenth century an increasingly weak Spanish king, Charles II, turned the attention of the rulers of Europe to the problem of who would be his heir. King Charles was the last of the Habsburgs to sit on the Spanish throne and his death would spark a dramatic change in the balance of power in Europe. Negotiations began to find an heir acceptable to King William and the French monarch Louis XIV but Charles II had his own preference. On his deathbed he declared his grand-nephew, and Louis XIV's grandson, Philip Duke of Anjou, as his successor. This would give Philip both the Spanish and French thrones, placing the balance of power strongly in favour of the House of Bourbon. Louis was, of course, in favour of this development so he supported Charles's new will thus forcing England, the Dutch Republic, Austria and the Holy Roman Empire to reform the so-recently disbanded Grand Alliance to temper Louis' increasing grasp on Europe. The resultant war became known as the War of the Spanish Succession.

With troops disbanded after the end of the Nine Years' War, recruitment began in earnest to fill the regiments of William's armies in anticipation of conflict in Europe. Kit re-enlisted in her old regiment of dragoons, under the command of Lord John Hay, and was immediately shipped off to Holland. Kit was now considered a veteran of war and an experienced soldier. As a result she would have been respected by her fellow soldiers and looked up to by raw recruits. Kit did not have to wait long before she found herself back in the throes of battle. Between April and October 1702, Kit was involved on the front lines of the sieges of Keisersweert, Stevensweert, and Ruremond, allowing the allies to march as far as Maastricht. Perhaps the fiercest of assaults came in the Principality of Liège where Kit describes with glee the brutality of the hand-to-hand combat and the joy of the booty taken by the victors.

> Three days together we battered the citadel… we cleared the palisades, mounted the breach sword in hand, and made a cruel slaughter… Few of the garrison escaped with their life, and not one of those who did carried off with them rags enough for a cut finger.[10]

Kit lamented the lack of booty she was able to secure during this assault, due to the Grenadiers having already plundered the place. She was, however, able to secure a large silver chalice and plate, which she later sold for one-third its value. This was clearly a part of the business of war that Kit found appealing.

In between the clashes with enemy forces and taking booty, Kit continued to inquire after her husband, although not with the same single-mindedness as she had in the beginning. Fate was about to take a hand. The Duke of Marlborough planned a grand campaign to march his troops, consisting of 90 squadrons of horse and 51 battalions of infantry, to be joined by the 28,000-strong army of Prince Eugene of Savoy, to secure Vienna and the Imperial throne, thus turning the tide of the war. This massing of troops would bring Kit face to face with her missing husband.

After six weeks and 250 miles of marching, on 22 June 1704, Kit and her fellow troopers found themselves in the Schellenberg Heights, in sight of the River Danube.

The Danube was of high strategic importance as a route to Vienna. The battle for Schellenberg Heights was to be a bloody and important one for the allies and for Kit alike. Here Kit received her most severe wound to date when a musket ball ripped through her tunic and embedded in her hip. Despite this wound, Kit watched the rest of the battle propped against a tree shouting to her comrades 'kill, kill, kill the bastards'. She was later taken to hospital where surgeons were unable to extract the ball and it remained an open wound for the rest of her life.

In total, the allies lost 3,000 troops, with the Royal Scots Greys suffering seven casualties and with seventeen wounded. But they were still able to claim victory and with it the spoils of war, including tents, plate, cannon, copper, munitions, oats and sacks of flour, in which Kit was able to share. Local towns and villages were razed by troops, devastating the area. Kit expressed no regret for those 'poor inhabitants'. Instead she talks of raiding shops for plate, spoons, and mugs.

Finding Richard

The Duke of Marlborough gathered all his troops together with his Prussian allies ready for his grand plan to settle the war once and for all. He had kept his plan secret from all but a few to hamper the French spies he knew were trawling his troops for information. Kit and her regiment marched the long distance across the muddy terrain, following the Rhine south towards the Danube. The allied ranks were now swelled with German, Danish and Prussian troops. Unbeknown to her, amongst these thousands of troops was her beloved Richard.

The battle had produced many prisoners of war for the allies. Kit was part of the detail charged with escorting these prisoners to be housed in Breda. Their sheer numbers meant they had to be housed in workhouses and private homes. Many prisoners were ill fed and lacked shirts and shoes. Kit was performing this duty when she observed the soldiers of another regiment being reunited with their loved ones. Among these men returning from battle she recognised her husband. After twelve years of searching, crossing an ocean and fighting her way through the bloody battlefields of two wars, Kit was finally to be reunited with her beloved. To her great dismay, she found him in the arms of another woman. Kit was heartbroken but her passionate nature meant her heartbreak quickly turned to anger at his infidelity.

Richard had found himself in the ranks of Lord Orkney's regiment. Kit wasted no time in confronting him and his Dutch mistress and, at first, appeared to have some pity for a woman seduced by the promise of marriage. Perhaps Kit felt an affinity for her, having previously been the victim of such villainy herself. However, her compassion was short-lived and when Richard's lover later attempted to entice him back to her side, Kit reacted violently. Before this, it was Richard who was to receive the sharp end of Kit's wrath. But now Kit faced a dilemma. She had achieved her aim and had the money still secreted away, now augmented with the plunder she had gained in various battles, so she could conceivably buy both herself and Richard their passage home and reunite the family. Kit was, however, enamoured with military life and had no wish to give it up. Kit agreed to take Richard back, under the condition that she was not forced to give up her new life and identity. She continued in her disguise, refusing to share a bed with her husband – but also banning him from sharing it with anyone else. Instead they fought side by side as 'brothers'; as usual Kit got her way.

The next few years saw Marlborough's army attempt to push their way through the Moselle Valley and penetrate French territory. At 2 p.m., on 23 May 1706, Marlborough's troops, with Kit and Richard among them, finally met the enemy at Ramillies, 28 miles south-east of Brussels. This was to prove an important battle in both the campaign and Kit's personal war. Injured and vulnerable, her secret was finally revealed to all and the 'pretty dragoon' was no more.

When Brigadier Preston and Lord John Hayes found out that one of their best men was in fact a woman, they quizzed her bunkmate to see if he had been aware of her deception. Kit's bunkmate swore he had never suspected a thing. Her techniques had obviously worked. They then questioned Richard, who they correctly suspected was in fact Kit's husband. Kit was never rebuked for her deception but she was immediately discharged. Her story amused and enthralled her superiors; her dedication and loyalty to her husband were seen as a testament to the fortitude and forbearance of the British people. They had no doubt that it was love and loyalty to her husband that had sent her onto the battlefield. The idea that a woman could wish to serve her country never occurred to them.

Lord Hay ordered that Kit was to be paid a full wage during her convalescence and would be given a generous payment, a silk gown and material to make shifts as gifts for her to re-enter civilian life. Kit admitted it was her love of army life that had prevented her from revealing herself when she had found Richard. She had refused sexual relations with her husband as she had no wish to become pregnant, as this would have been impossible to hide. But now they were free to be together and their new celebrity among the regiment meant their remarriage was a huge affair. They were married on the battlefield with their friends, comrades and superiors all present. The party was a welcome distraction for the troops who kissed the bride and gave her a piece of gold to start her on her new life.

Life as a Sutler

So began a new chapter in Kit's life. Now a wife and a cook in Lord Orkney's regiment with her old/new husband, she became pregnant almost immediately. The child was born in the winter of 1706, but sadly lived just a year-and-a-half. Kit does not tell us the sex of the baby, nor does she mention her other children back in England. Cooking proved an insufficient way to earn wages and Kit sorely missed the profits from marauding after battle so she decided to become a sutler, those whose duties included acquiring food, liquor and supplies for the troops. This involved considerable risk as she was required to be forward of the troops to buy supplies. But to Kit, this was part of the adventure and she was determined that Richard would have everything he needed, no matter the danger.

The first conflict with Kit in her civilian role was the siege of Menin. This battle was a success for the allies but came at a great price in blood. Among the men who died was Lord John Hay, Kit's former colonel, a man she had greatly admired and who had supported her remarriage to Richard. Despite Kit's civilian status, she was still determined to make her contribution to the cause. She boiled a pot of stew, which she carried 5 miles, through an enemy village, to her husband and his fellow troops. However, Kit's devotion to Richard was soon tested when one day not long after, she returned to her lodgings to find her husband with his Dutch mistress. Kit's reaction was immediate and vicious: 'My rage was so great, that I struck at her with a case-knife I had undesignedly brought out in my hand, and cut her nose off close to the face, except a small part of the skin, by which it hung.'[11]

The attack caused the victim to be permanently disfigured but her ordeal did not end there. Kit reported the pair to Richard's superiors, who took a dim view of infidelity among the troops. His mistress was condemned as an adulteress, a crime for which she was sentenced to punishment on a turning stool, or whirligig. The turning stool consisted of a wooden cage that was spun faster and faster until the occupant either passed out or vomited. Richard's mistress was then frogmarched out of the town gates. Richard was also reprimanded and imprisoned for a time of Kit's choosing. Her memoirs do not record how long she, as the injured party, had him incarcerated but she did eventually forgive him and he returned home to his wife.

Tragedy struck on 11 September 1709 on the field at Malplaquet. Richard had been subdued before this fight. He was getting older and the hard life of a soldier had taken its toll. Orkney's regiment were ordered to manhandle six cannons onto the battlefield. Kit had remained on the sidelines with a flask of beer ready to administer to her husband. Malplaquet was the bloodiest of Marlborough's victories with over 36,000 deaths listed in the 'butcher's bill'. Present on the battlefield that day was Captain John Blackader of the 26th Cameroonian Regiment who described the horrific scene

> This morning I went to view the field of battle... In all my life I have not seen the dead bodies lie so thick as they were in some places about the retrenchments, particularly at the battery where the Dutch Guards attacked.[12]

Richard's regiment was decimated and when he failed to return from the field with the other survivors, Kit flew into a fit of anguish and raced to the battlefield to find him among the scattered bodies. Kit reportedly turned over 200 bodies before she finally found her husband's. She became prostrate with grief, refusing to leave her tent for days, neither eating or sleeping. On occasion, she would run from the tent to Richard's grave where she would dig with her bare hands to 'have another view of the dear man'. Kit's actions and devotion endeared her to the regiment, especially one Captain Ross who was reported to have carried her off the battlefield during her despair. His patronage gave her the nickname 'Mother Ross'.

Despite her extreme grief Kit was not to stay single for long. She was courted by Grenadier Hugh Jones – a mere ten weeks after Richard's death. Perhaps she could foresee the misery of life as a single woman within the camp. She would need the support and protection that being a soldier's wife would give her. She married him just one week later but extracted from him a promise not to share her bed until they returned to the garrison. Yet again she was determined to be the power in this new relationship and childbirth on the battlefield could prove deadly to both mother and child.

Her life as Mrs Jones was not to last long; just one year later, Jones received a musket-ball to the thigh at the siege of St Venant. Kit nursed him, as she did her dear Richard, but he died ten weeks later and Kit was left alone again.

Kit's fortunes were as low as they had ever been. She and her husband had been relocated to Aire with the other injured soldiers but after his death, she was now alone in unfamiliar territory. She was without money, a position, a husband or friends. She was neither in the military, nor married to a military man. Using her reputation within the camp, she was able to garner a contribution to her upkeep of one crown per week from the commander and the leftovers from the kitchen in return for helping the cook. It must have been devastating to this proud woman who had once enjoyed the comradeship and respect of her military family to be an outsider, a camp follower with scant respect. As a 'man' she had fought alongside these men, bled with them, celebrated wins and mourned losses but now, as a widow, she was without a position in this society, and forced to live off charity and the goodwill of others. This reduction in economic and social status when not part of the military was a common complaint among these women warriors. Flora Sandes, who was the only recorded female combatant to serve in the trenches of the First World War, considered the horrors of war as more than made up for by the 'romance, adventure and comradeship'.[13] Finally, Kit realised her life in the military was over and so, in 1712, she decided to return to England.

A Return to Civvy Street

In order to return to England, Kit applied for and was granted funds to finance her trip home. Not satisfied with the ten shillings she received from her commanding officer, when she arrived in Dunkirk Kit resolved to apply for a pension for her services directly to the Duke of Marlborough. Marlborough had already been stripped of his position as Commander-in-Chief at the end of 1711, however, Kit believed he would be the best person to approach due to her service under his command and the interest in her story he had previously shown. Kit's memoirs claim she had a close relationship with the duke, who agreed to see her and presented her with a gift of a guinea – but he was either unable or unwilling to assist her in any other way. She was not willing to accept defeat and Kit continued her petition for her services to be recognised upon her return to London. This time she approached the Duke of Argyll, who was fascinated by her story and agreed to support a petition to Queen Anne. Her persistence paid off and she was eventually granted a bounty of fifty pounds and a pension of a shilling per day for life. Equally importantly, her service to her country was recognised.

Kit's return to civilian life was difficult. She had to fight to receive the bounty that was promised and the shilling per day was later reduced to just five pence per day. Her life was a strange mix of aristocratic patronage and bar-room brawls. She often hung around the homes of the nobility and ex-officers and used her reputation to garner gifts of money or food. Alternatively, she could often be found in bars where she would tell tales of her exploits, any perceived slight would be met with her fists. She returned to Dublin in an effort to rebuild her pre-war life. After a ten-year absence, she found the Pig and Bagpipes was now in the possession of another and Kit had no way of proving her ownership. Her possessions, which she had given to the care of friends, she had no hope of ever having returned to her. Most tragic of all was the fate of the children. Her eldest child had died aged eighteen and her youngest child, whom she had left as a baby, had been abandoned by the nurse and placed in a workhouse. Interestingly, Kit claims to have given birth to another daughter after her return to England although, like her other children, she shares very little information about her besides the complaint that she caused her mother 'great trouble and vexation'.

Kit attempted to rebuild and perhaps recreate her life before by returning to the pub business. As landlady of her new premises her fortunes appeared to be on the rise when she met her third husband, Fusilier Davies (his first name is unknown). After they married, Kit followed her husband to England where she took over the running of a pub in Willow Walk, Tothill Fields, Westminster. However, her third marriage was not a happy one and appeared to be her downfall. Davies was a drunk who squandered the money she made and in the final years of her life, she was again reduced to begging for money from officers and the nobility in Hyde Park. Kit was ever loyal though and in July 1739 she was nursing her husband through an illness when she herself caught a cold, which turned later into a fever. She died on 7 July 1739, aged seventy-two, in the Royal Hospital for Chelsea Pensioners where she requested her body to be interred among the pensioners. She was given full military honours at her funeral, with three grand volleys fired over her grave – giving her the distinction of being the first female Chelsea Pensioner almost three centuries before women were officially admitted to the institution.[14]

The tale of Mother Ross has endured throughout the centuries and is often remembered as a love story. Her pursuit of her husband into war and across Europe for over a decade, and the heartbreak of discovering him with his Dutch mistress is certainly the stuff of romantic novels. The lost-love theme is a common one among tales of women soldiers and sailors, and was often a theme of folk ballads. The concept of a woman choosing to go to war is only understandable to some through their connection to a man. Only love is a powerful enough emotion or acceptable enough reason for a woman to break the taboos of her gender. This idea was so ingrained that it was often tacked on to the story to help sell the tale and reassure the reader that the heroine was heterosexual.[15] Kit's tale shows many signs of deviating from this pattern. Although she argues strongly that finding her husband was her motive for leaving her family, it does not explain her continued absence from her home. In 1697, Kit described herself as 'resigned to the loss of her dead husband', therefore, neither her continued service, nor her re-enlistment in 1702, can be put down to any romantic inclination, instead it appears to be a genuine love of the soldier's life that motivated her.

In her biography, Kit describes in detail the daily rigours of camp life but she does not restrict her musings to 'domestic' topics. She also includes detailed descriptions of battles and campaign strategies, showing a clear understanding of the politics of war. She also displays genuine enthusiasm for the bloody aggression of battle and is clearly at times caught up in its bloodlust. What is conspicuous by its absence is any detailed description of those she has left behind. She rarely mentions her mother or children and never mentions her siblings by name. Although Kit was a remarkably resourceful woman, unafraid of hard work, physical labour or the darker side of life, it seems compassion and a strong maternal instinct was not part of her makeup. She was a master of reinvention, beginning with the transition from farm girl to pub landlady and businesswoman, but perhaps her greatest invention was Private Christopher Walsh. He was brave and gallant, heroic in battle, popular with the ladies, and ballads were sung about his courage on the battlefield. Kit's entry in Marion Broderick's *Wild Irish Women* simply describes her as a 'soldier'. Looking at her life, I think she would have enjoyed this testimony. More than a wife, a mother or a businesswoman, Kit clearly defined herself by her military service.

Notes

1. Defoe, Daniel, *Life and adventures of Mrs Christian Davies commonly known as Mother Ross on Campaign with the Duke of Marlborough* (reprinted by Leonaur, 2011), p. 24
2. Holland, Anne, *The Secret of Kit Cavenaugh – A Remarkable Irishwoman and Soldier* (Cork: The Collins Press, 2013), p. 155.
3. Defoe, p. 14
4. Ibid, p. 21
5. Ibid, p. 11
6. Broderick, Marian, *Wild Irish Women – Extraordinary lives from history* (Dublin: O'Brien Press, 2012), p. 94
7. Holland, p. 68
8. Defoe, p. 11
9. Almack, Edward, *The History of the Second Dragoons Royal Scots Greys (1908)* (reprinted Breinigsville, PA: Kessinger Publishing, 2010) p. 32

10. Defoe, p. 41

11. Ibid, p. 69

12. Diary of Captain John Blackader as found in *The Autobiography of the British Soldier from Agincourt to Basra, in his own words,* Lewis-Stempel, John (London: Headline Publishing, 2007), p. 69

13. Wheelwright, Julie, *Amazons and Military Maids – Women who dressed as men in pursuit of Life, Liberty and Happiness* (London: Pandora Press, 1989), p. 101

14. *The Soldiers Companion or Martial Recorder, Consisting of Biography, Anecdotes, Poetry, and Miscellaneous Information Vol. I* (London: Edward Cock, 1824)

15. Stark, Suzanne J. Female Tars: Women Abourt Ship in the Age of Sail, D(London, Pimlico, 1996), p. 100

2

MARY READ
AKA MARK READ – FEMALE PIRATE OF
THE CARIBBEAN

In an honest service there is thin commons,
low wages, and hard labour;
in this, plenty and satiety, pleasure and ease, liberty and power.
No, a merry life and a short one shall be my motto.

Black Bart Roberts[1]

The beginning of the eighteenth century was part of the golden age of sail when the Royal Navy was considered the greatest naval force in the world, and piracy was the scourge of the trade routes from Europe to the New World and the shores of the West Indies. Ships transporting goods, slaves, and taxes in the form of precious metals, gems and spices to and from the colonies were floating treasure troves to blood-thirsty pirates such as the notorious Blackbeard and Black Bart Roberts. On 10 October 1720, *The Boston Gazette* published a news item that described the crimes of two pirates who were terrorising crews off the coast of the Bahamas. It detailed two proclamations issued by the governor of the Bahamas; one was regarding an attack on the sloop *Recovery* by Captain John Lewis, but far more unusual was the second proclamation, which described the crimes of John Rackham, commonly known as Calico Jack, and his crew who among other crimes stole the sloop the *William*; it was not the nature of his crimes that scandalised the public but the declaration that his crew consisted of twelve men and two women. These women, identified as Mary Read and Anne Bonny, were declared with the rest of Rackham and his crew as 'pirates and enemies to the Crown of Great Britain'.[2]

We know that Mary Read was born in London but the exact date of her birth is unclear. Captain Charles Johnson suggests in his book *A General History of the Pyrates, From Their First Rise and Settlement in the Island of Providence, to the Present Time* that she may have been born as early as the 1670s. However, investigation by modern historians suggests she was probably born as late as 1690. Whatever the exact date, Mary was the illegitimate daughter of a widow. Her mother married a sailor when she was very young and soon became pregnant. But tragedy struck when her husband was lost at sea before she gave birth to their son. The young mother and child were forced to seek help from her wealthy in-laws, who agreed to support her with a crown per week. However, this financial security was threatened when the young Mrs Read had a liaison, possibly with another sailor, which resulted in her becoming pregnant again. Concerned that the scandal of an illegitimate child could result in her losing her income, her home and possibly even custody of her son, Mrs Read retreated into the country to have her child in secret. Her plans for the future were unclear, perhaps she would seek adoptive parents for her second child or perhaps begin a new life with her family somewhere she was not known. Whatever plans she may have had were derailed when her infant son, Mary's brother, died. Grieving, heavily pregnant and in danger of losing her only means of support, Mary's mother came up with an audacious plan. When her baby was born, she would simply pass off the child as her dead son and continue to receive financial support from his grandparents. When a daughter was born, she did not alter her plan, so 'Mary' would simply become 'Mark.' The popularity of non-gender specific dresses for all children under six years helped to pass off Mary as a boy and her mother continued to receive support from her mother-in-law, until she died. Before then, she would visit the child whom she doted upon, completely unaware that her beloved grandson had actually died in infancy.

Mary continued to be presented to the world as male but as she grew older her mother informed her she was not like the other boys. Cross-dressing in her formative years must have had a some kind of psychological effect on her. She learnt early in life that being male afforded her greater freedom and more financial opportunities. At thirteen, after the death of her 'grandmother' and therefore the end of their income, Mary was sent out into the world to find work. Still dressed in her male attire she found employment as a footboy to a French lady. With her pretty, effeminate looks, and dressed in her footboy's livery, she was the ideal fashionable servant to a family of quality. She remained in this position for a number of years (possibly until she was sixteen or seventeen) until the death of her employer prompted a change of direction. Mary decided that the life of a servant was too restrictive and that her best chance to find fame, fortune and adventure was the sea and so 'Mark Read' joined the crew of a British man-of-war. Dressed in loose-fitting trousers, a loose shirt, a jacket and with a handkerchief tied around her neck, she blended in well with the many other young teenage boys often found on board ship. Slight in stature, fast and limber, they were employed to climb the masts and work the rigging. However, Mary was disappointed with her situation. The conditions on board an 18th-century ship were crowded, wet and unsanitary yet despite this, offered low wages. In his book *Under the Black Flag: The Romance and the Reality of Life among the Pirates,* David Cordingly describes how the decks would have been clustered with a 'confusing jumble of tarred rope, mildewed sails, spare masts and spars, muddy anchor cable, hen coops, hammocks, seamen's chests, wooden crates of various sizes, and numerous barrels containing water, beer, salt pork and gunpowder'. Although Mary had plenty of experience with her masculine persona perhaps the danger of discovery in such close quarters had also made her nervous. Like other female sailors such as Hannah Snell and Mary Ann Talbot, she soon discovered that the sleeping quarters gave very little opportunity for privacy and it was difficult to see to personal hygiene. Mary quickly decided that the Navy was not for her and so left the crew as soon as they landed in Holland and sought her next adventure in the British Army.

The uncertainty of Mary's birth means it is unclear when she enlisted and what battles she would have taken part in. Johnson claims Mary was in Holland at the time of the signing of the Treaty of Ryswick, 20 September 1697, which ended the Nine Years War, a major conflict fought in three theatres across Europe, as well as in Britain, Ireland, and North America. However, it has also been suggested that she was involved in fighting before the signing of the Treaties of Utrecht, which would have placed her in combat during the War of the Spanish Succession, a conflict that saw the monarchs of Europe challenge the Spanish king, Charles II's choice of his grand-nephew, Philip Duke of Anjou, as his successor. The resultant conflict brought turmoil to Europe for fourteen years.

Mary first enlisted as an infantry soldier and later moved to the cavalry. Mary was ambitious and ultimately wanted to gain a commission as an officer but it soon became apparent that without money or connections, this was not going to be possible. She did, however, gain a reputation as an exceptional horseman and duellist who discharged herself well in battle. While serving in Flanders, Mary found herself sharing a camp with a handsome Flemish soldier. She would often seek his company and even volunteer for dangerous missions to fight alongside him. Her interest was noticed by fellow soldiers and rumours about her sexuality began to circulate. It is interesting that her fellow soldiers thought 'a homosexual' before they considered 'a woman' as an explanation for her conduct. When her feelings became obvious to the object of her affections, Mary decided it was time to reveal herself to him as a woman. This was the first time that Mary had ever disclosed her secret to anyone and it was dangerous as she risked not only romantic rejection but also expulsion from the military and her way of life. Fortunately, Mary's Flemish lover (we never discover his name) was pleased to find out that his dear friend was, in fact, a woman and he was eager to make her his mistress. However, Mary, perhaps learning from her mother's mistakes, was unwilling to cross this line without the benefit of marriage. Instead they continued as brothers-in-arms until the regiment reached its summer quarters.

When they were settled, Mary and her fiancé purchased some female clothing and with Mary dressed as a woman, possibly for the first time in her life, they revealed her true identity and their intention to marry to their superiors. This appears to have been a surprise to their officers and fellow soldiers, who claimed to have had no knowledge of Mary's true gender; the couple were granted honourable discharges and given blessings for a happy marriage. Their extraordinary tale meant their wedding was quite an event in the camp, with their fellow soldiers coming out in droves to watch their marriage. The newlyweds were given a generous donation by former comrades and 'Mary traded her breeches for petticoats and her gun for mugs of ale'[3] as they used the money to begin a new venture as landlords of the Three Horse Shoes Inn in Breda, Holland.

For the first time Mary was living the traditional life of a woman. She was married and her business was a success, attracting former brothers-in-arms and those who came to see the famous woman soldier. However, the sudden death of her husband left her new life in tatters. Not only was she grieving his loss, Mary found she was unable to manage the Three Horse Shoes. She decided to give up her business and her home and revert to her old ways of cross-dressing to rebuild her life. There were definite economic reasons for her decision but it must have also been devastating for Mary that her only foray into life as a woman had ended so tragically. The death of her husband must have seemed to reinforce the lesson her mother taught her as a child – that life as a man meant freedom, opportunity and economic security whereas life as a woman could mean the threat of starvation. It seems only logical that Mary would decide to return to the comfort that her life as a man had given her. She cut her hair, dressed in her male attire and attempted to return to her life of soldiering.

The very public nature of Mary's revelation of her secret meant she was unable to return to her old regiment. Instead, she decided to join a small band of soldiers in a remote outpost, hoping she would not be recognised. Her hopes of accumulating a new fortune were quashed when the war came to an end; there is no booty to be had in peacetime. Mary decided to leave Holland and so she boarded a merchant ship to seek her fortune in the West Indies. This decision would change the course of her life, as she found herself the dangerous world of privateering and eventually crossed paths with the infamous woman pirate Anne Bonny.

Mary's journey into piracy began when her ship was attacked during her journey to the West Indies. Mary was still concealing her female identity but as the only English-speaking sailor on board, she caught the attention of the pirate captain who had boarded the ship. He offered her a place in his crew. Piracy was a profitable business in the early eighteenth century and was particularly rampant in the Caribbean colonies. The War of the Spanish Succession had seen many English, French and Spanish ships with supplies for their troops being attacked by enemy vessels. In order to turn the tide of the war in their favour, governments would issue letters of marque to private ship owners. These were contracts that allowed them to attack, disable and plunder vessels belonging to their enemies. These privateers were legalised pirates. The end of the war also saw an end to their contracts, but the ships and crews remained. Far from giving up their profitable business, the end of those contracts released them from any obligation they felt to restrict their plundering to the ships of their enemies. These were men (and women) who felt no allegiance to any country and with the battle to control the Caribbean islands still underway, there was no law and order to control them. Perhaps Mary felt drawn to the freedom and profit offered by this lifestyle, and the war had clearly hardened her to the conditions aboard ship that she had previously found unbearable. Her experience as a member of a hijacked crew had also taught her how easy such a job could be and she discovered that life with a pirate crew was very different to her service in the Royal Navy.

William Snelgrave was, for a time, a prisoner on board a pirate ship and had noted the surprising degree of organisation and democracy that was often absent from the strict discipline on a naval or merchant ship. Officers were elected rather than appointed, and the authority of the captain was restricted to command during battle. All other decisions, such as deciding which targets to attack, were put to a vote and if the crew did not agree with a plan that was put forward, then it was not put into action. The quartermaster, a relatively minor position on merchant and naval vessels, was elevated to second in command. He was responsible for dividing the spoils, arbitrating in disputes and punishing minor offences. While a naval crew were subject to the harsh discipline of a captain, major offences on a pirate vessel were dealt with by a jury of twelve crew members. Even the captain was subject to the rules on board ship and should he contravene them, he could be ousted by the crew. Bartholomew Roberts, a notorious pirate later known as Black Bart, had articles drawn up by consensus of the crew that each recruit, including him, had to sign. They all pledged 'to stand by one another ... to ye last drop of blood in ye piratical practice, and to share ye purchase according to ye custom of Blades of Fortune'.[4] However, one of the rules that seems to have been prevalent among naval and pirate crews involved the prohibition of women on board the ship. Women were considered by many as weak, hysterical and unable to cope with the conditions on board ship. They were also considered a distraction to men and it was said that having a woman aboard would bring bad luck to the crew and bring forth 'supernatural winds'.[5] Due to this belief, Roberts made a proclamation that 'if any man were to be found seducing [a woman], and carried her to sea disguised, he was to suffer death'.[6] The nature of his declaration seems to suggest women had previously been smuggled on board often enough to warrant a ban. However, Suzanne Stark's study *Female Tars: Women Aboard Ship in the Age of Sail* shows women did go to sea as the wives of seamen, and as prostitutes, but as sailors they were still a rarity and most hid their identity. So we may never be sure how many there truly were.

Pirates of the Caribbean

On 5 September 1717 the English king, George I, issued a royal proclamation, which offered a pardon to all pirates who surrendered to the Crown,

> And we do hereby strictly charge and command all our admirals, captains, and other officers at sea, and all our governors and commanders of any forts, castles, or other places in our plantations, and all other our officers civil and military, to seize and to take such of the pirates who shall refuse or neglect to surrender themselves accordingly.[7]

The increase in Britain's trade with America meant an increased number of potential targets for the pirates, so this increased the British government's determination to stamp out the scourge. The cost of lost ships and their cargo had brought piracy to the forefront of British politics. Realising they were outmanned and unable to police all the oceans, the British Government decided on an alternative method to end piracy. The offer of clemency was a way to curb these outlaws' crimes without the heavy cost of an armed assault. Mary was one of many who decided to take advantage of this offer of clemency and she surrendered herself to the Governor of the Bahamas. She settled for a brief time on the island of Nassau, a pirate stronghold, which is believed to be the inspiration for the novel *Treasure Island* by Robert Louis Stevenson, and is also vividly depicted in the TV series *Black Sails*.

On Nassau, Mary and the rest of the crew attempted a brief stint as honest citizens (it is unclear if she did this in a male or female guise) but this foray into life ashore did not take, and after a second royal proclamation on 21 December, Mary ventured into another new career – that of pirate hunter. The Crown had decided to enlist the help of those experienced sailors who had been granted a pardon to catch those who refuse to surrender by offering large cash rewards; it declared

...for every commander of any pirate-ship or vessel the sum of one hundred pounds; for every lieutenant, master, boatswain, carpenter, and gunner, the sum of forty pounds; for every inferior officer the sum of thirty pounds; and for every private man, the sum of twenty pounds;[8]

Mary joined the crew of Captain Woodes Rogers, Governor of Providence Island, West Indies, and the man who would later officially declare Mary Read to be an enemy to the Crown. The crew of Rogers' ship contained many former pirates. Unfortunately for Rogers, these were not people used to blindly following orders and he soon had a mutiny on his hands. Mary was among those to rebel against the captain's authority and she quickly turned from a pirate hunter into a pirate again. She was later to claim at her trial that she was forced into piracy and that 'the life of the pirate was what she always abhorred'[9] but witnesses of her behaviour suggested she was, in fact, very active and enthusiastic, and her actions at this time seem to corroborate witness testimony over her own claim. Her time with Rogers' crew was to be her last foray into an honest life for it was here that she encountered the famous pirates Anne Bonny and Jack Rackham.

Anne Bonny and Calico Jack

In 1719 Anne Bonny and her lover Jack Rackham, known as Calico Jack because of his flamboyant way of dressing, including wearing calico, unbleached cotton, were established but small-time pirates. They commandeered a small ship they had encountered and, in an effort to augment their own small crew, they offered the sailors on board a place among the pirate crew. One member who took up this offer was an attractive Englishman, who soon caught the eye of Anne Bonny, who was drawn to his clean-shaven look and delicate voice. Mary attempted to keep her true identity secret from Anne, as she had with her previous crew members, but as Anne's attentions grew more pronounced Mary revealed her true gender.

Mary's relationship with Anne is the subject of much speculation. There are many who believe the two women had a sexual relationship and some even speculate that Jack may have been aware of this, or even involved with both women. It is clear Mary and Anne became close after they discovered they had a lot in common. They were both products of extramarital affairs and both had male identities thrust upon them at a young age.

Anne was the daughter of prominent Irish lawyer William Cormac; she was conceived as a result of his affair with his housekeeper, Peg Brennan, while his wife was recovering from the birth of their first child. When Mrs Cormac discovered the relationship, she dismissed Anne's mother and had her arrested on a trumped-up charge of theft. Peg discovered she was pregnant while incarcerated and had Mrs Cormac not relented and had the charges against her dismissed, Anne would have been born behind bars. After her birth on 8 March 1702, her parents maintained a long-distance relationship. Her father had been cut off from his family fortune in disgrace but, despite their separation, the forgiving Mrs Cormac continued to financially support her estranged husband for many years. Anne's change in circumstances came when she was five years old, when her father decided he wished to forge a closer relationship with his daughter. He introduced Anne into his home as his new apprentice; she was disguised as a young boy. Like Mary, her upbringing had more freedom than the average young girl's. She was allowed to run and play but she had suppressed her femininity before she really understood it herself. When Anne's father's estranged wife discovered her existence and presence in his home she was furious;

Mrs Cormac cut off all financial support. With his law practice failing and his reputation in tatters, Mr Cormac decided to reunite with his mistress. The couple and their daughter set off for a new life in America.

As a teenager Anne was an attractive young lady with red hair, green eyes and a fiery temper. She reportedly once attacked a servant, who upset her, with a knife and beat another man, who attacked her, unconscious. Anne's early experiences had apparently freed her from typically female submissive behaviour. She no longer dressed as a boy but she still fought like one. Even Anne's parents were not immune to her temper when, at sixteen, Anne fell in love with a man of whom they did not approve. James Bonny was a roguish sailor who was rumoured to have criminal connections. Her father threatened to disinherit Anne unless she broke off the romance. She responded by eloping with her lover and in her anger at her father, attempted to burn down her family's plantation.

Anne and James took to the seas, where they developed a reputation as voracious pirates. In reality, James was not the fearsome character he pretended to be and was better known as an informant. Soon Anne's capricious nature began to show and she tired of James. It was then that she met the flamboyant ladies' man Jack Rackman, also known as Calico Jack. Jack was a small-time pirate who had cemented his reputation when, in 1718, as quartermaster to the infamous Charles Vane, he orchestrated the crew to mutiny against their captain. Jack commandeered the vessel, marooned his former captain and began his campaign to plunder small ships along the coast of Jamaica. He was known as a relatively temperate thief who would refuse to use torture or murder during his crimes. After looting one ship he not only returned the vessel to its captain but also arranged for a passenger, a Jamaican tavern keeper, to have safe passage home.

In May 1719, Jack decided to take advantage of the offer of clemency and sailed to New Providence in the Bahamas. When he became involved with the young Anne Bonny, she was visibly pregnant with James Bonny's child. When the child was born, Anne abandoned both the child and James and ran off with Jack on his ship the *Revenge*. It was soon after this that they commandeered the merchant ship on which Mary Read was part of the crew. Jack offered her a place in his crew and Mary, disillusioned and bored with the honest life and still dressed as a man, jumped at the chance of adventure and profit. When she discovered Mary's true identity, Anne was initially disappointed but she agreed to keep Mary's secret from Jack and the rest of the crew. However, Jack's jealousy of the man he saw as his romantic rival became so vicious that he threatened to cut her new lover's throat, so Anne was forced to share Mary's secret to calm his temper.

Mary and Anne developed a close relationship based upon their similarly unconventional childhoods. Some sources suggest that the two women had a sexual relationship and some even suggest that the three formed a ménage à trois (without an actual ménage), although this seems to be pure speculation. There is also some confusion about whether Mary continued with her masquerade or whether she abandoned her disguise at this point. There seems to be no need for Mary to continue it as she was in no danger of losing her position aboard the ship, and witness statements at her trial suggest that her gender was no longer a secret, although Johnson writes that she remained in disguise until she again fell in love.

At the beginning of 1720, the *Revenge* cruised around the coast of the Caribbean islands attacking small lone ships, looting their cargo and recruiting from the captured crews to enlarge their own. Mary was noted as one of Jack's best fighters, possibly due to her military combat experience. The pirate crew's tactic of firing across the bows of their prey and demanding surrender was often successful as the *Revenge* crew did not have the blood-thirsty reputation of some of their contemporaries, such as Blackbeard or Charles Vane, and they typically allowed the captured crew to later sail away. As a result, they remained relatively small in the pirate world and if it were not for the unusual presence of two women in his crew, the name of Calico Jack would probably have been lost to history.

Mary's life aboard ship became complicated when she developed an attraction to a fellow crew member. Just as she had with her Flemish husband, Mary was left with the choice of revealing her feelings or keeping her secret; however, as mentioned, witness statements at her trial suggested that her feminine identity was not quite as well hidden as Johnson would have us believe. Several witnesses came forward to state they were victims of the *Revenge* and recognised two women among their attackers. Perhaps Mary had simply become complacent about her disguise as she felt secure in her position on board the *Revenge*. When Mary made the decision to romantically pursue her fellow crew member she was aware that as an enforced member of the crew, he was unhappy with his life as a pirate. So Mary attempted to insinuate herself into his good graces by expressing a displeasure she did not feel about pirate life. When they eventually became close friends and messmates Mary decided it was time to reveal her secret to him when she 'suffered the Discovery to be made, by carelessly shewing her Breasts'.[10] They quickly became lovers (her earlier fears of sex before marriage were apparently no longer an issue) but, according to Johnson, had to keep this secret both from their fellow crew members and Jack, who Johnson claimed would have become jealous.

Despite these precautions, the affair caused problems for Mary when her lover became embroiled in an altercation with another crew member and was challenged to a duel. Her lover accepted, despite his lack of skill, which meant he was almost certain to lose the fight and possibly his life. Knowing he would never back away from the challenge, Mary devised a plan to save him without sacrificing his pride; she would kill his enemy first. She engineered an altercation with the same crew member and, when he challenged Mary, she ensured this encounter would happen two hours before the one with her lover. Mary killed the challenger.

As the year continued, the crew took several prizes and continued to increase their numbers but time was running out on the 'golden age of piracy'. In November 1720, pirate hunters Captain Jonathan Barnet and Captain Bonneville were sent by Captain Woodes Rogers, Governor of the Bahamas, to combat the pirate scourge. Barnet spotted a 12-ton sloop, the *William*, 'lying dark and silent' at Negril Point off the western end of Jamaica.[11] The *William* had been stolen from Nassau by the pirate crew three months earlier. When they spotted Barnet, Rackham ordered his crew to quickly raise the sails to escape.

Unfortunately for the crew, a consignment of stolen rum proved to be their downfall. On the morning of their capture, the crew were reportedly below decks sleeping off the effects of the night before while Mary, Anne and Jack were alone on deck. When Barnet began to give chase, Mary attempted to rouse the crew, with little success, and, according to one story, when they failed to respond, she fired her pistol killing one crew member and wounding several others. Johnson's version of this tale may be fanciful; it is unlikely the entire crew were so drunk they had passed out and left only three people to defend the ship. However, many witnesses testified at their trial that the two women did fight fiercely, although to no avail. Rackham was forced to surrender and he and his crew, including Mary, were arrested. Johnson claims that Mary's true gender was soon discovered by her captors, however, an earlier report published in *The Boston Gazette* had specifically named Mary as part of Rackham's criminal crew – showing that her identity had already been discovered.

> Whereas John Rackun, George Featherstone, John Davis, Andrew Gibson, John Howell, Noah Patrick &c, and two Women, by name Ann Fulford alias Bonny, & Mary Read, did on the 22nd of August last combine together to enter on board, take and steal and run away with out of this Road of Providence, a Certain Sloop call'd the *William*.[12]

Upon their arrest the two women were separated from the male prisoners, although they were charged with the same offences. The four charges were:

1. That they 'did piratically, feloniously, and in a hostile manner, attack, engage and take, seven certain fishing boats' and that they assaulted the fishermen and stole their fish and fishing tackle.

2. That they did 'upon the high sea, in a certain place, distance about three leagues from the island of Hisponiola ... set upon, shoot at, and take, two certain merchant sloops' and did assault James Dobbin and other mariners.

3. That on the high sea about five leagues from Port Maria Bay in the island of Jamaica, they did shoot at and take a schooner commanded by Thomas Spenlow and put Spenlow and other mariners 'in corporeal fear of their lives'.

4. That about one league from Dry Harbour Bay, Jamaica, they did board and enter a merchant sloop called *Mary*, commanded by Thomas Dillon, and did steal and carry away the sloop and her tackle.[13]

At the trial, several witnesses were called to testify about the crew's many crimes and to show the willing part Mary and Anne had taken in them. One such witness was Dorothy Spenlow, who testified that she was attacked by the crew, who stole her dugout canoe and provisions. She stated that Mary and Anne 'wore men's jackets, and long trousers, and handkerchiefs tied about their heads'[14] but that she had immediately recognised them both as women because of their breasts. Thomas Dillon, captain of the *Mary*, also testified that both women were present and active in the attack on his ship, stating 'they were both very profligate, cursing and swearing much and very willing to do anything on board'.[15] This discredits Johnson's claim that Mary's identity was still a mystery to the crew as it is inconceivable that her victims would be able to recognise her as a woman, while those with whom she shared close quarters every day did not. It is likely Johnson used this device to add drama to his tale. It also contradicted Mary's defence that she was an unwilling participant in such crimes and she and her 'husband' (her on-board lover) were planning to leave as soon as they were able to.

Calico Jack and ten of his crew members were found guilty and sentenced to hang. After his execution, Calico Jack's body was put into an iron cage and placed on display on a small island off the coast of Port Royal, known as Deadman's Cay, as a warning to others. The witnesses' testimony about the two women's active part in the crimes sealed their fate and they were both unanimously found guilty of piracy and robbery. Sir Nicholas Lawes, president of the court, declared:

> You Mary Read, and Anne Bonny, alias Bonn, are to go from hence to the place of execution; where you shall be severally hanged by the neck till you are severally dead. And God of his infinite mercy be merciful to both your souls.[16]

As soon as she was sentenced, Mary told the court that she was pregnant and, as it was against English law to execute a pregnant woman, her sentence and Anne's, who also 'pled her belly' were delayed until after the birth of their children. In the end, Mary did not face the gallows; she died of fever in the early months of 1721. Her child also died and they were buried on 28 April 1721 in the parish of St Catherine in Jamaica, where their graves can still be seen today. There is no record of Anne's fate, although her father did attempt to mount a defence when he discovered her conviction. It is not known if he was successful or if her sentence was carried out.

The story of Pirate Read is such an incredible one that even in Johnson's fanciful account *A General History of the Pyrates, From Their First Rise and Settlement in the Island of Providence, to the Present Time* he describes it as a 'story no better than a Novel or Romance'. However, transcripts of the trial of the two female pirates Read and Bonny stand as proof of their existence and of their crimes. How much of it was truth or myth is very difficult to determine as there are few contemporary sources available that detail the daily lives of pirates. The sources that do exist, which include the colonial governor's reports, trial records and accounts of attacked ships, paint a gruesome picture but are understandably biased. Pirates themselves strove to encourage this blackening of their reputations as it ensured they met less resistance from their victims. The story of Mary's beginnings and her service in the military are unusual but plausible. Mary did attempt to hide her gender, although she appears to have become complacent when she boarded the *Revenge* and struck up a friendship with a woman who did not feel the same need to hide her gender. Their crimes may have been small in this most lawless of times but their legend has endured.

Notes

1. Sanders, Richard, *If a Pirate I must be: The true story of Bartholomew Roberts, King of the Caribbean* (New York: Skyhorse Publishing, 2007) p. 1
2. Cordingly, David, *Spanish Gold: Captain Woodes Rogers and the True Story of the Pirates of the Caribbean* (London, Bloomsbury Publishing 2011) p. 184

3. *History's Famous Women Pirates – Grace O'Malley, Anne Bonny and Mary Read* (2012) (Charles River Editors) p. 38

4. Sanders, p. 37

5. Stark, Suzanne J., *Female Tars: Women Aboard Ship in the Age of Sail* (London: Pimlico, 1996) p. 1

6. Sanders, p. 38

7. River, p. 58

8. Ibid, p. 40

9. Cordingly, David, *Women Sailors and Sailors' Women: An Untold Maritime History 2001* (New York: Random House, 2001), p. 81

10. Johnson, Captain Charles, *A General History of the Pyrates, From Their First Rise and Settlement in the Island of Providence, to the Present Time* (London: 1724) p. 134

11. Druett, Joan, *She Captains: Heroines and Hellions of the Sea* (New York: Simon and Schuster, 2000) *p. 91*

12. Cordingly, *Women Sailors and Sailors' Women p. 83*

13. Cordingly, David. *Under the Black Flag: The Romance and the Reality of Life among the Pirates* (New York, Random House, 2006) p. 63

14. River, p. 88

15. Cordingly, *Under the Black Flag,* p. 64

16. *History's Famous Women Pirates – Grace O'Malley, Anne Bonny and Mary Read,* Charles River Editors, p. 86

3

JENNIE HODGERS
AKA ALBERT D. J. CASHIER –
'THE SMALLEST SOLDIER IN THE
US CIVIL WAR'

I had expected to meet an amazon. A woman who had fought in
the death grapple of a nation and had lived and toiled as a man
through half a century should be big, strong and masculine. And
when I entered her hospital ward there rose and came to meet
me, in her faded soldier's uniform, just a little frail, sweet-faced
old-lady, who might be anybody's grandmother[1]

In the small village of Saunemin, Livingston County, Illinois,
in the early 1900s, the elderly Albert D.J. Cashier had lived
quietly for forty years. As a veteran of the Grand Army of the
Republic, Cashier had fought proudly for the North in the
American Civil War. He drew a small soldier's pension, which
he supplemented by performing odd jobs for the inhabitants
of the village. Cashier was considered eccentric by his friends
and neighbours and was known to be particularly obsessive
about his privacy. He had several locks fitted to his door to

protect against intruders. The locks were frequently changed in case anyone had managed to obtain a key. He was also known to nail the windows of his home shut if he ever left the house overnight. But despite these peculiarities, Albert was known and respected by his neighbours. As a veteran of the Civil War, he was granted the privilege of marching in the annual Decoration Day parade through the town with fellow members of the Grand Army of the Republic. Had he not had an accident that led to hospitalisation, he probably would have died quietly in his home, remembered only by his friends and neighbours.

In 1911, Albert's life was dramatically changed while he was employed at the home of the former State Senator, Ira M. Lish. While doing some yard work for the senator, Albert was standing in the driveway when Lish backed his new Model T Ford out of his garage, accidentally hitting the old soldier. Albert was knocked unconscious in the accident, which also resulted in him breaking his leg near his hip joint. Lish was horrified by the injuries he had caused and immediately called for his own doctor to treat Albert. It was during this examination, whilst Albert was still unconscious, that the truth of his identity was discovered. The veteran soldier, who had lived as a man for over half a century was, in fact, a woman named Jennie Hodgers.

Jennie Hodgers was born in humble circumstances, on a small farm in Clogherhead, County Louth, Ireland, on Christmas Day 1843. It was shortly after her birth that the potato crop, the main produce of Irish farming, was struck by the 'late blight'. This disease resulted in a nationwide failure of the crop from 1845 to 1849 and the worst European famine of the nineteenth century. This had a devastating effect on the rural population of the country in particular, and farmers like the Hodgers found themselves facing starvation. In such circumstances, all members of the family, even the youngest, were expected to contribute to the family income. Jennie's stepfather came up with a creative solution to attempt to keep his family fed. Jennie was uneducated and illiterate but even at seven years old, she was unafraid of hard physical labour. However, as a girl she was limited in the work that would be available to her. A boy would not only have more employment opportunities but also an increased income for doing the same jobs. Her stepfather decided that to generate enough income to support the family, Jennie would have to become a boy. As a result, the young Jennie was dressed in male clothing and sent out to look for work. She remained in this disguise throughout her young life and worked in several different jobs until the death of her mother left her so devastated that she decided it was time to leave her family, the farm and her country to seek a better life in America. At the point she made this monumental decision, Jennie was only twelve years old.

When Jennie left the farm, she had no resources to pay for her journey but the strong-minded youngster was determined nothing would stop her from starting a new life in America. She stowed away aboard a ship headed across the Atlantic, all the while dressed in her male attire. Jennie was not the only Irish emigrant hoping to trade the famine for the opportunity that America offered and those, like Jennie, who could not find the money to pay for passage would often risk arrest and deportation by stowing away aboard ships. In 1849 Her Majesty's Colonial Land and Emigration Commissioners issued a pamphlet, which estimated that 219,450 migrants made the journey from Ireland to the United States.[2] The true figure would be dramatically increased if unofficial migrants, such as Jennie, were included. It is not recorded whether Jennie faced any problems from the authorities during her journey but we do know she managed to maintain her male disguise; an identity she had then held for five years. It was at this point that Jennie began to call herself Albert D.J. Cashier. Albert began his new life in Belvidere, Illinois, where he drifted through several jobs including labourer, farmhand, shepherd and factory worker. In Ireland Jennie had already discovered the benefits her male persona gave her in employment opportunities and this proved no different in her newly adopted country. As a young woman, she would have been limited to domestic service or lowly paid jobs in mills and factories but, in addition to higher wages, being Albert also offered Jennie a degree of protection in a country where she had no friends or family. Jennie worked hard and although she drifted from job to job for a number of years, she was able to forge for herself a new life and identity. However, her peaceful life was soon interrupted when she found herself, with rest of her new countrymen, embroiled in the destruction of war.

The bombardment of Fort Sumter, South Carolina, by the Confederate Army on the morning of 12 April 1861 did not directly result in any deaths but it did signal the start of a brutal conflict that would see citizens face their fellow countrymen across the battlefield. At this time the North and South of what we now know as the United States of America represented two very different socio-economic areas. The South had retained its predominantly agrarian economy, with self-sufficient plantations producing crops such as tobacco, sugar cane and cotton. These were predominately produced by using slave labour. The North had a far more industrially based economy, manned by the influx of immigrants from Europe and, in particular, Jennie's homeland of Ireland. These differences inevitably led to a divergence in the social, cultural and political beliefs of the people in the two areas, with issues such as taxes, tariffs and state versus federal rights at the centre of many disputes. But the most burning issue that the two sides clashed on was slavery. Although proportionately few families in the South actually owned slaves, the culture of slavery was so prevalent slaves could be rented, traded or used as currency to settle a debt. The northern states such as Pennsylvania, Massachusetts and New Hampshire had abolished slavery in the 1780s. As the abolitionist movement grew stronger and the divide became more apparent, violent clashes, such as those dubbed the 'Bleeding Kansas conflicts', occurred. In 1859 abolitionist John Brown was hanged for treason after he recruited a small 'army' of twenty-one followers, including his sons. These abolitionist activists systematically attacked slave-owning residences in the Kansas area. Brown's arrest and subsequent execution led to him being hailed as a martyr by supporters of the abolitionist cause. For many slave-owning states, the election of slavery opponent Abraham Lincoln to the office of president was the last straw; so eleven states, including Virginia, Arkansas, North Carolina and Georgia, voted to dissolve their state contracts with the United States and form the Confederate States of America. But it was the attack on Fort Sumter that proved to be the flashpoint of hostilities between the states above and below the Mason-Dixon Line and marked the official beginning of the American Civil War.

The northern industrial states, led by the newly elected President Abraham Lincoln, responded to the attack by calling on 75,000 Union volunteers to repress this 'domestic insurrection'. In July 1862, as the length and severity of the conflict become more apparent, President Lincoln requested an additional 300,000 troops to be mustered for the Union Army. It was in August of that year that Albert, like many working class young men, answered this call to arms. He joined the newly formed 95th Illinois Infantry Regiment, under the command of Captain Elliott N. Bush. The regiment fought as part of the 2nd Brigade of the Army of Tennessee and would become known as one of its hardest fighting regiments during the upcoming conflict. Before the discovery of Jennie's presence in the regiment, the 95th already boasted two other notable members: Patrick. F. Sughrue went on to become sheriff of the notorious Dodge City in Ford County, Kansas, while the self-educated escaped slave and lecturer on abolition, Captain Hezekiah Ford Douglas, was one of the few black men to reach such a rank and to command his own company.[3]

As with all soldiers, Jennie had to go through the recruitment process. Union Army medical officers were supposed to perform full medical examinations on all new recruits but, at the time of her enlistment, the need for additional troops was so strong that the reality was often a cursory examination to rule out any obvious deformities. As a result, her examination was less than thorough and Jennie had little difficulty in joining the army. Another female-in-disguise Union soldier Emma Edmondson, who enlisted under the name Frank Thompson in June 1861, described a medical examination so perfunctory that the doctor looked no further than her hands, noted they were callous-free and instantly sanctioned her enlistment. Jennie's enlistment medical was just as cursory, in which the medical officer reportedly 'hastily passed along the line, taking a look at each individual as he passed'.[4] Jennie was declared fit and she immediately signed up for three years' service, as Private First Class Albert Cashier. The 95th Illinois Infantry Regiment company book describes Private Cashier as a nineteen-year-old farmer, 5 foot 3 inches tall, with auburn hair, blue eyes and a fair complexion.[5] As the presence of Emma Edmondson proves, Jennie was by no means the only woman who used a male disguise as a means to enlist. It is estimated that up to 400 women slipped through to serve on the front lines in this particular conflict. Jennie's own sergeant, Charles Ives, reported witnessing two other women who had also made the same attempt. Unlike Jennie, these women were not successful in concealing their femininity and were discovered almost immediately. In a newspaper interview, Ives described a scene in which the women were caught while fruit was being passed out to the new recruits. Apples were thrown in their direction, and forgetting they were in uniform 'made a grab for their aprons' rather than catching the fruit. The next morning the two soldiers were missing from duty with no explanation.[6] Although this story smacks of embellishment, it is probable that the women's identity was discovered by their inability to emulate their male comrades' gait and gestures; Jennie, however, had had many years of experience in hiding her true gender so it was never doubted by her peers.

Even with her years of experience in male disguise, the enforced close quarters of the army camp would have still proved a challenge for Jennie and in her quest for privacy she was noted as introverted and shy. Most quarters were double bunked and so she was often forced to share with one of her male colleagues but on the rare occasions when a single cot became available, Jennie was always the first to request it and she would briefly retreat into her own space. She would seek privacy for bathing and dressing and would always keep her shirt buttoned up to her chin, in a possible bid to hide her lack of an Adam's apple. But this behaviour would not necessarily have been considered suspicious by her camp mates. As Sergeant Hermain Weiss of the 6th New York Heavy Artillery explained, soldiers would often sleep in 'boots, overcoat and all' and another female soldier was able to conceal her identity at the 6th by using this very method.[7] Only on very rare occasions would it have been required to undress. Harry G. Weaver, another soldier in the 95th, stated to a pension committee in 1914 that there was never any suspicion by any of her comrades of Albert's true identity and he declared 'I never did see any part of his person exposed by which I could determine the sex'.[8] Her short stature, and small hands and feet, were often noted by her comrades and Jennie was often teased about her lack of beard. However, these attributes actually could have helped her promote her image of a young teenage boy. As a result, Jennie's true gender remained undiscovered throughout her service and she was simply considered 'one of the boys'.

Private Cashier began training with the 95th Regiment at Camp Fuller, Rockford, Illinois, in September 1862, alongside troops of the 74th, 92nd, and 96th Illinois Infantry. Jennie was mustered into Company C, under the command of Captain Jason B. Manzer, where she was trained under the new 'Revised

Army Regulations and Tactics'. These new regulations taught troops both the theoretical part of war as well as the practical elements of drills and dress parades. While at Camp Fuller, the troops were swamped with generous gifts from locals of 'eatables and luxuries palatable to the taste'[9] that supplemented their normal rations of coffee, sugar, and meat known as 'hard tack'. Once they left the comparative luxury of the camp, Jennie and her fellow troops lived in far less comfortable conditions, living on 'hard cracker[s] without butter, coffee without milk, potatoes desiccated, and pork and beans'.[10] On 19 January 1863, Jennie's regiment with troops from the 11th Iowa, 18th Wisconsin and the 2nd Illinois Artillery, made their way down the Mississippi River, aboard fifteen steamships to join the army of General Ulysses S. Grant. Jennie was on board the *Maria Denning* for the journey, which was 'filled above with soldiers, and crammed full below decks with horses, mules, army wagons and artillery'.[11] Their journey was slowed down by the fact the steamships were susceptible to enemy fire during the day, so could only sail after dark. The troops finally arrived at Milliken's Bend a week later, where they marched the 15 miles to their final destination at Vicksburg. The march was not uneventful and Jennie found herself involved in several skirmishes with Confederate troops along the way. She had already begun to establish her reputation as an enthusiastic soldier with a fearless nature, and was often selected for reconnaissance missions. Former Sergeant Ives later described his comrade Al's war exploits in an interview with the *Omaha Bee,* 30 May 1923

I remember one time when our column got cut off from the rest of the company because we were too outnumbered to advance...

'Al' hopped on the top of [a] log and called: 'Hey! You darn rebels, why don't you get up where we can see you?' Another time Cashier gained distinction by climbing a tall tree to attach the Union flag to a limb after it had been shot down by the enemy.[12]

During another reconnaissance mission, Jennie found herself surprised by enemy troops who succeeded in taking the young soldier captive – but she was not one to go quietly. When her opportunity came she attacked a guard, took his weapon from him and fled to the safety of the Union lines, where she arrived flustered but uninjured after her ordeal.

When the Union troops arrived at the city of Vicksburg, it was under control of Confederate General John Pemberton. The fortress city was of great strategic importance because of its position above the Mississippi River. Controlling this river would open up a major supply line for the Union Army, simultaneously cutting off the supplies for Confederates, and split the forces of the South in half. Lincoln had declared the importance of its capture to his officers stating, 'See what a lot of land these fellows hold, of which Vicksburg is the key! The war can never be brought to a close until that key is in our pocket.'[13] On 18 May 1863 the Union forces laid siege to the city in an attack that Jennie and her comrades knew could determine the entire outcome of the war, but victory was not to come easily. Pemberton's troops had entrenched themselves in the city by digging more than 500 'caves' into the hills. It took six weeks of shelling by Union troops, including the 95th, to weaken their hold. With no hope of any outside help and supplies running low, Pemberton finally surrendered on 4 July 1863. Among the surrendered Confederate troops was a private of the 3rd Missouri Cavalry who was later discovered to be a woman named Ellen Levasay. Women warriors fought on both sides of the conflict and we may never know the true extent of their contribution.[14]

The conditions suffered by troops on both sides of the siege were horrendous; fifty per cent fell victim to an appalling epidemic of dysentery. Jennie was one of them. Of the casualties suffered by the regiment, more were due to illness than injury. The conditions in military field hospitals had been greatly improved by the introduction of the private relief agency created by federal legislation, the U.S Sanitary Commission in 1861 and were generally clean, well ventilated and organised. For Jennie, the result of this was that a visit to the hospital ward for treatment could result in discovery so she was faced with a dilemma – should she have treatment and risk exposure, or risk her life to guard her secret? In the end, the resourceful and persuasive soldier was able to persuade medical officers to treat her as an outpatient in her own tent. It is not recorded how Jennie managed this feat or whether it was considered odd by any of her comrades but the sheer numbers of patients seeking treatment must have assisted her in getting her way. The Vicksburg siege was a difficult one in the history of the 95th. It took the lives of twenty-five soldiers, with a further 124 wounded and ten missing in action. The Vicksburg battlefield monument has more than 36,000 names listed in tribute to the Illinois soldiers who fought there, including the name Albert Cashier.[15]

After Jennie recovered from her illness in Vicksburg, she was able to continue to serve undiscovered for the full three years of her enlistment. In total, Jennie and the 95th were involved in more than forty battles and skirmishes during the Civil War. She was one of 30,000 Union troops who took part in the Louisiana Red River Campaign, which lasted from March to May of 1864 and is considered the last decisive Confederate victory of the war. She participated in the Battle of Guntown on 10 June 1864, a tragic campaign that resulted in heavy losses for the 95th Regiment; the Battle of Nashville, and the Siege of Mobile, in Alabama. Mobile was a campaign that ended just two days before the death of President Lincoln by assassination at Ford's Theatre in Washington D.C. Over the course of the war, a total of eighty-three soldiers and officers of the regiment were lost on the battlefield, but 177, a far greater number, died of disease. Jennie Hodgers had managed to come through the war uninjured and undiscovered.[16]

Private Albert Cashier received an honourable discharge from the military at Camp Butler in August 1865, after three years exemplary service. Jennie returned to her pre-war home of Belvidere, where troops received a hero's welcome. She continued to live as Albert but Jennie soon began to crave a quieter life so began to drift from town to town across Illinois. She took jobs including church janitor, cemetery worker and farmhand, and continued this way for several years until, in 1869, she finally settled in the small village of Saunemin in Livingston County. Here she found employment as a farmhand, general handyman and street lighter. Albert settled into the village well and was respected by the townsfolk of Saunemin. He is remembered in local history archives as someone who was 'well liked, kept himself clean and neat, marched in patriotic parades in complete Civil War uniform, chewed a little tobacco, and was considered an asset to the community'.[17] Jennie lived here happily and quietly for forty years. She would march each year in the Decoration Day parade through the town with fellow members of the Grand Army of the Republic, she would give cookies and ice cream treats to the local children and always participated in local politics by exercising her right to vote (a right that would have been revoked, regardless of her military service, had the authorities realised her true gender). Despite her respected place in the community, Jennie maintained an aloofness from her neighbours who noted her many eccentricities and her fierce defence of her privacy. She did, however, count among her friends the Chesebro family who not only employed her as a handyman but would often invite the veteran soldier into their home to share a meal. Joshua Chesebro also assisted Jennie to build the one-roomed house that she called home for most of her post-war life.

As she aged, Jennie found it increasingly difficult to work and subsequently to pay her bills. She finally decided to seek financial assistance by claiming the military pension her service had entitled her to. Jennie had never previously sought to make such a claim as the process required her to submit to a physical examination to determine her level of disability, an action that would, of course, exposed her long-kept secret. But as her needs increased she decided that the risk was worth the reward. The illiterate veteran was unable to complete her application herself (she signed all relevant documentation with an X) and so asked for assistance from another neighbour, Patrick Lannon, who in 1890 applied to the Department of the Interior's Bureau of Pensions on her behalf. He was able to secure Jennie the sum of eight dollars per month, an amount that was increased to twelve dollars per month in April 1899 as her health began to decline. Lannon was somehow able to get Jennie both pensions without the need for her to submit to a physical examination. Instead, fifteen friends and former employers signed a statement declaring that Albert was 'enfeebled, destitute and dependant on charity'.[18] One name found on her application was Senator Lish, the man who would later hit Jennie with his car and lead to her final exposure. Blanton and Wike, in their study *They Fought Like Demons: Women Soldiers in the American Civil War,* suggest the description of Jennie's condition by her neighbours was an exaggeration of the truth but their willingness to put such a claim to paper proves how highly regarded Albert was in the community.

While the Chesebro family may have remained ignorant of Jennie's true circumstances, the Lannon family were soon to make a remarkable discovery about their friend and neighbour. In 1910 the increasingly ailing Albert became sick and so, concerned for her elderly neighbour, Mrs Lannon sent her own family nurse to assist him. For the first time in sixty years, Jennie was unable to hide her true identity. The visiting nurse was so shocked by her discovery that she reportedly ran from Jennie's home crying 'My Lord, Mrs Lannon, he's a fully-fledged woman.'[19] It must have been a terrifying experience for the independent Jennie to be in such a vulnerable position. She was used to taking care of her own life and making her own decisions, even in extreme circumstances, but now she was at the mercy of the two women whose awareness of her secret could spell disaster. Jennie told her extraordinary tale to Mrs Lannon and, after speaking at length with Jennie, she decided to respect 'Albert's' privacy and keep the secret. Unfortunately, this incident foreshadowed the beginning of the end of Albert Cashier's comfortable existence in Saunemin as Jennie's health continued to decline. It was just a year later that she was involved in the fateful car accident that would eventually lead to her worldwide exposure.

After this accident, with Jennie lying unconscious on his driveway, the senator was faced with a similar quandary as Mrs Lannon had a year earlier. Lish had called for his own doctor, Dr C.F. Ross, and Jennie's neighbour Nettie Chesebro, to treat her injuries when the discovery of her gender was made. When she awoke, Jennie begged Lish not to expose her secret and tear apart the life she had built, and Lish agreed. It is interesting that so far no one seemed to censure her for her deception and supported her right to live as she wished, even knowing about her military service. Lish felt compassion for Jennie's plight but keeping her secret would not be as simple as before. Lish immediately swore the doctor and nurse to secrecy, then arranged for Jennie to be treated at the Soldier and Sailor's Home in Quincy, Illinois. She was admitted as a patient on 5 May 1911 with age-related disabilities, weakened mental facilities and a leg broken near the hip joint. Concealing her true gender from the hospital staff would have been impossible under such circumstances, yet records show it was Albert Cashier who received treatment in Quincy, not Jennie Hodgers. Lish had apparently used his connections to persuade the hierarchy at the home to preserve Jennie's secret and although some staff must have been aware of her true gender, patients only knew of Albert. Jennie soon settled into the home and for the next two to three years appeared content as she socialised and happily exchanged war stories with the other veterans, and for a short while 'Albert' was allowed to continue living her life in anonymity. Sadly in 1913, Jennie's physical and mental health deteriorated and she began to grow increasingly erratic in her behaviour. On 27 March 1914, Adams County Court declared Albert and seven other residents of the veteran's home 'insane' and committed them to Watertown State Hospital for the Insane. On her day of admission, Jennie was bathed by the nursing staff; once stripped, they realised that their new patient was, in fact, a woman, approximately seventy years old. Jennie was no longer in any position to protect herself, and her secret was finally revealed.

The story of the female Civil War veteran was quickly picked up by the press and her tale was published to great public interest. Local newspapers scrambled to get the story of 'the smallest soldier that served in the Civil War'[20] who had fought for the North in more than forty battles. Reporters came in droves to interview 'Albert' and she enjoyed a short burst of fame. Jennie was happy to discuss her life as Albert and her military service but refused to reveal her real identity or any of her background; she was Albert Cashier. A reporter from the Quincy *Whig* visited her at the infirmary and wrote about his encounter:

This little woman does not know that the story of her secret has now been chronicled in every newspaper over the country, and is still under the belief the Colonel Anderson, and one or two attachés of the hospital, together with ex-Senator Lish, are the only ones who know that she is a woman. She chatted freely yesterday with the reporter but was elusive of answering pointed questions ... Since the story of her extraordinary life appeared in print, many pictures of her have been taken and probably at the present time one-third of the veterans in the home have photographs which will be preserved by their children and grandchildren as souvenirs.[21]

The general public's reaction to Jennie's revelation was positive. One section of society particularly amazed but supportive of 'Albert' was the former soldiers of the 95th Regiment – the men she had fought, marched and slept alongside for four years. The members of her regiment were proud of her involvement and celebrated her actions. In a letter between former corporal Robert Horan and Charles Ives, who had been First Sergeant of Company G, the pride and affection for Cashier is made clear:

> I did go to the reunion. Had a good time. Some 75 or 80 was thare... I heard a letter from Wash Robb also from you. Also Mr. Sebring of Jasper about Cashier. Most all of the Boys had seen his name in the papers... I also showed them a photo [of] Cashier taken in 64, I also showed a photo of him as he looks to day at Quinsey [*sic*].[22]

However, another section of society was not so positive in its reaction to the news that they had been tricked by Jennie's disguise. The Federal Bureau of Pensions immediately launched an investigation into her entitlement to an army pension. At first, they refused to believe that she was, in fact, the same Albert Cashier that had served and fought for the Union Army. Several of her former comrades came forward to give testimony that Jennie was, in fact, the same person who had served alongside them and therefore should be entitled to the pension. However, the Bureau did not easily give in. A theory was put forward that 'Jennie' was the twin sister of 'Albert'. As evidence of this, it was claimed that 'Albert' had once told a sergeant that he had a twin sister and that their mother had dressed them both as boys when they were children. There is, however, no evidence that a twin sister ever existed. This is just one of the many conflicting tales that Jennie told after her secret was discovered. She told members of the Chesebro family that she had assumed her male identity to follow a lover into battle. Again, there is no proof that such a lover existed. Jennie may have been attempting to muddy the waters of her life story or these tales may have simply been a symptom of her increasingly failing mental health. On 10 February 1915, the Pension Bureau finally accepted that 'Jennie' and 'Albert' were one and the same person and decided in favour of Jennie retaining her pension.

Back at Waterdown Hospital, conditions for Jennie took a turn for the worse as the doctors saw Jennie's cross-dressing as a symptom of her mental deterioration. She was forced to wear 'suitable' women's clothing, against her wishes, for the first time in half a century. Unused to wearing skirts or dresses she would often trip and fall, and Jennie hated the garments so much that she would try to wrap the skirt around her legs to simulate trousers. Her friends and former colleagues strongly objected to her treatment at Watertown, which former Sergeant Ives described as 'bureaucratic insensitivity'. After a visit to his former brother-in-arms he stated 'I left Cashier, the fearless boy of 22 at the end of the Vicksburg campaign… When I went to Watertown, I found Georgia Hodges [*sic*], a frail woman of 70, broken, because, on discovery, she was compelled to put on skirts. They told me she was awkward as could be in them.'[23] One day Jennie tripped over her hated skirt and injured her hip. She never recovered from her injuries and the once vibrant soldier and proud American citizen slowly deteriorated. Private Albert D.J. Cashier was pronounced dead on 10 or 11 October 1915, aged seventy-one, from complications resulting from injuries sustained in a fall. He was buried in full uniform in Sunnyslope Cemetery in Saunemin in an official military service of the Grand Army of the Republic. The tombstone at his grave is inscribed: 'Albert D.J. Hodgers Co. G 95 Ill Inf Civil War'. Later, in the 1940s or 50s, a birth name was added to the inscription: 'Born Jennie Hodgers in Clogherhead Ireland 1843–1915'.

After her death, Jennie left an impressive sum of $418 in her estate. The executor of her will, W.J. Singleton, vice president of the Illinois State Bank, went to great lengths to identify any heirs to her estate but the mysteries of her origins proved too complex and after nine years, the money was returned to the State of Illinois. Mary Rooney of Philadelphia initially contacted Captain J.E. Andrews at the Illinois Soldiers' and Sailors' Home claiming to be Jennie's heir but was unable to adequately prove kinship and Singleton's request that Mrs Rooney bring proof to Livingston County Court went unanswered. Another claimant, Joseph Rooney, possibly related to Mary, claimed to be Jennie's nephew but despite eight years of correspondence between lawyers representing the estate and Mr Rooney, he was also unable to prove his claim of kinship. The estate was closed and Livingston County retains the money to this day.[24]

At the end of the war, several stories of female combatants began to emerge. As with the tale of Private Cashier, these were often well received by the general public. Ida Tarbell, a reporter with *The American Magazine,* wrote to the Adjutant General, General F.C. Ainsworth, on 21 October 1909, requesting an official number of women who enlisted and served in the Civil War. The reply she received was,

> No official record has been found in the War Department showing specifically that any woman was ever enlisted in the military service of the United States as a member of any organization of the Regular or Volunteer Army at any time during the period of the civil war. It is possible, however, that there may have been a few instances of women having served as soldiers for a short time without their sex having been detected, but no record of such cases is known to exist in the official files.[25]

However, investigation of Civil War military service records show that several soldiers were discharged from service for 'sexual incompatibility', meaning they were discovered to be women. Private John Williams served with the 17th Missouri Infantry, Union Army, for one month in October 1861 until 'he' was discovered to be a 'she' and immediately discharged. The Confederate Army enlisted Mrs S.M. Blaylock into the 26th North Carolina Infantry, Company F. Her CMSR states:

> This lady dressed in men's clothes, Volunteered [*sic*], received bounty and for two weeks did all the duties of a soldier before she was found out, but her husband being discharged, she disclosed the fact, returned the bounty, and was immediately discharged April 20, 1862.[26]

Some of the more famous female Civil War veterans include Francis Clayton, also known as Private Jack Williams, and Sarah Emma Edmonds, also known as Private Franklin Thomas. Both of these women served their time in the Union Army. Clayton's husband had enlisted in the Missouri Regiment so she decided to serve by his side. Francis Clayton fought in eighteen battles, sustained three wounds and was taken prisoner by the enemy. She was so dedicated to the cause she continued to fight even after she witnessed her husband's death at the Battle of Stones River on 31 December 1862. Edmonds story is just as compelling. The daughter of an abusive father, Edmonds left home to avoid an arranged marriage and disguised herself as Franklin Thompson to avoid detection. Edmonds enlisted in the 2nd Michigan Infantry under her assumed identity and served for three years as a male nurse and delivering mail She claimed to have worked as a spy for the Union where she would have to cross enemy lines undetected. Edmonds contracted malaria in 1863 and was forced to desert for fear of discovery during her treatment. After her recovery, she returned to duty as a female nurse with the United States Christian Commission, where she served under her own name until the end of the war. These women were by no means the only women to serve their country during the Civil War. In 1888, Mary Livermore of the U.S. Sanitary Commission stated the estimate that 'a little less than four hundred' women had served was conservative:

I am convinced that a larger number of women disguised themselves and enlisted in the service, for one cause or other, than was dreamed of. Entrenched in secrecy, and regarded as men, they were sometimes revealed as women, by accident or casualty. Some startling histories of these military women were current in the gossip of army life.[27]

Jennie's case was of course very different from many other women who had disguised themselves in order to serve. As with the English sailor and Caribbean pirate Mary Read, her cross-dressing began in childhood and was not initially her own choice. The question must be asked whether this enforced prepubescent cross-dressing affected her psychologically. Would she have still made the choices had her masquerade not been forced upon her before she had developed her own sexual identity? Or was Jennie's reluctance to return to female identity in her later life evidence of transgender characteristics? Without her story in her own words, we may never be certain. Unlike many other female soldiers such as Hannah Snell, Christian Cavenaugh or the doubtful tales of Loreta Velasquez, she never published her life story. She never sought money, fame or recognition for her exploits. History will remember her as the longest-serving documented female soldier in the US Civil War but to many, she was simply 'Albert', a soldier, a neighbour and a friend.

Notes

1. *The Hartford Republican* 6 June 1913 as found in www. newspapers.com/the_hartford_republican/ accessed 1 March 2017
2. *The Illustrated London News* July 6, 1850 as found in viewsofthefamine.wordpress.com/illustrated-london-news/ the-tide-of-emigration-to-the-united-states-and-to-the-british-colonies/ accessed 1 March 2017

3. Davis, Rodney, 'O, Private Albert Cashier As Regarded by His/Her Comrades', *Illinois Historical Journal Volume LXXXII/Number 2/Summer 1989*, p. 108

4. Blanton, DeAnne and Lauren Cook Wike, *They Fought Like Demons: Women Soldiers in the American Civil War*, p. 28

5. Tsui, Bonnie, *She Went to the Field: Women Soldiers of the Civil War* (Globe Pequot Press, Connecticut, 2006), p. 65

6. Davis, p. 110

7. Blanton, and Cook Wike, p. 47

8. McPherson, Marcus, *Women Soldiers in the Civil War: 26 True Stories of Female Soldiers who fought in the Bloodiest American War*, 2015, eBook p. 527

9. Wood, Wales W., *A History of the Ninety-Five Regiment Illinois Infantry Volunteers From Its Organisation in the Fall of 1862, until its Final Discharge from the United States Service in 1865* (Chicago, Tribune Company's Book and Job Printed Office, 1865), p. 20

10. ibid, p. 20

11. ibid, p. 54

12. Davis, p. 110

13. Ibid, p. 112

14. Blanton, and Cook Wike, p. 17

15. Hall, Richard, *Patriots in Disguise: Women Warriors of the Civil War* (New York, Marlowe & Company, 1994), p. 22

16. Wood, Wales. W, *A History of the Ninety-Five Regiment Illinois Infantry Volunteers From Its Organisation in the Fall of 1862, until its Final Discharge from the United States Service in 1865* (Chicago, Tribune Company's Book and Job Printed Office, 1865), e-copy, p. 18

17. Hall, p. 23

18. Tsui, p. 70

19. Certificate of Dr. C.F. Ross as found in Davis, Rodney. O, 'Private Albert Cashier as Regarded by His/Her Comrades', *Illinois Historical Journal Volume LXXXII/Number 2/ Summer 1989*, p. 108-112

20. Tsui, p. 63

21. as found in Hall, p. 24-5

22. Davis, p. 110

23. Tsui, p. 66

24. There is some dispute among historians over the exact amount of Cashier's estate. Blanton and Wike claim that $282 remained after funeral expenses were paid. p. 174

25. As found in Women Soldiers of the Civil War *By DeAnne Blanton Prologue Magazine* Spring 1993, Vol. 25, No. 1

26. ibid

27. 1888, Mary Livermore of the U.S. Sanitary Commission as found in 'Women Soldiers of the Civil War' *by DeAnne Blanton Prologue Magazine* Spring 1993, Vol. 25, No. 1

4

HANNAH SNELL
AKA PRIVATE JAMES GREY – FEMALE MARINE

Hannah in briggs [breeches] behaved so well
That none her softer sex could tell;
Nor was her policy confounded
When near the mark of nature wounded [shot in the groin].

Oh, how her bunkmate bit his lips,
And marked the spreading of her hips,
And cursed the blindness of his youth
When she confessed the naked truth![1]

This raucous poem was published to the amusement of readers some time in the latter half of the eighteenth century. It described the exploits of a celebrity soldier who had graced the stages of several London theatres. Private James Gray had returned to England on Saturday 9 June 1750 after serving four years with the Royal Marines in the East Indies and was celebrating with friends and colleagues at St John Winter's pub in Downing Street, Westminster. Many had just received their discharge from service and final pay, and so the ale was flowing when Gray stood up to make an announcement. In the very theatrical way in for which he was known, he proclaimed:

> It is very probable, likewise, that not one of you will ever see your friend and fellow-soldier, Jemmy Gray, anymore... Why, gentlemen, Jemmy Gray, you will find before we part, cast his skin like a snake and become a new creature... Had you known, Master Moody, who you had between a pair of sheets with you, you would have come to closer quarters. In a word, gentlemen, I am as much a woman as my mother ever was and my real name is Hannah Snell.[2]

Her former colleagues and friends, after initially denying the truth of her words, applauded and praised her actions, declaring they had never suspected that the competent, respected soldier was a woman in disguise. The above-mentioned Master Moody even proposed marriage to his old bunkmate, an offer she cheerfully turned down.

Hannah had been ingenious in orchestrating her revelation. She had ensured she was surrounded by witnesses who could testify about her identity as the soldier James Gray, while her sister and brother-in-law were also present to verify her true name and gender. But perhaps most cunningly of all, Hannah had waited to make her announcement until after she had been discharged, sold her two suits of clothes and collected her back wages from the Navy, the not inconsequential sum of £15. Now she was ready to reveal herself to the world and resume her life as a woman. But it was not the drudgery of her pre-war life that she sought, instead she intended to use her experiences to seek fame and fortune. To this end, just a few weeks after the incident at St John Winter's pub, she approached journalist and printer Robert Walker and offered to sell him the tale of her exploits. Hannah was able to give a first-hand account of battling French forces at the Siege of Pondicherry, where she reportedly received twelve wounds and was forced to operate on her own injuries; she described conditions on board the *Swallow*, shelling by French warships, and storms so violent that the ship and its crew almost perished. There was also a harrowing tale of being flogged at the hands of her fellow crewmembers. *The Female Soldier; or, the Surprising Life and Adventures of Hannah Snell* was published later that year and was such an instant success that a second edition was published just two weeks later. Ballads and poems were printed in newspapers and sung in taverns and she achieved a modest celebrity status across the country as she appeared on stage in her full dress uniform, where she would entertain audiences by telling tales of her exploits, singing raucous songs and performing drill. However, the very nature of Hannah's celebrity, and the reputation of Walker as a 'literary hack' throws some doubt upon some of the more outrageous claims found in her biography. When looking at the life of Hannah Snell, we must ask ourselves what could have motivated a young woman to leave her normal life and enter the harsh and dangerous world of the Royal Navy – and how much of her story can we truly believe?

Hannah was born on 23 April 1723 in the parish of St Helens, Worchester. She was the eighth child in a family of nine. Her father, Samuel Snell, was a hosier and dyer at a time when the textile industry, which had sustained the area for 200 years, was in decline. The Snell family began to see the effects of this decline in the deterioration of their neighbourhood. An increasing number of large families had begun to occupy the small cottages that were built to the rear of their home in Friar Street. This increase in population was exacerbated when the new city gaol was relocated to just a few doors from Hannah's home.[3] The cramped overcrowded streets combined with the notoriously unhygienic living quarters of the prisoners to create conditions perfect for the spread of contagious diseases. A particular fear was of the highly infectious typhus, known colloquially as 'gaol fever'. Epidemic typhus is a devastating disease that thrives in conditions of overcrowding and poor hygiene. Transmitted by lice and fleas, the conditions in Britain's prisons in the 18th century meant the disease was prevalent there. Sufferers would experience headaches, loss of appetite, fever, chills and nausea. As the disease progressed, the patient could suffer from kidney failure, and gangrene of the extremities and the genitals, but death was usually from cardiac failure.[4] The danger Hannah and her family faced living so close to the city gaol was a significant one. In 1730, prisoners from Ilchester gaol brought the infection with them to the Blandford Court during their trials. As a result, several officers of the court – including the High Sheriff, the Sergeant-at-law, the crier of the court, the judge Lord Chief Baron Sir Thomas Pengelly, and two of his servants – succumbed to the disease. There were also reports of 100 deaths in the nearby town of Taunton, although there are no official records of these deaths so they may be anecdotal.[5]

Hannah's childhood was typical of a tradesman's daughter. She was given a rudimentary education, taught to read but not to write (shown by her signing the affidavit based on her biography with an X). This was not uncommon for a female child in her situation, as education for its own sake was still a low priority for the lower classes and was practically unheard of for women in early 18th century. Hannah would have had little access to books for recreation; instead, her reading would have been limited to household accounts to ensure that she was not cheated by local tradesmen.

Walker's depiction of the Snells in Hannah's memoir paints a picture of a family steeped in military tradition with all but one of her siblings enlisting, or marrying men who served either on land or at sea. He traces these 'seeds of heroism, courage and patriotism'[6] back to an incredible tale of Hannah's grandfather who supposedly rose from the rank of private soldier to Captain-Lieutenant via a field commission after an incident of battlefield valour at the taking of Dunkirk. He served in the ranks of the Welch Fusiliers in Queen Anne's War, where he fought at Blenheim and then at Malplaquet, where he was mortally wounded. Interestingly, this would have seen Hannah's grandfather on the same battlefield as another famous cross-dressing soldier, Christian Walsh, whose husband died on the field at Malplaquet. No records have been discovered to corroborate Sam Snell's service, or his death at Malplaquet, so this story could be could be a piece of complete fiction – or perhaps such tall tales were told to Hannah and her siblings as children, which may have had a profound effect on their ambitions. Hannah, in particular, seemed to believe that the battlefield was a place of adventure and glory. As a child, she would play a game of soldiers with her friends who would march up and down the streets of Worcester in a mock troop formation, calling themselves the 'Young Amazon Snell's Company'. Little did young Hannah know that one day she would be able to turn her dream of marching and fighting for her country into a reality.

By the time Hannah turned seventeen, she had lost both her parents and, like many working-class girls at the time, Hannah chose to leave her home in Worcester and travel the 138 miles to London, to seek work. Unlike many who attempted to seek a better life in the capital, Hannah had family to assist her. She arrived at the home of her sister and brother-in-law, Susannah and James Gray, in Ship Street, Wapping, on Christmas Day 1740. At that time Wapping was a relatively rough parish located on the docks near the Tower of London, where James Gray worked as a carpenter. Susannah was Hannah's half-sister, the daughter of their father's first wife, Elizabeth Marston, but their relationship was a warm one and Hannah settled into a comfortable life with her family. We have no record of how she was employed at this time as records from the early 18th century rarely focus on the common man or, indeed, woman. Low levels of literacy and education among the lower classes meant written records, diaries and letters that describe everyday life are mainly restricted to the gentry; as a result, the life of a lower class 18th-century woman is inevitably murky and mysterious to us today. However, it is likely Hannah would have been expected to earn a wage and contribute to the household expenses. As an unmarried woman, she may have engaged in one of the cottage industries such as sewing or weaving, or perhaps worked outside the home in domestic service with a more prosperous family. Hannah may have been dissatisfied with the limitations placed on her prospects. As a woman she was barred from many trades and even those open to her, offered significantly lower wages to female employees than those paid to men. Hannah's dissatisfaction may have led her to consider the military as a career that could offer her skills and experiences denied in traditional female roles, so Hannah's path soon began to deviate from the norm as she embarked on a career that would take her across oceans to see first-hand the gruesome side of war.

Before she decided to rebel against the restrictions of the accepted female role, however, Hannah followed the predictable path of a woman of her position and class and became a wife and mother. As a pretty girl with pale skin and a good complexion, a fact often remarked upon even during her masquerade as a man, she soon attracted the attention of a Dutch sailor, James Summs. *The Female Soldier* describes a marriage between Hannah and Summs on 6 January 1744, although no record of the marriage is to be found. It is possible the union was of an unofficial nature, as was common among the lower classes and this is reinforced by Hannah not using the surname Summs. She refers to herself throughout her memoirs and her subsequent stage career always as Hannah Snell, which seems to suggest a formal marriage never took place. Their relationship did, however, result in the birth of a daughter who was born on 5 September 1746 and christened Susanna in honour of Hannah's sister.[7] Hannah was deeply disappointed in the character of her husband, whom Walker describes as 'the worst and most unnatural of husbands'. He would '[keep] criminal Company with other Women of the basest Characters, but also made away with her Things in Order to support his Luxury and the daily expenses of his Whores.[8] The marriage further deteriorated when Hannah discovered she was pregnant and Summs abandoned his wife just two months before his daughter's birth, taking with him most of their possessions and leaving mother and child in abject poverty. Hannah was forced to return with her newborn daughter to the home of her sister for comfort and shelter. Sadly, little Susannah lived only seven months so as well as the pain of Summs' betrayal, Hannah was mourning the death of her child. Susannah was buried in St George's Parish, Middlesex, 'at [Hannah's] own expense'.[9]

With her dream of a happy domestic life in tatters, Hannah was left with an uncertain future. Her experiences with Summs had soured her view on the prospect of marriage offering her happiness, and her employment prospects were limited. As many women warriors before and since, Hannah decided that the best way to break free from these restrictions was to throw off the confines of her gender altogether and assume a male identity, with the idea of following her brothers into that most masculine of professions, the military. Hannah began her transformation into a man by taking a suit of clothes from her brother-in-law's closet. There is no specific description in *The Female Soldier* of the manner in which Hannah disguised her female body but other women such as Christian Cavenaugh, also known as Mother Ross, describe the process in great detail. Presumably, she used similar methods such as suppressing her breasts by using material wrapped around her torso and perhaps cutting her hair. She had also decided to use her brother-in-law's name, James Gray, which was common enough not to arouse suspicion or make her memorable. Her smooth skin would have given her a youthful appearance and so she presented herself to the world as a young teenage boy. Satisfied with her transformation, Hannah left her sister's home, and London, with only a few coins to her name and set out to search for adventure and a new life. Walker claims her disguise was so convincing that soon after leaving London, heading for Coventry, Hannah was accosted by recruiting officers of the British military.

However, there are many problems with Walker's version of Hannah's story. The illiterate Hannah dictated her tale to the newspaper publisher, who was well known for his love of sensationalism. The final publication was entirely under his control. He instantly saw the financial potential in Hannah and rushed to publish the first edition of *The Female Soldier,* forty-six pages long. The second edition, however, was far more involved at 187 pages, and included a diatribe on the loss of 'the love of glory' in society. Walker also included a new section that described her involvement in quashing Jacobite rebels and, unfortunately, Walker appears to have altered some of the dates of Hannah's life in order to include this section; this has led many to doubt the validity of her entire tale.

Walker claimed Hannah made her journey to Coventry on 23 November 1745 while the country was in the grip of an invasion. The Jacobite troops of Bonnie Prince Charlie had landed in Scotland on 25 July 1745 in an attempt to dethrone George II. The Young Pretender, as the prince was known, had gathered supporters among the Highland clans of Scotland and with these troops had successfully taken Carlisle on the very day Hannah had apparently left her family. He then proceeded south, with his sights set on London. At this time of conflict, there were many recruiters roaming the streets and local taverns 'beating up for soldiers'. In her disguise that gave her the appearance of a young man, Hannah was approached by a Corporal Samuel Bishop, who attempted to persuade her to enlist. When this failed, he forced money into her hand, which he would later claim before a magistrate she accepted; taking the 'the king's picture' meant she was now obligated to serve her country. Hannah's response was not to reveal she was a woman, which would have removed her from the situation, but instead to accept it and immediately enlist.

> She, not affrighted at their threats, told them she was as ready and willing as any of them to serve her king and country, and then boldly enlisted with Captain Miller, and took from him one guinea and five shillings in silver, and was the next day, November 27th, sworn in before a magistrate.[10]

'Private James Gray' was now a member of General Guise's Infantry Regiment, in Captain Miller's Company, under the command of the very Corporal Bishop who had enforced her enlistment. However, rather than feeling any resentment about her predicament, Walker describes a woman enjoying new-found freedom from social constraints who 'made her resolve to pursue her fate, let whatever should befall her, and fully determined to keep her sex concealed'.[11] She laughed and drank with her new comrades in the local tavern and even took it with good humour when she was called on to pay the bar bill as the newest recruit. During her stay in the city, Hannah began to question those around her about the possible whereabouts of her estranged husband, without success.

Three weeks later, the eighteen new recruits, including Private Gray, supposedly travelled north to Carlisle to join Colonel Guise's regiment and help suppress the Jacobite rebels. Here Walker describes Hannah's harrowing, violent experience while under the command of a villainous Sergeant Davis, but this tale does not stand up to scrutiny.

Davis was reportedly engaged in the seduction of a local young woman when he decided to use Gray as a means to convey messages. Walker claims that instead of carrying out her sergeant's wishes, Hannah instead revealed Sergeant Davis's less than virtuous intentions and the young lady was supposedly so grateful that she turned her attention to the handsome young soldier Hannah appeared to be. On seeing he had been thwarted in his seduction, and presuming Hannah had deliberately supplanted herself in the lady's affections, Walker then claims Davis sought revenge by falsely accusing the young soldier of neglect of duty. Hannah was sentenced to be flogged and apparently received 500 lashes as punishment, an excessive amount for such a crime and highly unlikely to be accurate.

Post punishment, Hannah reportedly returned to duty, hardly surprisingly, in an uneasy atmosphere, which was further aggravated by the arrival of a new recruit. George Beck was a carpenter from Worcester, who had previously been given shelter in the home of Susanna and James Gray. Hannah became afraid that Beck would recognise her and see through her disguise, especially as she was using her brother-in-law's name. This dread of discovery, plus the threat of further unfair treatment by her sergeant, prompted her to take drastic action; she deserted her regiment.

Extracting Fact from Fiction

It is here that we must address the discrepancies of Walker's account of Hannah's life in *The Female Soldier* by considering the facts that can be corroborated. Firstly, Walker claims it was the death of Hannah's child that precipitated her actions but this does not tally with death records. Susanna Summs, daughter of James and Hannah Summs, was buried on 31 January 1747, two years after Walker's account has Hannah joining Colonel Guise's regiment. His description of the manner of her enlistment also needs further examination. It is true recruiters did use such aggressive tactics to fill recruitment quotas, and would often be paid a bonus for every soldier they could deliver into the ranks. The courts were also often used as means to force service on those who were unwilling. However, Walker appears to have created this entire scene to establish Hannah as a brave heroine who was willing to serve her country, while limiting accusations of deception on her part; Hannah did not set out to deceive but, when pressed, she was ready and willing to serve King and Country. There is no evidence that such an encounter ever occurred, and this entire episode does not appear in the first version of *The Female Soldier.*

Perhaps the least credible section is Walker's description of Hannah's encounter with the 'villainous' Sergeant Davis and her subsequent flogging. A punishment as severe as 500 lashes would have been a death sentence; indeed, a sentence of 200 lashes had been known to result in the recipient's death. It is also inconceivable that Hannah would have been able to maintain her disguise under such circumstances. Her shirt would have been stripped from her, revealing her breasts to those watching. Walker's explanation that she faced the castle wall, which prevented discovery of her real gender, seems highly improbable. In fact, there are many accounts of female soldiers and sailors who were discovered in exactly this way. In 1771 records show that Charles Waddle was sentenced to two dozen lashes (a more conservative and realistic punishment compared to Hannah's supposed 500 lashes) but upon being strung up for punishment, his shirt was removed to expose the torso and Waddle was discovered to be a woman in disguise. Waddle's punishment was immediately rescinded and she was discharged from the service. Rather than being punished for her deception, Waddle was given clothing and money and 'treated kindly' by the Admiral.[12] In 1787, George Thompson was revealed to be Margaret Thompson in similar circumstances, when her sentence of three dozen lashes for theft was about to be carried out. Thompson was actually innocent of theft; a search of her sea chest had produced an array women's clothing, her own property, but that was understandably presumed to be stolen. Again, her punishment was never carried out once her female identity was discovered.[13]

Inconsistencies and uncorroborated facts are strewn throughout Walker's publication but are especially prevalent in Hannah's supposed early career in General Guise's regiment. It must be remembered that Walker's publication was a commercial venture, designed to sell as many copies as possible. Just as sometimes occurs in 'true stories' today, this meant embellishing the tale for dramatic effect, something Walker was well known for doing. Despite this, we should not dismiss Hannah Snell as a fraud as there are many parts of her life and service that can be, and have been, verified.

A *Little Tar of Note*

The true story of Hannah Snell's military life and transformation actually began in the autumn of 1747, just a few months after her infant daughter's death. Hannah had left her sister's home in her brother-in-law's clothes and made her way directly to Portsmouth. Here 'James Gray' enlisted into Colonel Frasier's regiment of the Royal Marines and was later drafted into the crew of the sloop the *Swallow*. Just three weeks after enlisting, Hannah and the crew of the *Swallow* were bound for the East Indies and war with France. As many female sailors in disguise discovered, enlisting was a relatively trouble-free venture. Many of those who found themselves in the Navy were there as a result of press gangs or of unscrupulous recruiting officers who would ply them with alcohol before tricking them. Many of her fellow crew members deserted rather than endure life in the Navy at war. As a young, healthy, enthusiastic volunteer, 'Gray' would have been a welcome addition to the crew. The *Swallow* set sail as part of a fleet of ships under the command of Admiral Boscawen, from Portsmouth, on 23 October 1747. Hannah was one of six new arrivals aboard that day. It is at this stage that evidence begins to corroborate Hannah's tale as Private James Gray is listed among the muster records of the *Swallow* along with Lieutenant Richard Wyegate, and Privates John Hutchins and Dougal McDougal.[14] Hannah was given the duty of mess boy to Lieutenant Wyegate, where her skills as a cook and seamstress soon made her a firm favourite among the officers on board. In times of attack her battle station was on the quarterdeck and, as one of the after-guard, her business was to fight and 'do what mischief she could with the small arms which they had on board'. She took her turn on watch every four hours and soon, with 'her natural intrepidity and peculiar sprightliness she became, with a very little instruction, a little tar of note.'[15]

Admiral Boscawen's fleet of ten naval ships, with 2,000 soldiers including 800 marines on board, was on a mission to recapture the English settlement of Madras, which had recently fallen under the control of the French. Madras was one of the three major trading towns, with Calcutta and Bombay, which the English (later British) East India Company had established on the Indian continent. During the seventeenth century, the East India Company had established dominance over trade in the area. However, the establishment of the French East India Company in 1664 saw a rival to that monopoly. While the French colonies were centred around Pondicherry on the east coast, the English settlements were mainly further north, around the area of Madras. The two companies had initially distanced themselves from the conflicts in Europe and remained neutral but as England and France found themselves on opposite sides of the War of the Austrian Succession, this ceased to be possible. British Commodore Curtis Bennet attacked the French fleet in 1745 and so began a series of counter-attacks, which culminated in the French attack on Madras on 7 September 1746. French troops laid siege to the city with artillery. Over the years, the British had sorely neglected the city's defences and French troops quickly took possession of it. The British surrendered possession of the city on 21 September and were forced to retreat. They regrouped at Fort St David, to the south of Pondicherry, where they awaited reinforcements.

The *Swallow,* with Hannah on board, set out on its journey from Portsmouth to deliver these reinforcements and to take back the city for the British. After they set sail, they were almost forced into port at Torbay, Devon, by bad weather. This was an omen for the rest of their voyage. There was a further setback at the Bay of Biscay, when a hurricane forced the fleet to separate. During the three weeks it took to repair the ship, Hannah and many of her colleagues were quartered ashore, where her nursing skills were required when her superior, Lieutenant Wyegate, became seriously ill.

After the repairs were completed, the *Swallow* continued on her journey but the streak of bad luck had not yet ended and just a few hours after they left harbour for the next stage of their journey towards Cape Town, they were hit by a third storm so violent that the *Swallow* was separated from her from her escort ship, the *Vigilant.* This time, the ship was so badly damaged that all hands, including Hannah, were forced to work the pumps to keep her afloat. The *Swallow* finally reached her destination and joined the rest of Boscawen's fleet on 6 May. All on board were safe and well, but this had been a tough test for the new marine.

The *Swallow* was only three times the size of a London bus and housed a crew of 110. In the sleeping quarters below deck, hammocks would have hung just a few inches apart, as was true on the HMS *Victory*, the largest ship of its day. This would leave no room for privacy. How did Hannah manage to conceal her gender in such cramped conditions? The truth is there were many women who managed just this. Research into the seventeenth and eighteenth centuries show at least twenty cases of cross-dressing women who managed this feat on Royal Navy and merchant ships, as well as an undisclosed number of women who were never discovered. Most who were revealed to be women did so either voluntarily, as Hannah did, or were discovered in circumstances beyond their control, such as flogging or injury. But they were, in fact, able to pass as men for long periods of time. One of the main ways they did this was to pose as adolescent boys. The Royal Navy and Merchant Navy vessels were often crewed by boys as young as nine or ten because they were quick, agile and able to climb the masts and rigging. Posing as boys, these women were able to explain away their smaller frames and lack of beard. The uniform of a sailor also aided their disguise as it consisted of baggy shirts and trousers, a waistcoat or jacket, and a handkerchief tied around the neck. Hair was often worn long and tied back. If Hannah was able to sufficiently conceal her breasts, there is every possibility she would appear to be a teenage boy.

The most difficult aspect of concealment was personal hygiene. Sailors were not known for regularly washing so Hannah would never have been required to be naked near the rest of the crew. Toilet facilities on board ship were primitive in the extreme. Sailors would defecate through a hole in a platform at the figurehead of the ship, known as 'the head', or they would urinate straight into the sea. Hannah would have had to be careful to use the head privately. She may have even used a similar tube-like device as the one used by another woman warrior, Christian Cavenaugh, which was described in her biography as 'a silver tube with leather straps which she placed in her breeches'.[16] Neither Hannah nor Cavenaugh mention how they dealt with menstruation, however, in her study *Female Tars – Women Aboard Ship in the Age of Sail* Suzanne Stark suggests the poor diet and rigorous lifestyle of the 18th-century sailor may have stopped menstruation altogether in these women. Any bleeding that did occur could have been put down to a case of venereal disease, which was common among seamen of the time.

So far Hannah's experience in the military was limited to the dangers faced at sea but after spending only twelve days ashore during their six-month journey, she would finally face the battlefield. The crew docked at the English settlement of Fort St David on the east coast of India, and the *Swallow's* marine unit set up camp 2 miles outside the fort, where they were joined by the battalions of the East India Company and 3,000 Indian troops. Their delay in arrival had allowed the French time to secure their fortifications and those in charge of the attack began to express their doubts about their chances of success. But these fears never reached the ears of the troops and on the morning of 8 August, Hannah began the march in her battalion towards the fortifications at Pondicherry, carrying her own supplies that included tent poles, a hatchet, a camp kettle and her musket. The fort at Ariancoupan, situated 4 miles from their ultimate goal, was the first target. Hannah's battalion laid siege to it for nine days before the French surrendered. Unfortunately, success at Pondicherry was not to be as quick. When Hannah's company finally arrived at their destination, their first task was to dig trenches. With her comrades, these dirty, mud-filled channels would be her home for the next month while they were bombarded, night and day, by mortar and gunfire from the battery of twelve French guns. James Miller, a fellow British soldier in those trenches, described the deplorable conditions they faced:

> We have had very bad weather of late, the Rains have been so great that our Trenches fill'd with water and Mud, being almost unpassable, being so deep that it takes us to the waist and are oblig'd to stand in them twenty four hours and to pass and repass everything to the assistance of our Brother Soldiers. The Duty is very hard upon us, having scarce a night's rest in the week.[17]

Hannah was involved in several skirmishes during the bloody siege, where she witnessed the deaths of many of her battalion at close quarters, took the lives of several enemy soldiers, and was shot herself. In total, she received six musket balls to the right leg, five to the left and one to the groin. Unable to stand and bleeding badly, Hannah was carried to the military hospital for treatment but could not allow the surgeons to extract the musket balls, particularly the one to her groin, without risking discovery. Even in this time of war, with her years of loyal service behind her, discovery would have meant immediate dismissal for Hannah. Rather than risk this outcome, Hannah chose to operate on her own wounds in the confines of her tent using only lint, salve and her own fingers.

> She probed the wound with her finger till she came where the ball lay, and then upon feeling it thrust in both her finger and

thumb pulled it out. This was a very rough way of proceeding with one's own flesh, but of two evils, as she thought, this was the least, so rather choosing to have her flesh torn and mangled than her sex discovered.[18]

There are many other women warriors who, during times of injury, were forced to 'operate' on their own wounds to avoid discovery. American Revolutionary soldier Deborah Sampson removed a musket ball from her thigh in similar circumstances. However, in this case, it seems unlikely that Hannah would be able to successfully remove twelve musket balls alone, as is described, and we may have again come across Robert Walker's tendency to embellish. It is likely Hannah's wounds were minor and caused by only one or two musket balls, although any gunshot wound is a serious enough injury to deal with under such conditions. Whatever the number and extent of her injuries, Hannah was able to successfully treat them herself and she soon recovered without revealing her secret to anyone.

After her recovery, Hannah and several other marines were transferred to the crew of the *Eltham*, a man-of-war class ship. The *Eltham* sailed from Fort St Davis to Bombay on 24 October 1748. The ship was not in good repair and leaked badly during its journey and as a result, the *Eltham* took nine weeks before it weighed anchor in Bombay. During the voyage, Hannah and her crewmates were in as bad a condition as the ship was, with almost half the crew taken ill with scurvy, a condition caused by a lack of vitamin C in their diet. Fresh fruit, vegetables and meat could not be preserved on long journeys so a ship would only have a limited supply.

Richard Walter, a ship's chaplain who witnessed the ravages of the disease on board a ship in the 1740s, describes its awful symptoms:

> Skin black as ink, ulcers, difficult respiration, rictus of the limbs, teeth falling out and, perhaps most revolting of all, a strange plethora of gum tissue sprouting out of the mouth, which immediately rotted and lent the victim's breath an abominable odour.[19]

This condition became so prevalent among ships' crews that it became known as 'the plague of the sea'. In 1795 British sailors began to be issued with a daily ration of lemon or lime juice to try to combat the disease, which led to the nickname 'limey' for British sailors.

Hannah's time on board the *Eltham* was made worse by a run-in with one of her superior officers. She had become known among her crewmates for her lyrical voice and was requested to sing by the First Lieutenant George Allen. Hannah refused, a decision that is never explained and the Lieutenant's response to this was swift and violent. He accused her of the theft of a shirt, a crime of which she was innocent, and had her clapped in irons for five days and given twelve lashes. This tale strongly reminds us of Walker's invention of the malicious Sergeant Davis, who supposedly had Hannah flogged with 500 lashes. However, there are many reports of brutal naval officers who abused their power in such a way. Most were members of the upper middle class or gentry and saw their crew as inferior people who could only be controlled by harsh discipline. As she was still considered a youth on board ship, Hannah may have been flogged in the 'kissing the gunner's daughter' position bent forward over a field gun, rather than standing up. The lashes were then applied to the naked bottom with a cat o' nine tails. The bare bottom may have caused issues for Hannah but being bent forward there is still a possibility she could have hidden herself from view. It is perhaps this experience that made Hannah decide it was time to return home.

Homeward Bound

On 19 October 1749, the *Eltham* began its long journey back to England and Hannah began her return to her home, and her female identity. However, the journey took a tragic turn almost immediately when Hannah's friend and master, Lieutenant Richard Wyegate, for whom she had worked for most of her service, died just a day after they left the port at Fort St David. Hannah's friendship with the Lieutenant had granted her a modicum of protection from the derision of some of her crewmates and the abuse of some of the more brutal officers. It is perhaps his illness that had allowed the disastrous encounter with First Lieutenant Allen to occur. Hannah was a skilled seamstress, which made her a valued crew member and she was soon placed in the service of Third Lieutenant Samuel Wallis who 'proved very kind and indulgent to her during the whole voyage'.[20] But her skill with a needle and laundry, along with her lack of beard, soft voice and small frame earned her the nickname Miss Molly Gray among several of the new crewmembers and Hannah became increasingly uneasy about discovery. She would attempt to overcompensate for her feminine reputation by indulging in heavy drinking sessions and frequenting taverns and brothels while in harbour. Despite her nickname, her crewmates would later claim they had no suspicions about her true gender.

During the voyage, the *Eltham* needed to make several stops for repairs and to take on supplies. During one of these stops, in a tavern in the port of Lisbon, Hannah finally met with an acquaintance of her estranged husband. This sailor claimed Summs had served with many crews since his disappearance and had been seen in Cork, Amsterdam and Genoa. While ashore in Genoa, Summs had embarked on his usual alcohol-fuelled exploits when he fell into argument with 'a person of some distinction'. This man was fatally stabbed during the altercation and Summs was reportedly executed for the crime by being sewn into a heavy hessian sack, weighted down with stones, then thrown into the sea to drown. The sailor went on to tell Hannah that before his execution, Summs had lamented his ill treatment of his wife and '[begged] her pardon and forgiveness for all the injuries he hath done her'.[21] The sailor was apparently unaware he was actually speaking to the wife in question at this time. There is no record of James Summs's crime or execution but this manner of putting someone to death is not an official execution but a method used by pirates and those seeking revenge, so it does not necessarily follow that it did not take place. Either way, Hannah was apparently free from her quest to find her husband and was ready to return home.

On 7 May 1750, the *Eltham* set sail on the final leg of its voyage, arriving in Portsmouth on the 25th of the month. After two nights of drinking at the Jolly Marine & Sailor in celebration of their return, Hannah and ten members of her regiment set off for London; she had five shillings 'conduct money' in her pocket. After three days of travel Hannah arrived at her sister's home, still in the uniform of James Gray, and knocked on her door, unsure of the welcome she would get. While not one soldier, sailor or officer had recognised her in her disguise, Susannah Gray apparently immediately recognised her sister and 'threw her Arms about our young Marine's Neck, and almost stifled her with Kisses'.[22] Just two weeks later James Gray would stand before his fellow marines and make his bold declaration. On advice from her comrades, Hannah petitioned the Duke of Cumberland, Captain-General of the British Army, for a war pension in recognition of both her service and the injuries so sustained. On 16 June, she personally hand-delivered the petition to the duke in his carriage in St James Park. She was apparently dressed in a man's suit at the time suggesting that she still not keen to return to all of her pre-war habits. The news of her unusual request became public when it appeared in the *Whitehall Evening Post* one week later. The story that appeared, however, is much distorted from that which she would later tell herself.

Last week one Hannah Snell, born at Worcester, who was seven Years in the Marine Regiment by the Name of James Gray, went to the East Indies in Admiral Boscawens's Squadron, and was at the siege of Pondicherry, presented a Petition to his Royal Highness the Duke of Cumberland, praying some provision might be made for her now she is discharged the service. His Royal Highness referred her petition to General Fraser; to report it to him, and make her a suitable Provision according to her

Merit. It seems her sweet heart being impressed into the Marine Service, she put on Men's Cloaths, and entered in the same Regiment, went to the East-Indies in the same Ship with him, and was his messmate while he lived (he dying in the Voyage) and was a Servant to one of the lieutenants. She behaved with great Intrepidity as a Sailor and Soldier, and her Sex was never discovered by either her Sweetheart or any of her Comrades till she made the Discovery herself by the above-mentioned Petition.[23]

The invention of a 'sweetheart' is perhaps understandable as it was the only way in which the 18th-century public were able to understand the desire of a woman to enlist. Dubbed by historian Suzanne Stark the 'lost-lover theme', there were many popular ballads and tales with such a subject throughout the century. In truth, women like Hannah had various reasons to go to sea. They had increased social freedom and independence, were no longer subject to the men in their family, and any money they earned was their own. If their marriages were as disastrous as Hannah's was, this alone could have been enough of an incentive. Perhaps it was to correct the notion that she was following a man that motivated Hannah to tell her own version of events. *The Female Soldier; or, the Surprising Life and Adventures of Hannah* was published later that year. For a short time, Hannah enjoyed some fame. Ballads were written about her, such as the following, that was printed in newspapers and sung in taverns

Hannah in briggs, behaved so well
That none her softer sex could tell;
Nor was her policy confounded

When near the mark of nature wounded;
Which proves what men will scarce admit.
That women are for secrets fit.
That healthful blood could keep so long
Admist young fellows hale and strong
Demonstrates, though a seeming wonder,
That love to courage truckles under.
Oh, how her bedmate bit his lips,
And marked the spreading of her hips,
And cursed the blindness of his youth,
When she confessed the naked truth!
Her fortitude, to no man's second,
To woman's honour must be reckoned.
Twelve wounds! 'Twas half great Caesar's number,
That made his corpse the ground encumber.
How many men, for heroes nursed,
Had left their colours at the first.
'Twas thought Achilles' greatest glory
That Homer was to sing his story;
And Alexander mourned his lot
That no such bard could then be got-
But Hannah's praise no Homer needs;
She lives to sing her proper deeds.[24]

The ladies and gentlemen of the higher classes loved to read about scandalous breaches of acceptable etiquette and would turn out in droves to see Hannah appear on stage in full uniform, where she would regale them with tales of her high seas adventures, sing songs and perform military exercises. Portraits of the young marine dressed both in uniform and in female attire were sold on the streets. Between 29 June and 6 September Hannah performed her show sixty times in the London New Wells Theatre. She shared the stage with acrobats, dramatic recreations and novelty acts, such as herself. Eighteenth-century diarist and clergyman James Woodforde describes his encounter with Hannah as she performed onstage in his Norfolk neighbourhood:

I walked up to the White Hart with Mr Lewis and Bill to see a famous Woman in Men's cloaths, by the name Hannah Snell, who was 21 years as a common soldier in the Army, and not discovered by any as a woman. Cousin Lewis has mounted guard with her abroad. She went in the Army by the name of John Gray. She has a Pension from the crown now of 18.5.0 per annum and the liberty of wearing Men's cloaths and also a cockade in her Hat, which she still wears. She has laid in a room with 70 soldiers and not discovered by any of them. The forefinger of her right hand was cut off by a Sword at the taking of Pondicherry. She is now about 60 years of age and talks very sensible and well.[25]

But fame did not necessarily bring fortune with it. Although Hannah was awarded a pension of £30 per annum, there is no evidence that she ever received this money. At Woodforde's encounter with Hannah, he also saw her selling buttons, garters and laces as many old soldiers who had hit hard times were reduced to doing. His pity at her circumstances led him to pay her 2s and 6d for a card of buttons worth only 4d. Hannah attempted to solicit help from the Royal Chelsea Hospital and was admitted as an out-pensioner on 21st November 1750.

She was not the first woman to have been granted the privilege of recognition as a Chelsea Pensioner. Christian Cavenaugh, otherwise known as Mother Ross, had been buried at the hospital with full military honours in 1739, eleven years before Hannah's petition. In deference to her war injuries, Hannah was granted five pence per day for the rest of her life but as her encounter with Woodforde shows, this was not enough to comfortably support the veteran marine.

Hannah married twice more but very little is known about her family life. On 3 November 1759, she married Richard Eyles in Newbury, in the county of Berkshire. The marriage produced two sons and Hannah is believed to have been heavily pregnant or a new mother at her wedding, as her first son was also born in 1759. Hannah's fortunes may never have been very high but she did somehow manage to educate her son George enough for him to become an attorney. She was widowed again in 1772 and she remarried soon afterwards to Richard Habgood. Tragedy was never far away from Hannah though and in her twilight years, she was committed to the Bethlem Royal Hospital for the insane, commonly known as Bedlam. She passed away on 8 February 1792, aged sixty-nine, and was buried in an unmarked grave at the Royal Chelsea Hospital among her fellow veterans, only the second woman to be given the honour of being buried there.

Hannah's life is one of controversy, intrigue, tragedy and triumph. The complicated issue of extracting the truth from the myth has caused some to doubt the validity of her tale. The details may be fuzzy but there is enough evidence to assure me that Hannah existed and she served, and so she should be remembered.

Notes

1. Extract from *The Female Soldier* as found in Stark, Suzanne J., *Female Tars – Women Aboard Ship in the Age of Sail* (London: Pimlico, 1998) p. 106

2. *Walker, R, The Female Soldier; or, the Surprising Life and Adventures of Hannah Snell* (London: R. Walker, 1750) in *The Lady Tars: The Autobiographies of Hannah Snell, Mary Lacy and Mary Anne Talbot* (Fireship Press 2008), p. 41

3. Stephens, Matthew, *Hannah Snell: The Secret Life of Female Marine, 1723–1792* (London: Ship Street Press 2014) expanded digital edition, loc 247

4. Britannica Online Encyclopaedia, http://www.britannica.com/article/611812

5. Creighton, Charles, *A History of Epidemics in Britain from the Extinction of the Plague to the Present Time Vol 2* (Cambridge: Cambridge Press, 1894) p. 92 – Creighton states that there is no mention of the epidemic among the town records from 1730.

6. Walker p. 2

7. Stephens, ebook loc 349

8. Walker p. 4-5

9. ibid p. 5

10. ibid p. 6

11. ibid

12. Stark, p. 101

13. Ibid, p. 111-12

14. Muster record The *Swallow* October – December 1747 as found in Stephens, ebook loc 399

15. Walker p. 10

16. Stark, p. 46

17. The diary of James Miller, 1745–50 as quoted in Stephens, ebook loc 505
18. Walker p. 22
19. http://www.bbc.co.uk/history/british/empire_seapower/ captaincook_scurvy_ accessed 31 March 2017
20. Walker, p. 26
21. Stephens, ebook, loc 1943
22. Walker, p.36
23. 23 June 1750 *Whitehall Evening Post*
24. Walker, p.46
25. Cordingly, David. *Women Salilors and Sailors' Women – An Untold Maritime History* (New York: Random House, 2001), p. 75

5

LADY JANE INGLEBY – TROOPER JANE

Our women are all on fire, striving through a gallant
emulation to outdoe our men and will make good our yielding
walls or loose their lives.
Anonymous chronicler at siege of Chester, October 1645[1]

On 2 July 1644, Sir William Ingleby of Ripley Castle,
Harrogate, answered the call of Charles I to raise troops
against Parliamentary forces. Ingleby mustered troops from
his manor and the local village of Ripley in preparation to
face the combined forces of Sir Thomas Fairfax and the
troops of the Eastern Association, known as the 'Ironsides'
who were then occupying the Royalist garrison of York. He
would be up against the Lieutenant General of Horse for the
Ironsides, the formidable Oliver Cromwell, a Parliamentary
rebel who was fast making his name as a skilful commander.
Unknown to either Ingleby's enemy, or his own troops,
standing by Sir William's side, dressed in the Ingleby family

armour, was his sister, Lady Jane, also ready to defend her king and her home.

The English Civil War, as in any war in which countrymen are in conflict with each other, tore the nation apart. It pitted the Crown against Parliament, neighbour against neighbour and brother against brother. It is thought that up to one in five of all men served on either side of the conflict throughout its duration and about 85,000 people lost their lives on the battlefield. But the nature of civil war meant danger was not restricted to those men who were called to fight. Approximately another 127,000 citizens lost their lives as an indirect result of the war. Infectious diseases were a particular danger as troops would march from town to town spreading disease as they went.[2] It was, as Ann Plowden describes in *Women All on Fire – The Women of the English Civil War*, 'a curiously domestic affair' as the women of England, Ireland, Scotland and Wales also found their lives affected by the conflict. Troops were gathered locally to defend their own neighbourhoods and while some wives were left behind to cope in their men's absence, others accompanied their menfolk to nurse the wounded or perform domestic chores in the field. These women were often encouraged to dress in men's clothing for their comfort, convenience and protection. The dangers they faced were considerable. After the battle of Naseby in June 1645, women camp followers of the Royalist Army were attacked by the Parliamentary Cavalry and 100 were killed and many more mutilated. The form of mutilation, slitting the nose, was particularly brutal and a punishment usually reserved in the seventeenth century for the punishment of prostitutes and whores. This was meant as a statement on their morals as well as their Royalist sympathies.[3] Women of all classes were also often used as spies by both sides because they were usually able to pass unchallenged through enemy lines. At the besieged Royalist town of Chester, the mayor was able to send his maid back and forth across enemy lines to gather information. In castles and manors across the country, great ladies commanded armies to defend their homes, including the Puritan Lady Brilliana Harley who was left to defend Brampton Bryan Castle in Herefordshire against Royalist invasion while her husband was an MP in Westminster and their sons were all away with Parliament's armies. Lady Brilliana was hailed as having 'masculine bravery, both for religion, resolution, wisdom, and warlike policy'.[4]

Alison Plowden describes Queen Henrietta Maria as 'the only Queen of England to have sheltered in a ditch while cannon balls whistled overhead and a man was killed not twenty paces away'.[5] Elsewhere on many battlefields up and down the country there were wives and daughters who crossed even further into the masculine role of taking part in warfare. These women, dubbed 'she-souldiers' picked up weapons and fought alongside their countrymen to defend their homes and their principles.

One such incident occurred in 1645 when the Parliamentarians took Shelford. A Royalist corporal was taken prisoner, and then was discovered by his captors to be a woman. She was by no means the only 'she-souldier' to take up arms at this time. The Scots were rumoured to have many women soldiers in their ranks when they marched on Newcastle in 1644. Ballads were sung of female fighters, including the popular 1655 ballad of the adventures of 'Mr Clarke', who served alongside her husband for years; these songs show the habit was widespread. In fact, Charles I was so mortified by the fact that he issued orders that should any woman 'counterfeit her sex' she would be subject to the 'severest punishment which Law and our displeasure shall inflict'.[6] However, the king's distaste for women who '[defied] Nature and Religion'[7] did not prevent many a woman from taking to the battlefield in defence of her home and family, including Lady Jane Ingleby.

Origins of Rebellion

Charles I had not been born to be king; that privilege had originally belonged to his brother Henry, who died in 1612 from typhoid fever. Charles did not have a close relationship with either of his parents. This was because, as a child, he had been left in Scotland with servants while his father took the English throne. However, Charles was determined to rule in a way of which his father, James VI of Scotland and James I of England, would be proud. From his earliest childhood, James had taught Charles that kings were 'little gods on earth', ordained by God and not subject to the will of the people. This concept, combined with the embarrassment Charles felt over his small stature and his legs, which were deformed by childhood rickets, produced a stubborn and insecure character.

In direct contrast to Charles's lonely childhood, the champion of the Parliamentarians and the king's main foe, Oliver Cromwell, had a very close relationship with his mother. He was educated at Cambridge University and was far from the 'common man' he is often portrayed to have been. Cromwell's grandfather was a knight of the realm, and Cromwell described himself as 'by birth a gentleman, living neither in any considerable height, nor yet in obscurity'.[8] But Cromwell had fallen from the social status that his grandfather had held, his family were now the poor relations. His grammar school education was progressive, described by historian Diane Purkiss in her study *The English Civil War: A People's History* as representing 'a chance for boys to be different from their fathers, to do something different from what their fathers had done, to climb an inch or two further up the social ladder than their fathers had'. These two very different characters would soon clash in a far-reaching struggle.

In August 1642, Charles I faced two rebellions in his kingdom, one in Ireland and one in his own Parliament. At this time in history, Parliament was not the permanent establishment it is today. The king would call his lords together when he required taxes to be raised and theoretically to seek advice, but Charles was not a monarch known for heeding the opinions of his nobles. He had dissolved his last Parliament before the war in 1629 and ruled by decree for eleven years. This period became known by his detractors as the 'Eleven Year Tyranny'. After a series of expensive and disastrously unsuccessful wars with France, the British monarchy was almost bankrupt, but Charles was reluctant to ask his Parliament to raise taxes. He saw the increasing number of questions being asked about the prudence of these conflicts as disloyalty from his noblemen. Charles was prohibited from introducing taxes without Parliamentary authority but in 1635, he attempted to circumnavigate this authority by extending the existing 'ship money', which was an annual levy for the reform of the Navy, to include inland towns as well as those on the coast. For many people this was a further example of Charles's increasingly tyrannical reign, which also included many unpopular church reforms largely influenced by his Catholic wife, Queen Henrietta Maria, which were resented by the devout members of the Protestant nation.

Scottish rebellion at the Glasgow General Assembly in November 1638 led Charles to gather his forces and march on the rebellious Scots. A lack of funds meant the troops were poorly trained and lacked confidence, so Charles was forced to sign the Treaty of Berwick in the conflict known as the First Bishops' War, without fighting a single battle. Angry at this failure, Charles called his first Parliament in eleven years, in November 1640, to raise funds for the army. But what would become known as the 'Short Parliament' had other ideas. Parliament insisted on discussing the many issues and grievances that had developed over the decade since the last Parliament before it would grant the king his requested funds. In a rage at their audacity in questioning him, Charles dissolved Parliament almost immediately without receiving his funds. On 20 August 1640, the Scots invaded England for the second time in a campaign known as the Second Bishops' War, and on the 28th of that month, at the Battle of Newburn, they took control of Newcastle upon Tyne. Charles was again forced to call a Parliament but this one would sit for twenty years.

In October 1641, an uprising by the people of Ulster would cause a fundamental split between the king and his Parliament, which would ultimately lead to war. The political crisis that the Ulster Uprising would cause in the English Parliament was to do with control, principally the control of the army. When Charles mobilised his troops without reference to Parliament, to many people this was the last straw. The two sides were the Royalists, known as the Cavaliers due to their long hair and wigs, and the short-haired Parliamentarians, known as the Roundheads. First blood was drawn at the battle of Edgehill on 23 October 1642. By the end of the year, each side had armies of between 60,000 and 70,000 fighting men in the field; but there were also the women, who were not counted in these figures, who served or fought in the sieges and skirmishes that would typify this war.

By 1644, two years into the Civil War, the two sides had reached an effective military stalemate. Charles and his Royalist supporters controlled most of the north and west of England, as well as Wales and Ireland, while the Parliamentarians had the advantage of the south and the financial capital of London. Without London, Charles could not hope to win but neither had the Parliamentarians been able to quash the king's forces. This would all change in the summer of 1644 in the battlefields of the north. In spring that year, William Cavendish, Marquis of Newcastle and a Royalist commander, led his army to York where he was besieged by the Parliamentary forces of Thomas Fairfax and his Scottish reinforcements. In response to this attack, the king's nephew, Prince Rupert of the Rhine, sought to gather an army for Charles to raise the siege because to lose York would be to lose the north, and perhaps the war, for the Royalists. Prince Rupert called on all the Royalist houses in the area to gather troops for the cause. Among those who answered this call was Sir William Ingleby of Ripley Castle, who gathered his troops from the village of Ripley. Ripley Castle had previous royal connections, having hosted James VI on his road to his English coronation in 1603, yet the Ingleby family (changed to Ingilby by Act of Parliament in the early 1780s) was no stranger to rebellion. Their commitment to the Catholic cause had once seen them labelled 'a threat to the State'. Sir William's ancestor, Francis Ingleby, had been an ordained Catholic priest who was hung, drawn and quartered on the Knavemire at York for attempting to start a rebellion in 1586, while nine of the eleven co-conspirators of the Gunpowder Plot can be linked to the family by either blood or close association.[9] But on 2 July 1644, the family saw themselves on the side of king and country as Sir William had declared his Royalist loyalties and been granted a baronetcy in 1642. Jane Ingleby, Sir William's sister, was also a staunch Royalist and when the troops rode into battle, Jane had ridden with them, dressed in her family armour and fought beside her brother and the Ripley troops.

The weapons and armour that troops would fight with during the seventeenth century were mainly provided by the lord who called them to battle. As a result, many castles held their own armoury, which is how Jane was able to obtain her suit of armour. A typical pike man in the Civil War era wore armour that weighed up to 11kg consisting of a breastplate, a back plate, a gorget, which was designed to protect the neck, and a pair of tassets, which acted as thigh defences. There was also a helmet, which did not cover the face. Jane may have worn something similar, although she would not have carried the 16-foot-long pike but perhaps a sword or musket instead. Jane was certainly comfortable with weapons, a fact she would demonstrate later in the day when confronted with the enemy in her own home. It is not known if Sir William was aware of his sister's action but it seems unlikely she could have accomplished it without his knowledge, and if he was indeed unaware of it before the battle, he must certainly have been aware of it afterwards.

Unfortunately for the Inglebys and the Royalist army, Prince Rupert and his reinforcements did not reach York in time and were instead intercepted en route by Cromwell's Parliamentary Army. At Marston Moor, just 7 miles from the City of York, the two armies came face to face. Cromwell's combined forces of Parliamentarian troops and Scottish allies numbered more than 27,000 while Prince Rupert commanded just 18,000, including the Ingleby troops. The two armies faced each other in similar formation, with infantry in the centre, flanked on each side by cavalry, and an exchange of artillery fire occurred. By 2pm that day neither side had made a definitive move to attack, which led Prince Rupert to be convinced that no battle would occur before morning. But he was mistaken and at 7.30pm, during a thunderstorm, he was surprised by the first attack of Cromwell's troops. The fierce Parliamentary cavalry troop, known as the 'Ironsides' by those who faced them, defeated the Royalist right wing cavalry, but the Royalist left wing, led by Lord George Goring, had more success and managed to hold back the enemy charge. However, this initial advantage of the Royalist troops was not capitalised upon and the Parliamentarian Army were able to regroup and mount a further attack. Eventually, in a battle that was the biggest and arguably one of the most important of the Civil War, the Royalist troops, including Sir William and Jane Ingleby, were defeated. The Parliamentary victory was possible because of Cromwell's skill as a battlefield tactician. He selected his commanders on ability, not class stating, 'I would rather have a plain russet-coated captain that knows what he fights for, and loves what he knows, than that which you call a gentleman and is nothing else'.[10] There were 4,150 Royalist casualties at Marston Moor, including a poodle named Boy who belonged to Prince Rupert. Rupert lost his horse in the battle but he survived after he hid in a bean field close to the battle, before fleeing. Cromwell's army did not escape unscathed, losing 2,000 men. Among the casualties was Cromwell's nephew; after a cannon shot broke his leg, he died when the limb was amputated.

After their defeat, Jane and Sir William fled the battlefield to the safety of Ripley Castle but they were not the only ones hoping to make the castle their home for the night. Elated by his victory but with casualties, prisoners and troops who required food and rest, Oliver Cromwell followed close on the two warriors' heels. He arrived just minutes after the Inglebys had returned, knocked on the narrow tower door and demanded entry for himself and his troops. Luckily for Sir William, Cromwell was at that time unaware of his participation at Marston Moor and was merely seeking shelter for himself and his men. But as a known Royalist, Sir William could not afford to be found by Cromwell because if his participation in the battle were discovered he could have lost his property or even been put to death. As the home of a Catholic family, Ripley Castle had within its walls a concealed room in which members of the clergy had hidden during times of Catholic persecution; a priest's hole. It is possible this hidden room had previously been used to hide the Catholic priest Francis Ingleby after his failed rebellion. That night the tiny room, hidden behind the wooden panels, would be a safe haven for Sir William. He was forced to remain there overnight while his enemy was sleeping in his home.

With her brother safely hidden away, Jane was left to face Cromwell alone. She had removed her armour but she had not left the battlefield unscathed. At this moment, however, her wounds were not the most immediate threat she faced. Jane opened the door to the tower, carrying with her two pistols for protection. She was in a delicate position. If she angered Oliver Cromwell, he may have ransacked the property, but if she offered him hospitality, she risked her brother's discovery. Jane could not refuse Cromwell and his troops entry but, as a woman alone, she told her visitor, she was afraid to allow a strange man and his army into her home. She allowed Cromwell's men to stay in the outbuildings and the courtyard of the castle, while the man himself was invited to come inside alone. Jane insisted Cromwell could only enter the library, where he would be permitted to spend the night. Her tenacity paid off and he agreed to her demands. Cromwell slept in a chair while Jane remained in the room with him, awake and with two pistols trained on him all through the night. Cromwell had no idea that his nervous hostess had actually faced him in full armour across a battlefield just a few hours before. Jane Ingleby's claim of feminine nerves reinforced her adversary's image of her as a fragile woman. By claiming it was her chastity she was protecting, rather than her home or her family, she was able to avoid any hint of political affinity on her part. Her bravery and quick thinking ensured both her home and Sir William remained safe. Not all were so lucky. Before Cromwell left early the next morning he made a point of executing the Royalist prisoners he had taken the day before, in the courtyard of a known Royalist residence. Some of those prisoners may have even come from the local village of Ripley.

Unlike many of the women warriors in this collection, Lady Jane Ingleby did not have to pass through any official enlistment process to join the military and her combat experience was restricted to one battle. So can she truly be considered a soldier and therefore a woman warrior? The army as it stood in the seventeenth century was not a cohesive unit as it is today but rather a collection of private militias called together in times of war. At the time of the English Civil War, this was even more disorderly due to the different allegiances of many different areas. While most men joined their local militia, some went further afield to fight for their cause, particularly if their allegiance did not match that of the local lord. In this way, Jane's actions were arguably no different from many other fighting men. The Soldier's catechism composed for the Parliamentary Army stated that the principles required in a soldier were 'that he be religious and godly', 'courageous and valiant' and 'skilful in the Militarie Profession'. It is clear from her actions at Marston Moor and in the library of Ripley Castle that Jane did meet two of these requirements; she was a religious woman who showed great courage in both joining the fight and in helping her brother at the risk of her own life. As for the third requirement, it can be argued that Jane had as much experience as many of the other troops on the battlefield that day, who were farmers and tradesmen by profession. In this way, I believe that Jane Ingleby does meet the criteria of a woman warrior and that she is, in fact, representative of many women whose actions and sufferings during this conflict are often overlooked.

Notes

1. Randle Holme's diary 10 October 1645 as found in Hughes, Ann, *Gender and the English Revolution* (Oxford, Routledge, 2012), p. 150
2. Ibid, p. 32
3. Ibid, p. 162
4. ibid, p. 152
5. Plowden, Alison, *Women All On Fire – The Women of the English Civil War* (Gloucestershire, Sutton Publishing, 2004), intro xiii
6. ibid, p. 78
7. ibid
8. Purkiss, Diane, *The English Civil War: A People's History* (London, Harper Perrennials, 2007), p. 18
9. Yvette Huddleston and Walter Swan http://www.yorkshirepost.co.uk/news/analysis/family-home-is-our-castle-1-2330173 Friday 2 January 2009
10. Lewis-Stempel, John, *The Autobiography of the British Soldier from Agincourt to Basra, in His Own Words* (London, Headline Review, 2007), p. 42

6

MARGARET BULKLEY
AKA DOCTOR JAMES MIRANDA BARRY – SURGEON AND SOLDIER

He always took care never to be seen... like any ordinary man[1]

Was I not a girl I would be a soldier[2]

London in the summer of 1865 was in the midst of a stifling heatwave. The general unsanitary conditions of the streets combined with the unusually high temperature to produce a vicious epidemic of chronic diarrhoea, which swept through the area killing thousands of unfortunate citizens. In July alone there were well over 500 deaths from this condition. One of these ill-fated casualties was 'a male person of about seventy years' who passed away at his home in Margaret Street, Marylebone. Dr James Barry was a British Army veteran who had recently retired from nearly half a century's service, during which he had gained the very senior position of Inspector General of Hospitals. He had made his name as an expert in epidemic diseases in the tropical climates of South Africa and the West Indies and he had famously performed the first recorded caesarean section in the British Empire in which both mother and child had survived. Despite these successes, he was to meet with an undignified end when he succumbed to the ravages of the disease. Had he been treated using the methods he had advocated, which included strict diet and hygienic conditions, a controversial opinion he shared with the more celebrated Florence Nightingale, he might have survived his illness.

Dr Barry was attended in death as he had been in life by his manservant, nicknamed 'Black John' by the media, and his small dog, Psyche. Dr Barry had left strict instructions that his body not be disturbed by post-mortem, an interesting decision for a physician who had understood the importance of practical anatomy in modern medicine. Although this request was honoured, his body was stripped and washed to prepare for burial by a servant, Sophia Bishop, who afterwards made a startling claim; that the celebrated doctor and veteran of forty-six years in the British Military actually was a woman and, according to the telltale marks upon her body, may even have been a mother.

When Bishop's accusation came to light and rumours reached the press, there was much discussion among Barry's former friends and colleagues over the validity of her claim. The *Manchester Guardian* printed the 'Strange Story' on 21 August, stating:

> An incident is just now being discussed in military circles so extraordinary that, were not the truth capable of being vouched for by official authority, the narration would certainly be deemed absolutely incredible... Dr Barry... [enjoyed] a reputation for considerable skill in his profession, especially for

firmness, decision and rapidity in difficult operations... It stands as an indubitable fact, that a woman was for 40 years an officer in the British service, and fought one duel and had sought many more, had pursued a legitimate medical education, and received a regular diploma.[3]

So how did a woman become a military surgeon fifty-two years before the first female doctor in the UK, Elizabeth Garrett Anderson, officially became qualified?

Birth and Origins

There has been much speculation since the discovery of her deception as to the true identity of Dr James Barry. Unlike fellow cross-dressing soldiers Hannah Snell and Kit Cavenaugh, we have no first-person account of her life and very few letters or papers written in her own hand. Over the years, many people have speculated about her parentage and origins – including some wild theories that Barry was the illegitimate daughter of the Duke of York, or even the Prince Regent himself. These theories are purely based on the fact that Barry seems to have been able to attract powerful mentors and protectors throughout her career, and many of her contemporaries dismissed the idea that a woman would have been able to climb to the most senior medical post in the British military without a powerful, invisible, sponsor. The truth, however, is both more mundane and more extraordinary; Barry was, in fact, Margaret Ann Bulkley, the daughter of an Irish Catholic grocer.

During his lifetime James Barry had always maintained that he was born in London and while it is true that the identity of Barry did spring forth in that city, Margaret Ann Bulkley was born in Cork, Ireland, in 1789. Her mother, Mary Anne Barry, was the only daughter of an impoverished gentry family and the sister of the Royal Academy artist James Barry. Margaret Ann's father, Jerimiah Bulkley, was a grocer. He was an ambitious man with pretensions to gentility who was determined his children would climb the social ladder to better things. To achieve this, Bulkley ensured his children were provided with a genteel education. His son John was encouraged to pursue a career in law, while Margaret was intended for a good marriage. As a result, the Bulkleys spent a good deal of money (far more than they could comfortably afford) on John's education. Margaret, although 'brighter, [more] imaginative, [and more] inclined to dedicate herself to a course'[4] than her impetuous brother, was limited to those subjects that increased her marriageability. As a woman, she would not be encouraged to flourish in a career regardless of her potential. Despite his grand plans, Bulkley's ambitions for his family were not to come to fruition. A combination of bad management and poor decisions by the male members of the family led to its financial ruin; both father and son were imprisoned and the Bulkley women were sent out in the world alone. Had the Bulkleys put their faith, and money, into Margaret's future, perhaps their situation could have been very different.

Trouble for the family began in 1798 when tensions between nationalists and loyalists in Ireland reached a boiling point. The Society of United Irishmen was joined by 1,000 of Napoleon's French soldiers to rebel against British rule in Ireland. The rebellion was quickly crushed, but the ramifications for Catholic families, such as the Bulkleys, were far-reaching. A systematic removal of Catholics from positions of authority followed. Although there was suspicion of their political leanings amongst their neighbours, this did not appear to have affected custom at the grocery store. However, Jeremiah did lose his coveted position as an inspector at the city's weigh house, with its yearly salary of £140. This loss of income was a great blow to Jeremiah, who had borrowed heavily to start his business and provide a respectable education for his children, but it was just the start of the Bulkleys' misfortunes.

In 1801, their eldest son John was apprenticed to an attorney in Dublin, a position which cost his parents the grand sum of £400, almost three times the loss of income Jeremiah had suffered when losing his inspector employment. The Bulkleys were already deeply in debt but decided that investing in their son's career would be a worthwhile risk in financing their future, as well as his own. However, it soon became clear that John was not to be relied upon to support his family. He quickly decided that a career in law was not for him and wrote to his parents telling them of his wish to leave his studies. Instead, John informed them, he had fallen in love with a lady of genteel family and begged his parents to further assist him to marry her. Believing his son would want to continue his career once he settled down and that the family connections of Miss Ward would assist him in his success, Jeremiah gave John the astonishing sum of £1,200 in the form of properties including a farm, a house and offices as a marriage settlement, as well as £300 in cash. This was a sum they could ill afford. In addition, many of the properties had loans secured upon them, of which the creditors, realising what Jeremiah had done, began to demand immediate repayment. Jeremiah's gamble had not paid off. After his marriage, John left the law and set himself and his wife up as genteel farmers. Again, his lack of commitment would see this new venture fail and the Bulkleys were left with mounting debts that would eventually leave them destitute.

For Margaret, watching her parents descend into poverty and the security for her future disappear must have been dreadful and frustrating. As a middle-class woman, she was entirely reliant upon the men in her family. Her father had expected that her brother would assist Margaret in gaining a suitable marriage, and then her husband would take over her care. Margaret, and her mother Mary Ann, were powerless as they watched their menfolk slowly destroy their fortunes and security. But, unfortunately for Margaret, this was not the worst ordeal she would face in her young teens. Some time between 1801 and 1803, the Bulkleys welcomed into their family a baby girl named Juliana. There is no official record of her birth and the circumstances surrounding her arrival seems to have been quite sinister. Although Juliana was raised as Margaret's sister, Michael du Preez and Jeremy Dronfield in their recent work *Dr James Barry – A Woman Ahead of Her Time* suggest Margaret had been the victim of a sexual assault, which resulted in the pregnancy that much later Sophia Bishop would claim to detect on her body. At the time of the attack, if it took place, Margaret would have been between twelve and fourteen years old.

The candidate suggested as the perpetrator of this attack is Margaret's uncle, Redmond Barry. Redmond was a barely literate sailor with a 'volatile' temperament, which was evidently not softened by forty years at sea. In 1801, after no contact with his sister in over thirty years, he arrived in Cork demanding food and shelter from the Bulkleys. Mary Anne had always been intimidated by her brother, whom she knew to have violent and criminal tendencies so, despite their own financial problems, the family accepted him into their home. However, just a short time later the Bulkleys not only forcibly removed Redmond from their own home but also ran him out of town by using their connections to deny him any shelter in the area. Mary Anne also appears to have contacted her elder brother, James Barry, a successful painter in London, who had also refused any assistance to Redmond. In a letter to his brother, Redmond seems to confirm there had been an unpleasant incident that had led to his expulsion when he asks: 'Consider if you weare in My Situation and I in yours how you would Approve of my behaviour.'[5] What great crime had Redmond committed to turn the Bulkleys against him? Had he forced himself on the young Margaret, which had resulted in the birth of little Juliana?

James Barry of the Royal Academy, Life and Legacy

Mary Ann and Margaret had been let down or betrayed by almost every male member of their family. Jeremiah's bad judgment and John's selfishness had led to the loss of their business and financial security, while Redmond had possibly attacked and raped his own niece. In 1804, Mary Ann reached her limits when another bad financial decision by Jeremiah forced them out of their family home, a property she had brought into the marriage, while John had sold the property his parents had settled upon him and now had financial problems of his own. In desperation, she was forced to turn to her last remaining male relative for help, her estranged brother, James Barry, RA. Although Mary Ann had the legal right to live in the property, due to a clause in her father's will, her brother held the deed. If they could persuade him to sign this over to young Margaret, they could protect the property from her father's creditors. Deciding to take the lead in seeking their own salvation, and leaving Jeremiah and John to their own fates, Mary Ann and Margaret travelled together to London.

It was decided that Margaret would have more chance of success in persuading her uncle to assist them. Perhaps this was because she was beginning to show signs of the Barry genes with 'the same fine, fair, reddish hair' as James had had in his youth and 'the same large blue-green eyes and arched eyebrows... long curved nose... and the protruding chin'.[6] James Barry had always been the more ambitious of the Barry brothers. A talented artist, he met the philosopher Edmund Burke while in Dublin, who persuaded him to leave Ireland and set up his studio in London. His work was met with critical acclaim and, in 1773, he was admitted to the Royal Academy and elected Professor of Painting at the RA in 1782. It was through his association with Burke, and many of the great thinkers of the Romantic movement that Barry developed his liberal beliefs. He was a great believer in social reform and would often use his art to express his beliefs. He spoke out in favour of the French Revolution and the liberating of America from British rule. Most usefully to young Margaret and her mother, he strongly believed in the right of women to have an education, a belief shared by many of his associates and friends that would benefit Margaret in the future. Unfortunately for Mary Ann and Margaret, before they sought his assistance, Barry's fortunes and health had taken a decided turn for the worse.

Margaret arrived at her uncle's home at 36 Little Castle Street, West London, in June 1804. If she had an image of a glorious champion who would swoop down and rescue her and her mother from poverty, she was sorely disappointed. Number 36 was an unloved, dilapidated eyesore amongst the handsome townhouses around it. '[Window] panes grimy and cracked, some broken... the railings were rusted, and the steps down to the servants' entrance were clogged with litter, including several skeletons of stray dogs.' This condition was due to the fact that Barry was in the midst of a mental decline, which made him neglect his own health and appearance. He was suffering from a deep paranoia and as a result, refused to have any servants in his home to assist him. His eccentric and reclusive behaviour meant he was often the victim of pranks and vandalism. There were rumours that he was 'an old wizard, or necromancer or jew'.[7] It was obvious to Margaret that her uncle had fallen upon hard times. His volatile temper had seen him alienate his peers, which had resulted in his dismissal from his professorship and expulsion from the Royal Academy (the only artist to this day to have such action taken against him). Barry's paranoia and general mistrust of the world extended to his own family. Despite assurances that the two women were not after any financial assistance, and an apparent bond that seemed to develop between the artist and his niece over an appreciation of his art, he refused to sign the document and Margaret left her uncle's home distraught about her future. Eventually, it would be her connection to her uncle that would lead Margaret to her destiny as a doctor and soldier; a fact that she would commemorate by taking his name as her alias.

The Bulkley ladies would have to find a way to make their own living, but neither woman had any discernible skills that would allow for respectable employment. Margaret's education, interrupted as it was, was insufficient to become a governess, one of the few respectable positions available for a young lady of her class. Mary Ann was neither willing nor able to request help from her wayward son John and she had decided to leave her husband Jeremiah to his fate in a debtors' prison. It would not be long, however, before James Barry RA would become the saviour of the Bulkley ladies, although not in the manner they would have wished. In the early months of 1806 James Barry, former member of the Royal Academy, passed away leaving an astonishing estate, valued at possibly as much as £6.5 million in today's economy. The two remaining siblings, Mary Ann and Redmond, would fight a long, drawn-out court battle for the estate, which would last many years and stretch Mary Ann's resources almost to breaking point. Eventually, the siblings were proclaimed joint heirs to the estate and just three years later, Margaret Bulkley would disappear and a teenage James Barry would enrol as a medical student at Edinburgh University.

Mary Ann offered Redmond a cash settlement in exchange for Barry's back catalogue of work. One piece she was particularly interested in was a painting called *The Birth of Pandora*, considered the masterpiece of his collection; Mary Ann believed the sale of this painting would save them from destitution. While Mary Ann was concerned with financing their future, Margaret was focused on extending her education and improving her future employment prospects. She hoped to gain a position as a governess with a respectable family but her education had been cut short by her father's financial ruin. To gain a position she would need excellent skills in written English, French and Italian, as well as knowledge of geography, history, pianoforte and drawing. Margaret proved a diligent student but despite improving her skills, she still found it difficult to find a position due her relatively low-born background and the lack of references. Genteel families preferred their governesses to be from their background and there was competition for such positions. Margaret's search for work was unsuccessful. The sale of the art collection produced a disappointing £1,416 that Mary Anne was required to share with her brother Redmond, and after repaying the money she had borrowed in expectation of the sale, the ladies were left with just £408 to begin their future.

An Audacious Plan

Another plan would have to be hatched to secure a future for Margaret and in this, she turned to an old friend and benefactor of her uncle whose influence and connections would help to bring about the transformation of Margaret Bulkley, grocer's daughter, to James Barry, medical student. General Francisco de Miranda was born in Caracas to Spanish immigrant parents in 1750 and was a well-known ladies' man and republican. His lifelong pursuit of the independence of South America from Spanish rule earned him the title the 'Liberator of Venezuela'. General Miranda was also a firm follower of the ideals of Mary Wollstonecraft who advocated the education and rights of women, a belief the general shared with his friend James Barry RA. Margaret first met Miranda in early 1808 when he allowed her the use of his vast library to enhance her studies. Patricia Duncker suggests in her novel *James Miranda Barry* that Miranda and Margaret's mother were lovers and that the relationship between the general and the young Margaret was of a paternal nature. There is no evidence to support this theory, except for Miranda's reputation as a philanderer, but it is true that he had a strong influence on the course of Margaret's life. In addition to access to Miranda's vast library, Margaret had also begun to take care of his young son, perhaps in an effort to gain some experience, and so she began to spend an increasing amount of time in his home. As it became more apparent that a governess position would be difficult for Margaret to obtain, Miranda and a select number of other 'great liberal thinkers' formed an audacious plan. Margaret had shown great interest in the medical textbooks and so it was decided that she would train in medicine and once qualified, Dr Margaret Bulkley would practice openly in the newly liberated Venezuela with the support of its new leader, General Miranda. It is not known who first formulated this plan but Margaret and Mary Ann saw it as their salvation and agreed. One major obstacle stood in their way – no university in Britain or the colonies would admit a female student, so Margaret would not be permitted to study; but a young James Barry could.

The persona of 'James Barry' was created with the help of second-hand suits and the sewing skills of the two ladies. Margaret was more fortunate than many other female soldiers in disguise in that she had her mother to assist her in her transformation. James Barry needed to be reasonably well dressed to blend in with the other students at university. They were unable to have any suits properly fitted, as they could not visit a tailor without attracting questions, so second-hand gentlemen's suits were purchased and adjusted to fit Margaret's small frame. Then Margaret had to learn to feel and appear comfortable in these new clothes. The wool stockings, heavy tailcoats, high collars and tightly knotted cravats proved a difficult adjustment but the biggest difficultly she found was becoming accustomed to the male underwear, 'baggy around the chest where they ought to be snug, while below the hips they clung insolently where they should be loose.'[8] Her long red hair, the ultimate symbol of her femininity, was shorn into the Caesar style that was fashionable among young men at the time. She chose the name James Miranda Barry to honour both her mentor and the uncle whose money was financing her new life. Soon Mary Ann and her 'nephew' were ready to depart. The two travellers set sail from Millar's Wharf, Wapping, bound for Edinburgh on Thursday 30 November 1809. On board ship the young person who would now be known to all as 'James Barry' practised his new persona. He modelled his stance on the 'heroic bearing' of General Miranda, which was a straight spine, shoulders back and chin high with the left hand tucked behind the back in a fist. The young Barry's high voice, smooth skin and obvious self-consciousness in his own skin gave the impression to those he met aboard of a youth on the cusp of manhood. Margaret Bulkley was left behind in London and Mr James Barry emerged ready to begin his new life in Scotland

Edinburgh and Education

In 1809 Mr James Barry and his guardian and 'aunt' Mary Ann settled into their new lodgings at 6 Lothian Street, in Edinburgh. The building was part of the old town, populated by intellectuals, artists and students. Edinburgh was an inspired choice for Barry to reinvent himself. At the start of the nineteenth century the city was known as the 'modern Athens', and its reputation as a centre of culture had attracted many great thinkers to its streets; men such as poet Robert Burns, philosopher David Hume and William Smellie, who produced the first Encyclopaedia Britannica in 1768. Edinburgh University was respected as a centre of learning and for Barry, this was a particularly appropriate choice as Edinburgh medical school was considered very progressive and attracted a student body from across England, Ireland and the colonies. On a personal level for the Bulkleys, in Edinburgh they had had no acquaintances living nearby who may have recognised the girl in her disguise, but the name 'Barry' may have been recognisable to certain artists and writers, which would give the young student a level of credibility among the intellectuals who had set up home in the city. Perhaps the biggest factor that contributed to the choice of university was the fact that as a practising Catholic, Barry was barred from entering either Oxford or Cambridge, even as a male student.

Barry arrived at the University ready to start this exciting new chapter in his life. He was not required to produce any proof of identity or personal information of any kind to be admitted. The 'seemingly fresh-faced young man' simply enrolled as a student of medicine and literature, and paid his five shillings for the use of the university library.

Barry appeared to all to be a boy of about eleven years old, although Margaret was actually nineteen or twenty years old. There were concerns expressed about Barry's perceived youth but there were no regulations to prohibit the enrolment of such a young student (the Royal Commission on Scottish Universities that prohibited those under the age of twenty-one from obtaining a degree did not come into being until 1830) and she was able to enrol without difficulty.

Barry embarked upon a three-year intensive course of study that included surgery, chemistry, botany, midwifery, *materia medica*, anatomy, theory and practice of medicine and clinical medicine. He was also expected to study written and oral Latin, and philosophy but, unlike the medical students of today, the anatomy training he undertook was not considered a necessary part of a medical doctor's training. In fact, many of Barry's contemporaries and forbears would complete their medical training having never examined the inside of a human body. Instead, their training was garnered entirely from text books. A university education was, at this time, considered unnecessary to become a doctor. You could, instead, choose to be apprenticed to a practising doctor and learn the craft 'on the job'. Edinburgh was considered highly progressive as it offered both practical and theoretical studies and Barry's education benefited from great lecturers who taught the latest theories and techniques. Perhaps the limitations that had been placed on Margaret's education made her determined to wrest as much as she could from her new opportunities because, as Barry, she decided to supplement her training with private practical dissection lectures from the 'horrid' Mr Fyfe. These small private lectures would take place in Fyfe's own home where young medical students would cram themselves into a candle-lit front room to watch the systematic dismantling of a cadaver in order to gain close quarters knowledge of human anatomy.

The practice of dissection, at this time, was still in its infancy; but these private lessons proved to be so popular with students that lecturers often performed two a day. Eventually the demand for cadavers began to far outweigh the supply. The Murder Act of 1752 decreed that the bodies of executed murderers were to be given to the surgeons for dissection. This was seen as an additional punishment for the condemned man, as it was believed by many that to desecrate the body affected the soul. For some, the prospect of dissection was even more fearful than the execution itself. Friends and family were known to attack the gallows that held the body of their loved one; they would steal the corpse to prevent it from being violated by dissection. In 1832, the Anatomy Act also gave surgeons access to the unclaimed poor but this perpetuated the idea that the indignity of dissection only happened to the lowliest in society and, as the practice of dissection grew more popular in intellectual circles, there was still a distinct shortage of legally available bodies. During his studies, it is entirely possible that Barry would have witnessed, or participated in, the dissection of cadavers that had been sourced through less legitimate means. Thieves known as 'resurrection men' would seek out freshly dug graves to source corpses that were less than three days old. Some more brutal men, such as the infamous Burke and Hare, would even take to murder to supply their lucrative business. It was perhaps fitting then that after committing sixteen murders for such purposes, Burke's body found its way onto the dissection table of Edinburgh Medical School following his execution in January 1829.

Margaret's deception necessitated that she maintain a distance from her fellow students. She was unable to cultivate any real closeness with her classmates for fear they would see through her disguise. She practised hard to conceal her femininity, she studied her male stance and posture, and would wear an 'all-embracing, all-concealing surtout' rather than the more fashionable shooting coats to conceal her feminine figure, but she was never able to fully shake off the appearance of general effeminacy.[9] One friend she did make during her studies was fellow student John Jobson, who later recalled that he had once attempted to teach Barry to box but that he had refused to raise his hands to the correct position and instead would inexplicably protect his chest at all times. Despite this, Jobson claimed neither he nor his peers had ever suspected Margaret's true gender and instead thought her a mere child attempting to fit in with her much older classmates.

Another person she was able to garner some form of companionship from was her new benefactor David Steuart Erskine, 11th Earl of Buchan, who had been an admirer of her uncle. On introduction to the young Barry, Buchan had taken an immediate liking to the precocious young man and decided to take him under his wing. His patronage gave Barry's identity legitimacy among his peers and professors. Buchan was vocal in his support of the case for the education of women, declaring his belief that women should be entitled 'an education no way differing from that of men'.[10] He does not appear to have been aware of Margaret's true identity.

In a letter to General Miranda, Margaret urges Miranda not to disclose her secret to Buchan.

> As Lord B---- nor anyone here knows anything about Mrs Bulkley's Daughter, I trust my dear General that neither you or the Doctor will mention in any of your correspondence anything about my Cousin's friendship and [care] for me.[11]

After three years' diligent study, Barry was ready to complete his examinations but before he could take this momentous step, the perception of his extreme youth almost brought all his hard work and application to nought. The university senate initially refused to examine a student they believed could be as young as twelve (Margaret was twenty-three years old at this time). She was again forced to use her connections to intervene on her behalf. Lord Buchan pointed out to the university senate that there were no regulations that dealt with a student's age. Without his intervention, all Margaret's plans could have come to nothing.

In July of 1812 James Barry stood before his professors and fifty-eight fellow students to take his final examination. This consisted of an oral presentation and a verbal defence of his dissertation which, like all other written and oral exams, took place entirely in Latin, a language Margaret had struggled to master. The subject of her dissertation was an unusual one, *De Merocele vel Hernia Crurali* by Jacobus Barry was a study of the femoral hernia, which was a condition almost entirely confined to women. Barry even went so far as to repeat the bold assertion that the wearing of corsets was a contributing factor to this condition. None of his peers seems to have questioned why an apparently young teenage boy would choose such a female orientated condition as a subject of study. Barry dedicated his dissertation to his two most enthusiastic benefactors, General Francisco Miranda and the Earl of Buchan, in gratitude for their assistance and support. Margaret also included an impertinent quote from Greek playwright Menander which declared 'Do not consider whether what I say is a young man speaking, but whether my discussion with you is that of a man of understanding.'[12] On the surface this appeared to be a rebuke aimed at the senate members who had questioned her abilities because of her perceived youth, but the assertion that a person's knowledge and understanding is more important than their physical traits takes on deeper meaning when it is understood that the speaker is, in fact, a woman. Margaret was challenging the prejudices of the senate and the establishment, probably relishing the moment when she would reveal herself to the world as Dr Margaret Bulkley, MD.

Dr James Barry was deemed qualified by the prestigious professors at Edinburgh University, who had no idea that they had just passed the first qualified female physician in the UK. However, her medical degree had not come cheap and the Bulkley's finances were completely depleted. They were now in so much debt that their creditors prevented them from leaving the city until their bills were settled. There were still further funds to find before Barry could obtain his diploma. The exams had cost £10, and there was a staggering £24 3s charge for the diploma itself, but he was now officially qualified and ready to begin the next stage of the plan and join General Miranda in the newly liberated Venezuela. Unfortunately, Barry's success had not been mirrored by the General.

While Barry had been studying hard, a coup had occurred in Venezuela in 1810, without Miranda's participation, and he was called to return to Caracas, ostensibly to assist with the new government. However, his long absence from his own country had soured many of his countrymen against him and his idealism was no longer acceptable to some in the new regime. One such revolutionary whose authoritarianism clashed with Miranda's ideals was Simón Bolivar, a former protégé of Miranda's. Bolivar betrayed his former mentor to the Spanish authorities, who immediately arrested Miranda for treason. He spent the rest of his life in a dungeon in Cadiz. With no position available for her in Venezuela, there would be no glorious revelation of the true identity of Dr Barry, as Margaret Bulkley, MD, and no legitimate position for a female physician. Margaret had lost her place in the world and so Dr James Barry would have to remain.

James Barry returned to London in October 1812. Now he believed improving his skills was the key to his future so despite their precarious financial position, he borrowed heavily to continue his studies. He signed on to study surgical practices with Richard Whitfield at a cost of £20. He also paid ten guineas for anatomy and surgery courses from the pioneering Sir Astley Cooper of Guy's Hospital and surgeon Henry Cline from St Thomas's Hospital. It was at St Thomas's that James Barry would develop his compassion for the lower-class patient. The hospital's motto *Miseratione Non Mercede* translates as 'for compassion, not for gain'; the hospital claimed to offer treatment for all 'without distinction, or regard to any other consideration than the extent and degree of the sufferings'.[13] This was provided, of course, that the patient could pay the 3s 6d admission fee, which was increased to 10s 6d if the patient has a 'foul' venereal condition. Patients also required a sponsor, either a family member or church warden, who was required to provide clean linen for the patient and one guinea for burial should they succumb to their illnesses.

Diet was a particular focus at St Thomas's, with all patients given specially prescribed diets depending on their condition. A full diet included beef, mutton and broth; milk diets of rice pudding, milk and bread were prescribed for gout and tuberculosis patients, and finally there were the minimum 'dry' and 'fever' diets. There were, however, no vegetables served with any meals as their health benefits were not yet fully understood. The quality of ingredients was also carefully controlled, with particular emphasis on flour and yeast. The beer that was served was brewed on the hospital premises so that 'no adulterous drug [could enter] its composition'.[14] Barry carried the lessons he learnt at St Thomas's with him throughout his career when he would continue to promote healthy eating among his patients, particularly the benefit of a milk-rich diet over a heavy meat-laden one. This procedure was also advocated by Florence Nightingale. At this point, Barry also began to pay close attention to his own diet and followed a regime of strict vegetarianism and virtual temperance for the rest of his life. St Thomas's also attempted to assist in the moral health of its patients by insisting they adhere to the strict discipline of the ward and its segregation of the sexes. The hospital even provided separate operating theatres for female patients to preserve their modesty. How would the hospital authorities have felt if they had realised one of their promising new student doctors was a woman?

Margaret was greatly expanding her knowledge at St Thomas's, but her studies there were expensive and the Bulkley women were already reduced to living on money borrowed from both their own friends and those of her namesake uncle. Her mother had failed to find a buyer for her uncle's masterpiece, the *Pandora,* at a price that would save the two women, and requests began to be made for repayment of their loans. The stress had stretched Mary Ann's nerves to the limit. Realising the situation was untenable Margaret formulated a new plan. She turned her eyes towards the military. Such a career would give her financial security, a purpose, and a chance to practise medicine in the real world, but it came with great risk. She would have to pass through the scrutiny of recruitment without disclosing her secret.

Dr James Miranda Barry, MD, Military Surgeon

In June 1813, James Barry, MD, entered the offices of the Army Medical Board to apply for the position of Regimental Assistant Surgeon with the British Army. He was interviewed at the War Office by the Deputy Secretary at War, after which he was provided with a letter of introduction (for which he paid a fee of 5 s), requesting that Barry be examined 'whether he is fitly qualified for the above station'.[15]

The establishment to conduct the examination was the Royal College of Surgeons. The RCS was established in 1800, in Lincoln's Inn Field, London, with a mandate to distinguish the trained surgeon from the barber-surgeon. At this time, there were few laws in place that prevented poorly trained practitioners from setting up shop. There were also many instances in which these barely competent men were appointed to surgical posts within the military establishment. The RCS was attempting to combat this by assessing the knowledge of military applicants by oral examination. Those who were deemed fit to pass were issued with a diploma proclaiming their proficiency. Each applicant was questioned on their education, the professors they studied under, and their knowledge of anatomy and surgery. They were also questioned about their age. This was a subject which, for Margaret, was a complicated issue. She was twenty-four but had the appearance of a fourteen-year-old boy. She gave her age to the examiner as eighteen and if there were any doubts about her statement, they gave no indication of it; she was charged a further 5 *s* by the college secretary, and 2*s* 6*d* by the porter. Enlisting was proving to be an expensive business.

In 1808, the Parliamentary Commission of Military Enquiry had granted sweeping reforms to the Army Medical Board to combat the appointment of unsuitable and barely qualified individuals to medical posts in the British Army. In 1810 all members of the board were replaced and more stringent regulations were put in place. These were all honourable intensions but, as Michael du Preez and Jeremy Dronfield explain in *Dr James Barry – A Woman Ahead of her Time,* in practice, the examination was 'childishly easy' to pass. Barry stood before the eight examiners, plus the master of the college, ready to demonstrate his skills and knowledge. Many were elderly and old fashioned in both dress and attitudes but two faces were familiar to Barry – his former teacher Henry Cline and surgeon George Chandler, whom he had worked under at St Thomas's. The culture of favouritism was still strong within the board, despite the attempts to stamp it out by the reform commission, and in this case, it may have worked in Barry's favour. Barry was subjected to terse questioning which, unlike his medical exam, was in English, to which he replied confidently. Any nerves Barry may have felt would have been misplaced as it was very rare for candidates to be failed; examiner George Chandler had only ever failed one candidate prior to Barry's encounter with him. He was soon deemed competent by the board and granted certification, which cost a further two guineas. The board then sent a letter to the War Office which stated,

> To the Right Honourable the Secretary at War,
> …We have examined Dr James Barry, and find him qualified to serve as assistant surgeon to any regiment in his majesty's service. We are your most obedient servants, etc. etc.[16]

For Margaret, this must have been a great vindication of her hard work and ability, but perhaps also frustrating in that she would never have been allowed to stand before them under her own name.

Just one more obstacle stood between Barry and his goal. The Army Medical Board examination took place in their headquarters in Berkley Street on the following Monday. In this final test, he would be quizzed on his hospital experience with particular emphasis on anatomy, medicine, chemistry, pharmacy and botany. This board was a much younger crowd, staffed by experienced, qualified physicians who, at the time of Barry's application, had already made vast improvements to the medical services of the armed forces since their appointment in 1810. They had reopened hospitals, improved the supply chain and appointed qualified staff to suitable positions. Again, Barry passed with relative ease and was granted the post of hospital assistant.

During her laborious enlistment process, Margaret had been subjected to various mental examinations but she had not had to endure a physical examination of any kind. As an officer (and supposedly a gentleman) her word that she was in good health was considered enough and therefore examination was deemed unnecessary and indeed, would have been considered as doubting the word of a gentleman. Of course, an examination to check gender was never considered necessary. It would be sixty years before officer candidates were subjected to a physical examination like the other ranks.

On 5 July 1813, hospital assistant James Barry, MD, began his first assignment at the Chelsea Military Hospital. The Army Medical Department that Barry joined did not have the same status that the Royal Army Medical Corps does today. Medical officers did not have official military status, instead they were linked to a comparative military rank – surgeons were the equivalent to the rank of captain, assistant-surgeons were at second lieutenant level, while hospital assistants (the rank Barry held) were considered below this but were still at the level of a commissioned officer. There were two career routes to take within the AMD; the staff and hospital surgery route, or regimental surgeon. Margaret chose to enlist in the role of staff officer, which almost guaranteed she would be able to serve overseas; it also enabled her to move positions frequently, which would be instrumental in maintaining her secret. Again, her choice would leave little room for close, personal relationships. In leaving London she was also leaving her mother, her final tie to her female identity. There is no evidence that she was ever addressed as Margaret again.

At York Military Hospital in Chelsea, Barry had his first taste of the conditions he would be working in as a military doctor. Under the direction of surgeons, he found himself dealing with overcrowding so severe that inmates were often forced to take shelter in any room they could find. They would bed down on the floor of the hospital chapel while they awaited treatment and those unable to procure even that, spilled out into the village streets. Irish soldier, James Ewart, described the scene in 1814 in which he estimated 11,000 sick and wounded were living rough outside the hospital, hoping for treatment and to be found eligible for a Chelsea pension.[17] The conditions for staff were almost as appalling as for the patients. Their bedding was 'damp and dirty' and the food often caused chronic constipation. It is probable that this reinforced the lessons Barry had learnt at St Thomas's about the importance of a good diet. However, the daily chaos that the tired and overworked staff worked in meant there was little danger of Barry's true identity being discovered. He simply worked hard, kept to himself and made few close acquaintances, a pattern he would repeat often in his career. Barry's youthful appearance again began to cause consternation among his superiors. He had been delayed in his assignment to a regiment due to doubts being expressed that he was eighteen years old, as claimed (Margaret was actually twenty-four). These doubts were again expressed when she arrived at Plymouth Military Hospital and, as Barry, she again called upon her old patron, Lord Buchan.

It became clear to Margaret that her perceived youth would continue to be a problem for the foreseeable future so she would need to come up with another solution to combat it. Instead of denying the charges against her, she decided to 'confess' that she was born in 1799 – making her only fifteen years old. She thereby perpetuated an image as a child prodigy, backed up by her continual demonstration of her skills as a physician. Once this reputation was established, Barry was no longer questioned about his age because what had been a potential barrier had been turned into a career-enhancing advantage.

A New Sponsor

On 7 December 1815, Barry was promoted to assistant-surgeon and appointed to his first overseas post, in Cape Town Garrison. To mark the occasion, he commissioned a miniature portrait of himself in uniform. Margaret's previous mentor, General Miranda, had perished in his Spanish prison cell just a month earlier, but it would not be long before she encountered another whom she would hold in the same esteem, His Excellency, Lord Charles Somerset, the Governor of the Cape of Good Hope.

Lord Charles had lost his wife of twenty-seven years, just a year after they arrived in the Cape. His grief at Elizabeth's loss was great, as was his anger at the three doctors who had failed to comprehend the seriousness of his wife's condition. They assured Lord Charles, right up until the end. that 'there was not the slightest cause for apprehension'.[18] Barry, aware of how important a good sponsor could be to his career, was determined to charm his way into Lord Charles's good graces. Armed with a letter of recommendation from Lord Buchan, he introduced himself as soon as possible and it was not long before Barry was able to prove his worth. Lord Charles's eldest daughter Georgiana was taken ill and Barry's reputation as a prodigy persuaded Lord Charles to seek this doctor's assistance despite his mistrust of the medical profession. Barry's treatment of Miss Georgiana demonstrated the methods that would characterise his career. Firstly, he found that patients responded better when they had confidence in their doctor's abilities so he ensured he exuded confidence to the point of arrogance. Secondly, Barry dismissed all previous treatments and medications that may have been prescribed. This prevented any harm from incompatible treatments but also had the additional effect of seeming to elevate his skills above the previous physicians'. If the treatment was successful, he was vindicated; if not, the case was obviously hopeless. Next, Barry would look at the conditions the patient was living in. He advocated open windows to allow air and sunlight into sickrooms, which were usually kept hot and stifling. Barry was unaware of germs but he was unwittingly practising many modern methods. In the case of Georgiana, Barry found a young lady of a sensitive nature, with no occupation, who was grief-stricken after her mother's death. Barry prescribed a change of scenery, more metal simulation and 'soothing of the emotions'.[19] In modern terms, Georgiana was depressed. The successful treatment of the Governor's daughter not only sealed the newly-arrived doctor's reputation in the Cape but his place at Lord Charles's table.

Reform and Courting Controversy

Just three months after he arrived in the Cape, Barry was appointed personal physician to the Governor and invited to accompany Lord Charles and his party on a grand tour of the Cape Colony. He was now part of the inner circle. The party travelled through the interior of Africa, where Barry was subject to an incredible array of sights and dangers he had never faced before. A lion entered their camp near Mossel Bay and snatched a young Khoi-khoi boy while he slept. Luckily, the boy was found just a few yards from the camp with only minor bites and scratches. But for Margaret there were greater dangers than the physical threat of animal attack; it was the risk of anyone discovering she was a woman and, in a rare moment of emotional vulnerability, she allowed someone close enough to her to possibly expose her secret.

During a stay in Knysna, the party was housed on the 25,000 acre estate of Englishman George Rex, which also housed several dozen of his slaves. Barry was a lifelong anti-slavery advocate and took particular interest in Rex's children, all of whom were born of his relationship with his former slave Johanna Rosina. Barry taught the children lessons and was physically affectionate in a way that was unusual for the standoffish person Barry had become but completely in character for the one-time governess Margaret. Perhaps she was beginning to realise that her decision to live as a man would mean she was unlikely to have a family of her own one day. The danger of the closeness she had allowed became apparent when the children began to call her the *Kapok Nooientjie*, which meant little kapok maiden. The children had probably noticed the kapok stuffing in her jacket that Margaret used to bulk up her figure and to make her appear more masculine. The nickname suggests the children had seen through her disguise and detected her true gender. (Alternatively, the nickname simply means Barry strutted around like a bantam.) Barry would never allow anyone that close to him again.

On 7 December 1817, after the party had returned to the governor's home, Barry was appointed as the official physician to his household, granted a home in the grounds of Government House, and a salary of 600 rixdollars. Barry was also appointed as the Second Member of the Vaccine Institution, which provided him with an additional salary of 1,200 rixdollars. Including his military pay of 7s 6d per day, this placed his annual salary at just over £270, an amount that would be approximately £200,000 today. The days of unpaid bills and financial instability seemed behind her; however, Margaret never forgot the lessons her early experiences of poverty had taught her and was always known to be frugal with her money.

Barry's standing with the Governor made him popular both as a physician and as a dinner guest. He attended civic dinners, balls, hunting parties and was an avid theatre-goer. His dress was known to be ostentatious, even amongst the colourful, upper-class society. Surgeon-General McKinnon, who was a dinner guest with Barry, described him as 'a pleasant and agreeable man. He neither cursed nor swore, but behaved himself like a gentleman.'[20] Barry also developed a reputation as a flirt who would always dance with the ladies at a ball. He had an air of flamboyance and pomposity, and would often be seen in a 'coat of the latest pea-green Hayne, a satin waistcoat' and a pair of breeches whose tight-fitting nature led to them being known as 'inexpressibles'.[21] On duty, he often wore a plumed cocked hat, long spurs and a large sword. While many sniggered at the short doctor, who wore 3 inch false soles to give him extra height and stuffed his jacked with cotton wool for extra bulk, they put this down to vanity rather than suspecting the truth. After the exposure of her secret, many came forward claiming to have known Barry's true sex all along, but the legitimacy of these tales is suspect, published as they were after his death and after his secret identity was revealed. As Barry, Margaret was no stranger to controversy, especially when piqued; on one occasion, she even found herself in a duel with a fellow officer while defending the honour of a lady. After her death, Sir Josias Cloete, who became friends with Barry after their altercation, wrote, 'I am the only officer in the British Army who has ever fought a duel with a woman.'[22]

In the autumn of 1818, Lord Charles was diagnosed with a severe case of typhus and dysentery. Under Barry's ministrations, he was able to make a complete recovery. This cemented Barry's place in the family's affections and his reputation in the Cape as a medical prodigy. As a result, he attracted many wealthy patients who were very vocal in their praise of the odd but highly skilled doctor, particularly of his bedside manner. But Barry did not restrict his medical attention to the ruling classes. He took particular interest in those whom he felt could not fend for themselves. On 18 March 1822 Barry was promoted to the post of Colonial Medical Inspector, meaning that in just ten years Dr Barry, the female in disguise, had risen to the highest medical appointment in the colony. As Inspector, Dr Barry would go on to create sweeping reforms in all the public institutions under his control including medical facilities, prison hospital wards, and leper colonies.

Barry's advanced methods included insisting on daily changes of linen and cleanliness, while being aware of the dangers of overcrowding, bad drainage and lack of ventilation, and the benefits of good nutrition and fresh air and exercise. He was, in fact, practising such methods long before the more celebrated advocate of hygiene in medicine, Florence Nightingale.

Barry also tackled controversial issues of administration, such as the selling of medication by unlicensed apothecaries. In instigating his policies, Barry was not afraid to ruffle feathers and often found himself at odds with the authorities, merchants and medical staff. In the case of legalising local sales of medicines, Barry had pushed the boundaries of his power and found himself being slapped down by those above him. Local apothecary, Karl Liesching, had complained to the Colonial Office when Barry had refused to grant him a licence to sell medicines. Before Barry's appointment as Colonial Medical Inspector, such a licence was not required. Barry had objected to the fact that Liesching did not hold a European medical degree, although he had trained as a chemist in the Cape. Barry's decision was overruled, to which he reacted with undiplomatic anger. Barry's tendency to overreach the boundaries of his responsibility and his inability to use tact when dealing with opposition, eventually led to the position of Colonial Inspector being abolished. Barry had often turned to Lord Charles during his spats with authority and his level of loyalty led to some people questioning the nature of their relationship. Contemporary Samuel Hudson recorded details of this scandal in his journal in June 1824, in which Lord Charles was publicly accused of committing 'unnatural practices' with his young doctor. It was, perhaps, the embarrassment of the scandal that led to Lord Charles's lack of support during the Liesching affair.

History in the Making

Barry was still out of political favour when the incident that would secure him a place in medical history occurred on Tuesday 25 July 1826. He was called out into a Cape Town mid-winter storm to the bedside of Wilhelmina Munnik. The wife of a wealthy snuff manufacturer, Wilhelmina was in labour with their first child but things were not progressing well. The midwife had supervised the labour for a day and a night but there was no sign of the baby's arrival and with the mother's energy reserves failing, the life of both mother and child were now in danger. It was decided that it was time to call in a surgeon to end her suffering. Barry had come to the family's attention after he lodged with Wilhelmina's widowed sister and was known to be an unorthodox but brave doctor and, above all, successful in his treatments. Barry arrived with his obstetrical instruments, which included scissors, specula and forceps, as well as extensive knowledge of surgery and midwifery. Upon examining the patient, he found the foetus was alive but unable to pass through the cervix and his hope that he could use forceps to assist the safe arrival of the infant soon faded. It was clear he would have to use more invasive methods. The usual procedure for a physician faced with such a scenario was to perform a craniotomy, the surgical perforation of the skull of a dead fetus to ease delivery. This was a 'horrific procedure that involved extracting the foetus piecemeal from the mother with sharp hooks, knives, saws and forceps'.[23] Such a procedure was designed to save the mother at the expense of the child. Barry decided to take a bolder and more dangerous route – he would perform a caesarean section in an attempt to save both lives. At this point, there were no verified cases of both mother and child surviving such a procedure within the British Empire.

With no effective anaesthesia or antiseptic yet available, any invasive procedure was a danger to the patient. Surgical training at the time was restricted to operations on the extremities as it was considered impossible to successfully treat the body cavities with the knife. Students were taught that 'the abdomen, the chest and the brain will be forever shut from the intrusion of the wise and human surgeon.'[24] Barry was also aware that in such a situation, infection could be the biggest danger to the patient and the stifling room, filled with relatives and servants in which Wilhelmina was housed, could be deadly. The room was cleared of extraneous people. The midwife and servants were kept to assist with the procedure and were instructed to hold down the patient by her arms and ankles. A leather strap was then placed in her mouth to stifle any cries of pain. An incision would then have been made of about 8–10 inches. The pain must have been unbearable for Mrs Munnik, but a healthy boy was soon brought into the world and the race to save the mother began. Barry again chose to go against accepted methods by suturing the wound. It was erroneously believed in those days that the muscles of the uterus would spontaneously close, which often resulted in death from blood loss or infection. Barry's decision saved the Mrs Munnik's life and the doctor was hailed as a hero by the family. Had those at the birth known that the saviour of the mother and child was in fact a woman herself, how much more astonished would they have been by her skills as a physician? The normally money-orientated Barry refused his fee and instead as payment requested that the child be named after him. James Barry Munnik was baptised on 20 August 1826 in the Evangelical Lutheran Church, Cape Town, with Barry standing as godfather. The name was passed down through the family until eventually it was held by General James Barry Munnik Hertzog, Prime Minister of South Africa and a promoter of apartheid, an incongruous connection as the original James Barry was a strong anti-slavery advocate. A miniature portrait of Barry is still a treasured possession of the family.

On 26 September 1828, the now full staff surgeon Barry was aboard the *Eliza Jane* bound for a new post in Mauritius. However, life on the island would not be as kind to the doctor as it had been in his previous posting. The governor was not impressed by Barry's reputation for bucking authority and appointed a junior assistant surgeon over him as the principal medical officer. Barry found that without the support of the governor, he was often passed over both as a physician and in society. He was later posted to Jamaica and to St Helena. His constant complaints to the authorities were met with derision and his career began to suffer. Barry even went so far as to write directly to the Secretary of State at the War Office with reference to a disagreement with the Assistant Commissary General over supplies, an action that led to arrest and court martial. Barry was eventually acquitted but his crime of superseding the authority of his superiors left him out of favour in the military community and he was even referred to as 'an embarrassment of the Government'.[25] Barry would never again enjoy the respect and the standing in the community he had enjoyed under Lord Charles. On 2 April 1838, after yet another clash with Governor General Middlemore, Barry was sent home to England under arrest and in disgrace. The exact nature of the crime is unknown as Middlemore's letter to Lord Genleg gives us no clue, but there is also no evidence that an official Court of Inquiry ever took place.

Despite Barry's obvious lack of diplomacy, his skills as a doctor cannot be questioned. Each time he departed from a posting, the condition of those who had been under his care notably declined and even those who stood in opposition to him never questioned his medical abilities.

For the next few years Dr Barry continued to serve his country in the West Indies, covering areas including Barbados, British Guiana, Trinidad and Tobago, Grenada, St Vincent, St Lucia, Dominica, Antigua, Montserrat, St Kitt's and Nevis, and Tortola. Here Barry was kept busy treating diseases such as yellow fever, prevalent among the troops in the area. As Margaret was beginning to age, her smooth face and shrill voice could no longer be put down to youth and there were those who began to suspect the truth. Dr McCowan, who served with Barry in Trinidad, wrote after his death 'he was always suspected of being female from his effeminate features and voice, and neither beard nor whiskers'.[26] This may be an overstatement but it is likely it became more difficult for Margaret to conceal her true gender. In 1845, the aging doctor was struck down with yellow fever and avoided treatment for as long as possible. Eventually Barry was forced to call for help from a fellow physician. It was clear that Barry believed the illness would be fatal as he gave specific instructions to the doctor that should he die, his body was to be covered by a sheet and not 'inspected or disturbed' before burial. It was clear that Margaret intended to take her secret to the grave. This proved to be unnecessary this time, and she made a full recovery and was able to continue her good work.

The Crimean War and 'The Lady with the Lamp'

In March 1853, the British government announced its intention to intervene due to Russia's attitude to Turkey in the Crimea. At the outbreak of war late that year, Barry was stationed in Corfu but immediately volunteered his services. So far his military service had seen him tackle tropical diseases, epidemics and the general health of those troops under his care, but he had not seen the casualties of war since the Jamaican uprising of 1832. His request to be posted to the front lines of the conflict was denied but authorities accepted his request that casualties be shipped to a hospital on Corfu, where he could provide medical care.

HMS *Dunbar* transported more than 500 casualties for treatment to Corfu in February 1855. Barry was forced to commandeer private houses and administrative buildings to help the overwhelmed hospitals. The medical teams saw patients with 'festering gunshot wounds, cholera, dysentery, malnutrition and acute frostbite'. But even in these makeshift wards, in this appalling situation, Barry demanded the same level of cleanliness and order, in stark contrast to the nightmare of conditions found in the Crimea. His reputation was consolidated by his success; of 462 patients, only seventeen died. Within a fortnight, fifty-three were back on full duty and a further sixty-three were back to 'slight duty' fitness.

By April, 213 men were passed as fit to return to duty but Barry attempted to ensure an extended period of convalescence before they returned to the front lines. He was overruled by Major General Macintosh and many were immediately shipped onto overcrowded troopships on their way to Turkey. Barry had one of his infamous outbursts of outrage at the apparent disrespect for the welfare of the troops and threatened to write to Lord Raglan, Commander-in-Chief of the British Army. Macintosh did not believe Barry's assertion that he had influence with such a high-profile man. Raglan's reply, although supporting Macintosh's actions, relieved him of his misconception:

> I am sorry to learn that Dr Barry, of whose zeal for service I entertain no doubt, should have thought fit to interfere in a matter... which rested with you alone.[27]

Dr Barry was not the only healer in the Crimea who was attempting to improve the conditions of the common soldier. The famous Florence Nightingale was also making her presence known to authorities in her attempt to bring order to the cholera-ridden, overcrowded and filthy tents that served as wards on the frontline. But despite their apparent similarities, they did not hit it off when they met in 1855. Despondent about being denied a frontline position, Barry decided to take leave in Scutari and volunteered at the military hospital at the sharp end of the war. There he encountered the other champion of the troops. Nightingale was at that time out in the sun, with only a cap to protect herself and Barry, in his usual tactless manner, proceeded to publicly scold her. Nightingale, herself known to be a stern figure, stated Barry was 'the most hardened creature I ever met throughout the army'.[28] After a lifetime of campaigning for reform, Dr Barry was never given the honour and fame that Miss Nightingale achieved. It can be argued that the difference between the two women was that Margaret, in her Dr Barry persona, never fully understood the need for diplomacy as Miss Nightingale did.

Decline and Death

Barry's final military posting was to Canada where the cold climate was very different from the tropical ones he was used to. However, this did not keep the ever-diligent Dr Barry from performing his duties. He visited his charges in the snow and continued a tireless campaign for reform and 'civilised soldiering', which in this posting included the need for separate rooms for married soldiers, water pipes, a library and the introduction of athletics. On 14 May 1859, Barry was again struck down by illness, this time with flu and bronchitis, and was forced to return to Liverpool to recuperate. Margaret was seventy years old at this time and after a medical board review, Dr Barry had to retire from the military after more than four decades of service. For Barry, the end of his career precipitated a slow decline in health and he died at 4 a.m. on 25 July 1865 at home, with only his servant and a dog for company. It was only after Barry's death that the truth of her true gender came to light.

Once Dr Barry's true nature was revealed there was, of course, much controversy. However, the reaction was far more hostile than it was towards many other women soldiers in disguise. Hannah Snell and Kit Cavenaugh were both celebrated for their exploits, and gained royal approval through official recognition and pensions. In contrast, Barry's revelation was met with denial, and his records were ordered to be sealed for 100 years. Was it because Barry had died out of favour, having upset too many members of the establishment? Or is it because while Snell and Cavenaugh had infiltrated the lower orders of the male preserve of the military, Barry had attained a position of high authority? Some former colleagues attempted to suggest that Barry was not a woman at all but 'an imperfectly developed man',[29] preferring to completely deny her gender rather than accept that she could be a woman, a doctor and a soldier. It is clear that Barry wished to die as he had lived for most of his life, as a man.

Notes

1. Letter to *Whitehaven News* 7 September 1865 from Dr McGowan who served with Barry in Trinidad as found in Rae, Isabel, *The Strange Story of Dr James Barry* (Aberdeen, The University Press, 1958), p. 92

2. Letter from Margaret Ann Bulkley to John Bulkley, undated (probably September 1808) as found in Du Preez, Michael & Jeremy Dronfield, *Dr James Barry – A Woman Ahead of Her Time* (London, Oneworld Publications, 2016), p. 50

3. as found in Rae p. 1

4. Du Preez & Dronfield, p. 5

5. ibid, p. 59

6. ibid, *p. 11–12*

7. ibid, p. 14

8. ibid p. 59

9. ibid, p. 75

10. ibid, p. 79

11. Rae, p. 5

12. Holmes, p. 39

13. Golding, Benjamin, *An Historical Account of St Thomas's Hospital, Southwark* (London: Longman, 1819), p. 224

14. Golding, p. 235

15. Dunne, Charles, *The Chirurgical Candidate or, Reflections on Education: Indispensable to Complete Naval, Military, and Other Surgeons* (London: Samuel Highley, 1808), p. 48

16. Du Preez, Michael & Jeremy Dronfield, *p.* 100

17. Gleig, George Robert (ed.), *The Veterans of Chelsea Hospital,* vol. 3 (London: Richard Bentley, 1819), p. 21-23

18. Letter from Somerset to Beaufort, 16 September 1815 as quoted in Du Preez, p. 122

19. Du Preez, p. 123

20. Rae, p. 26

21. Holmes, p. 67

22. Sir Josias Cloete to Sir William Macintosh, as found in Rae, p. 29

23. Holmes, 162

24. ibid

25. Rae, p. 79

26. Rae, p. 92

27. Holmes, p. 242

28. Du Preez, p. 340

29. Rae, p. 115

7

DEBORAH SAMPSON GANNETT AKA ROBERT SHURTLIFF – HEROINE OF THE REVOLUTIONARY WAR

She has served in the character of a soldier...
with activity, alertness, chastity and valour[1]

Towards the end of the American Revolutionary War (1775–83), in 1782, on a hospital ward in Philadelphia, the beds were filled to capacity. However, war injuries were not the reason most patients were there but rather a malignant fever that was sweeping through the state. Patients succumbed to their illness at such a rate that the undertaker was as much a presence in the hospital halls as were the doctors and nurses, and corpses would be removed from their beds for burial only to be immediately replaced with yet another patient. One such victim was a young soldier of the Continental Army who lay in his bed so motionless and 'insensible' that the too-eager undertakers mistook him for dead. As they stood over the soldier's body, arguing over his valuables, a frantic nurse attempted to stop the potential catastrophe. Dr Barnabas

Binney was called to intervene on the patient's behalf and during his brief examination of the patient, he heard an almost inaudible soft gurgle, which was enough to prove to him that this body was not yet ready for the grave. Binney then placed his hand inside the patient's tunic to listen for a heartbeat where he made the even more surprising discovery that although undoubtedly a serving member of the Continental Army, the patient was a young woman.

On 17 December 1760 in the small farming village of Plympton, Massachusetts, a daughter was born to the already financially embarrassed Jonathan and Deborah Sampson. The child was to be the fifth child in a family of seven, and was named after her mother. Despite the current humble circumstances of the family, young Deborah Sampson was born of a great ancestry. Her father was a descendant of *Mayflower* crew member John Alden, while her mother was the great-granddaughter of William Bradford, former Governor of Plymouth Colony. But unfortunately for the young Deborah and her siblings, the family's circumstances had drastically declined, and at the time of her birth, Deborah's father worked as a labourer. Work was often difficult to come by and so Jonathan would often be forced to travel far from home to support his family. There were hopes that an inheritance from his parents' estate would help solve his family's misfortunes, however, when the time came, Jonathan found himself cheated out of his share by his brother. Jonathan was unable to provide for his growing family so he chose to leave them to seek his fortune at sea; his family never saw him again. Deborah's mother was later informed her husband had perished in a shipwreck in 1765, but the truth is far more disturbing.

Jonathan Sampson had abandoned his wife and six children to poverty and in 1770 he began a new life in Lincoln County, Maine. He eventually 'married' a woman named Martha, who bore him two more children. In his work *Masquerade – The Life and Times of Deborah Sampson, Continental Soldier,* Alfred F. Young suggests Jonathan's crimes were not limited to the desertion of his poverty-stricken family; he may have been responsible for five or six murders committed on the Kennebec River in Maine. Although a Jonathan Sampson was arrested and indicted for these crimes, the case was never brought to court and it has not been definitively proved that this Jonathan Sampson was Deborah's father. However, we do know that his common-law wife Martha and he were dependent on the State charity known as Poor Relief for several years and they both died in poverty.[2] His legal family were left in a similarly appalling financial position.

Deborah's father left her when she was just five years old so she had very little memory of him, but the effect he had her life was immense. Around the time that he deserted the family in 1765, Deborah's grandmother died – leaving the family further devastated. Deborah's mother was overwhelmed, and unable to care for her six children so she was obliged to separate the family and have her children cared for elsewhere. It was not uncommon in 18th-century New England for orphaned children and families enduring financiay hardship to seek help in this way, by fostering out children into the homes of friends and relatives. For Deborah, this would prove to be just the first of many upheavals. Deborah was initially fostered by a Miss Fuller, an elderly maiden cousin of her mother's, where she remained until her carer died three years later. She was then fostered by the widow of a local pastor, who taught Deborah to read so that she could read aloud to her mistress from the Bible each night. Again, her residency was cut short when the widow passed away after just two years, and Deborah was forced to move. This time, at about ten years old, Deborah, found a home with security when she was bound as a servant to the family of Deacon Benjamin Thomas, where she stayed until she reached her eighteenth birthday.

Her time with the Thomas family was a happy one; the deacon treated her well and he had a progressive attitude towards women's roles. As part of her duties, she performed many manual chores that were unusual for a female servant including ploughing fields, stacking hay and carpentry, which the outdoor-loving Deborah preferred to the accepted notion 'that a good farm woman never strayed far from the kitchen'.³ He also allowed Deborah to attend classes, often with his own sons. To educate a servant, and a female one at that, was an enlightened move on the deacon's part. Deborah proved to be an enthusiastic student who 'devoured everything taught and bullied the boys into teaching her everything they knew'.⁴ Deborah also displayed a keen interest in the world, had political awareness, and would often be seen reading newspapers. She showed a particular interest in news about the War of Independence, which her nation was fighting against the British Crown. As Young suggests, during her education she may have also been exposed to strong female characters such as Joan of Arc which, with her unusual education, may have helped to develop in her a tendency to challenge the accepted norms.

This, combined with her own strong will and adventurous spirit, led her down a remarkable path.

A Patriot's War

Deborah Sampson's early years were spent in a world of increasing tension between the British Government and the thirteen American colonies under its control. The colonies began to resent the excessive control the British Crown exerted over them, especially on the subject of taxation. The Seven Years War against France and Spain had left Britain in a financial crisis, so the Crown looked to its colonies as a source of revenue to bolster its own flagging economy. The first direct tax placed upon the American colonies was introduced in 1765, the same year Deborah's life was turned upside down by her father's desertion, in the form of a Stamp Tax. This legislation placed a levy on all printed paper documents used in the colonies. The colonists argued it was unconstitutional, and there were violent protests in which tax collectors were attacked in the streets to intimidate them into resigning. Those who opposed the tax gave themselves the name 'Sons of Liberty'. One such protestor was Boston lawyer James Otis, who argued the taxation was a symptom of the oppression of the nation by the British:

> The colonists, being men, have a right to be considered as equally entitled to all the rights of nature with the Europeans, and they are not to be restrained in the exercise of any of these rights but the evident good of the whole community. By being or becoming members of society they have not renounced their natural liberty in any greater degree than other good citizens, and if 'tis taken from them without their consent they are so far enslaved.[5]

Although the tax was repealed a year later, the British Government were keen to show they were not intimidated by the rebellious colonists, so they issued a declaration that reaffirmed the authority of the British Government to pass any legislation of its choosing. For the next decade, they continued to use the colonies as a source of revenue. The 1767 Townshend Act, named for the British Chancellor of the Exchequer, placed taxes on lead, glass, paints, paper and tea. Objections to this form of indirect taxation spilled onto the streets on 5 March 1770, when British sentries in Boston were confronted by an angry crowd. Reinforcements arrived in the form of British soldiers, billeted in Boston expressly to guard British customs agents, who fired their weapons – resulting in the deaths of five people.

Although the officer in charge, Captain Thomas Preston, and eight of his men were arrested and charged with manslaughter, their subsequent acquittal was seen as a betrayal and 'the Boston Massacre' as it was dubbed, became a catalyst for Patriot leaders, such as Paul Revere, to draw supporters to their cause of rebellion against the British. Tensions continued to rise and there were protests such as the famous incident known as the 'Boston Tea Party', which saw the destruction of the cargo of a British tea ship, the *Dartmouth,* in protest over the taxation on tea. On 18 April 1775, these tensions came to a head when British troops began to march in their hundreds from Boston to the town of Concord on a mission to seize a cache of arms held by the colonial militia. Patriot leader Paul Revere rode through the night to sound the alarm. Although the famous line taught to American school children 'the British are coming' is the stuff of legend, the vital information he shared did precipitate the mobilisation of the colonial militia, which enabled them to intercept the 700 British troops. The two sides collided on the Lexington town green where the colonial militia were initially vastly outnumbered but were soon joined by 2,000 'minutemen'; so called for their ability to ready themselves quickly. After an intensive exchange of gunfire, the British were forced into a hasty retreat; the fight for independence had begun.

In 1778, France formally recognised the independence of the United States of America and entered into the war against the British. In that same year, Deborah reached her eighteenth birthday and her time as an indentured servant came to an end. With no father, husband or employer, she became what is known as a 'masterless woman', free to earn her own money and legally subject to no one. But there were still limitations on what she could achieve, with few occupations open to women apart from domestic service, shop-keeping and needlework. The world around her was undergoing violent changes as her countrymen fought for their right to independence but Deborah found own her life lacked any scope for adventure and, just like her nation, she was searching for a new identity. She remained with the Thomas family for a short while, and was able to eke out a living raising her own chickens and sheep and selling her own woven cloth.

In 1779 Deborah secured a post in which she could use her education when she was employed as a teacher for two summer school seasons. In 18th-century America, female teachers were often employed to teach female students and young male students to read, although they were paid half the wages of their male counterparts. As the children progressed in their education, the more advanced classes, such as maths, were taught by young male college graduates. Further education was still beyond the reach of most girls, with even girls from the higher classes banned from public schools until the 1780s. Deborah had managed to raise herself out of the position of a servant and had carved out a modicum of independence but teaching did not hold the same status that it does today and female teachers especially were considered little more than caretakers of 'an assortment of unruly boys and girls of all ages and sizes'.[6]

In New England public school teachers were paid with room and board at the homes of various citizens. For example, New England citizen Benjamin Thomas was paid £1 16s to have a teacher board in his home for six weeks in 1773.[7] In Deborah's district of Middleborough, the students were scattered across several areas so she was required to often move between various schoolhouses and to board with various families throughout the district to reach all the students in her charge. The result of this policy was Deborah's life had again taken on the transient quality she had experienced as a young girl; she quickly began to feel dissatisfied with this lifestyle and longed for more adventure. The traditional path for a woman of Deborah's class would have been to seek marriage, but she showed no interest in this route. She had witnessed the drudgery of Mrs Thomas's life as a farm wife and had no desire to follow in her footsteps. In addition, marriage would mean giving up the modicum of independence she had already achieved as a teacher and weaver. Instead, Deborah, never one to shrink from breaking the rules, found a way to push the boundaries of 'acceptable behaviour' to relieve the tedium of her life.

It was perhaps her experiences with the Thomas children that led Deborah to think boys have more fun and helped her formulate her bold plan. Over the course of several weeks she used her weaving skills to fashion cloth, which she then sewed into a suit of men's clothes – a coat, waistcoat and breeches. Using a long cotton strip, she flattened her small breasts and tied back her long hair in a style fashionable for men at the time. Dressed in this attire, Deborah made her first excursion into the world as a man. She headed straight for a place forbidden to any respectable woman, a tavern, where she drank alcohol, smoked tobacco and behaved in a manner society would have deemed unseemly for a young woman. Deborah had previously worked as a weaver for tavern owner Granville Temple Sproat, who had offered her room and board while she completed her work for him; although she may have witnessed the carousing of the tavern goers, she had been barred from taking part in any of the fun without serious damage to her respectable reputation. Deborah enjoyed her escapade so much that she repeated the experience as often as her limited funds would allow; but soon she took her scheme one step too far and her secret was discovered.

Between March and April 1782, Deborah was boarding at the home of Captain Benjamin Leonard while employed as a weaver when she decided to have another of her adventures. She had neglected to bring her male clothing with her and did not have sufficient money to make a trip to fetch them but the mischievous Deborah was not about to let this stop her from escaping for an evening. For the first time, she was going to require help in order to achieve her aim. During her time with the Leonards, Deborah had shared a room and bed with a young black servant named Jennie, whom she had regaled with stories of her exploits as a man. Jennie was so excited by her friend's animated tales that she agreed to help her to escape again. This was the first time that Deborah had shared her secret with anyone and Jennie's enthusiasm must have seemed like an endorsement. The first step in the plan was to procure for Deborah male clothing, which the young women did by creeping into the bedroom of their master's son and taking a suit from his wardrobe. Dressed in probably the most expensive suit she had ever worn, Deborah slipped out of the house and took herself off into the outside world. However, she had yet to solve the problem of her lack of funds, so Deborah devised an audacious and morally questionable plan.

At the beginning of 1781, morale in the Continental Army was at an all-time low. The rebel governors' lack of funds had meant many of their soldiers had not been paid. On 1 January 1,500 soldiers of the Pennsylvania Line, under the command of General Anthony Wayne, abandoned their posts at Morristown, New Jersey, in protest against these missing wages and insisted that their three-year enlistment had expired. Three officers were killed in the mutiny.

Such grievances were not isolated incidents and as a result, a request for an additional 37,000 recruits to the Continental Army was met with a lacklustre 8,000 volunteers. Recruitment officers would often troll the taverns for potential recruits but increasing reports of these mutinies and the failure to pay promised wages had begun to trickle down to these young men and reversed their inclination to enlist. Recruitment officer Captain Alexander Graydon described the difficulties faced during on such recruiting expedition,

A number of fellows at the tavern, at which my party rendezvoused, indicated a desire to enlist, but although they drank freely of our liquor, they still held off. I soon perceived that the object was to amuse themselves at our expense, and that if there might be one or two among them really disposed to engage, the others would prevent them. One fellow in particular, who had made the greatest shew of taking the bounty, presuming on the weakness of our party, consisting only of a drummer, corporal, my second lieutenant and myself, began to grow insolent, and manifested an intention to begin a quarrel, in the issue of which, he no doubt calculated on giving us a drubbing.[8]

Cash bounties began to be offered to help with recruitment but a scam known as 'bounty jumping' soon began to develop, which saw men enlist and then immediately desert only to re-enlist again in another county, thereby claiming multiple bounties. Deborah was aware not only of the political situation of the war and that recruitment officers were on the look-out for more troops, but also of the existence of this scam. On the night she snuck out of the Leonards' home, she decided that she too would profit from this flaw in the system. Instead of heading straight for a tavern, which had been her usual procedure, Deborah went to the home of Mr Israel Wood, which was being used as a recruitment office, and enlisted in the Continental Army under the name Timothy Thayer. The enlistment procedure required no more than her signature on the relevant documents and once this was completed, Deborah was presented with her bounty of $50. However, at this time Deborah had no intention of serving in the military and instead she pocketed the money and went to the Four Corners tavern,

2 miles east of Middleborough, where she proceeded to drink and behave in a 'noisy and indecent manner'.[9] In the morning, Deborah returned to the Leonards' home as if nothing had happened and 'Timothy Thayer' never reported for duty.

Unfortunately for Deborah, her exploits had not gone undetected; while investigating the whereabouts of the missing recruit Thayer, officers of the Continental Army interviewed an elderly woman who had been present at Mr Wood's home at the time of Deborah's visit. This lady, who had been sitting by the fire carding wool, had noticed that Thayer had a peculiar way of holding the quill when he had signed his enlistment papers and informed the authorities this was a peculiarity he shared with the local teacher Deborah Sampson, caused by the loss of the use of her forefinger in an accident. The officers immediately deduced that Deborah and Thayer were, in fact, the same person. Although she was never charged with a crime, Deborah was forced to repay the enlistment money and the truth of her exploits was exposed to her community. This incident was not a part of her life that Deborah was proud of and, as a result, it does not appear in *The Female Review*, Mann's biography of her life. But records of the event and the investigation appear in the September 1782 minutes of the Third Baptist Church, where Deborah worshipped. She avoided any formal punishment but the senior members of her church declared her exploits to be those of a loose woman and 'unchristian like'.[10] Deborah's membership of the church was withdrawn until she apologised for her actions, and gossip ran amok among her friends and neighbours who suggested that if Deborah were married and 'contained within a home' she would not indulge in such behaviour. Her mother agreed with this assessment and attempted to promote a match with a young man whom Deborah described as having 'all the *sang-froid* of a Frenchman, and the silliness of a baboon'. She rejected the match.[11] It is moot whether it was the drinking of 'spirituous liquor', the taking of money through deception, or the cross-dressing and breaking of gender taboos that most upset people. The story of the 'notorious character' of a would-be woman solder was the stuff of legend in the town of Middleborough, where it was described locally as 'a juicy bit of misogynist lore' in which 'tradition affirms that Samuel Leonard was so shocked at the idea of his clothes having been used by a woman, that he never wore them afterward.'[12] Deborah may have felt shame at having gained money by deception, and perhaps even regret over her subsequent expulsion from her church, but she had no such feelings about crossing the gender divide. She was a rebellious character who was not afraid to push the boundaries of society. Wearing breeches had given Deborah a freedom she had never experienced before and despite the negative reactions to her actions, she resolved to repeat the experience.

In May 1782 Deborah decided to again enlist in the military, only this time she was determined to serve her country. She left her home and marched to the town of Bellingham. To limit the possibility of again being recognised in her disguise, Deborah used a third party who, in return for payment, would sign up on her behalf in the town of Uxbridge. Deborah chose the name Robert Shurtleff after her beloved brother Robert Shurtleff Sampson, who had died aged eight, and used it to enlist in the 4th Massachusetts Regiment of the Continental Army, under the command of Colonel Shepherd and company commander Captain George Webb. This particular regiment had a reputation for having well-equipped and well-fed soldiers. Private Shurtleff was presented with an enlistment bounty of $60 and a 'receipt dated Worcester, May 23, 1782 for the bounty paid said Shurtleff by Noah Taft, Chairman of Class No. 2 of the town of Uxbridge, to serve in the Continental Army for the term of three years'.[13] She was then issued with a uniform consisting of

> ...a blue coat lined with white, with white wings on the shoulder and cords on the arms and pockets; a white waistcoat, breeches or overhauls and stockings, with black straps about the knees; half boots, a black velvet sock [for display around the neck] and a cap with a variegated cockade, on one side, a plume tipped with red on the other, and a white sash about the crown.[14]

There is no mention of any physical examination taking place during the enlistment process and Deborah had not even had to enter the recruitment office herself but she still had to pass as a man to officers and fellow soldiers. Neighbour and former employer Granville Temple Sproat described the young Deborah as 'tall, muscular and very erect and considered one of the best specimens of womanhood'[15] and at 5 feet 7 inches, she more than met the standard height requirement for the rank and file. In her youth Deborah had towered over most women in Middleborough, who averaged just 5 feet. Her height combined with her naturally low-pitched voice helped her pass for a teenage boy of around eighteen and 'Shurtleff' would have fitted right in with the troops who were at that time 'awash with undersized beardless boys'.[16]

Private Shurtleff was now ready and willing to fight for her nation but before her first battle, Deborah came up against her first threat to her disguise when she, with the rest of her regiment, were ordered to report for a smallpox vaccination. Knowing that she must avoid any medical attention if she was going to successfully go unmasked, Deborah refused the vaccination, preferred to risk catching the disease than to be discovered. Having survived this danger, Deborah was eager to enter the fight. She was one of sixteen new recruits assigned to the Light Infantry Company, which was the most active of all regimental companies. Light infantrymen were 'younger, more athletic and intelligent' and required more 'endurance, agility and initiative' and her superiors obviously saw potential in the tall teenage boy she appeared to be.[17] Deborah's new duties required her to march double time for up to 10 miles per day carrying her equipment, which, although lighter than the general rank and file, still included 30 lbs of arms and ammunition, a knapsack containing personal belongings, rations and a sidearm. Deborah developed a reputation as a vigilant soldier who performed her duties to the best of her ability and she seemed to fit in well with her regiment and was soon accepted as one of the boys. When her unit moved to Worcester to join the rest of the regiment, she was appointed as an aide-de-camp to General Paterson. As she slept alongside her male comrades, Deborah would later say she was comfortable that she would not be discovered '[for] they little suspected my sex'.[18]

By the summer of 1782, just a few months after Deborah's enlistment, the war was almost won for the Patriots, who had managed to force the British Army into the confines of

New York. A tenuous truce was declared but this did not stop the occasional clashes between parties scouting on the edges of the territory. In early June a detachment party, which included Deborah, were sent to the south by the Continental Army to gather intelligence on the movement of British troops. This was a dangerous mission and Deborah was aware that capture could mean death, or worse, if the enemy discovered the sex of the young soldier. The party was split into two groups to cover more ground and a rendezvous point was established in Harlem, behind enemy lines. The party had noted the position of the enemy troops and withdrew to White Plains within their own territory to reveal their information to their superiors. On 26 June, a fire fight broke out between the British Dragoons at Tarrytown, New York, and the Loyalists troops from Sing Sing. Deborah and her company were forced to retreat under heavy fire and were near defeat when reinforcements arrived and forced the British to retreat.

Deborah had managed to come through both incidents unscathed but her luck was not to last. Just a few days later, on 3 July, Deborah was among thirty volunteers who were instructed to flush out armed Tories in East Chester. An early morning fire fight at Vontoite resulted in the death of several Tories, one Continental soldier and the wounding of Private Shurtleff. Deborah had received two musket balls to the thigh and sustained a head wound. She would later declare,

I considered this a death wound, or as equivalent to it; as it must, I thought lead to the discovery of my sex. Covered with blood from head to foot, I told my companions I fear I had received a mortal wound; and begged them to leave me to die on the spot.[19]

Refusing to leave their wounded comrade, Deborah was carried 6 miles on horseback to the French Army hospital for treatment. As she drew closer to medical attention and possible discovery Deborah grew increasingly distraught and drew her pistol from her holster, preferring to take her own life than risk the shame of discovery. But Deborah did not pull the trigger, an act she put down to 'Divine Mercy'.[20]

By the time Deborah was admitted to hospital, she had already lost copious amounts of blood, but she still attempted to hide her thigh injury in the hopes she could pass through undiscovered. Her head injury was only a slight cut and after it was cleaned and bound, she and the other wounded were given two bottles of wine to share. But as she attempted to leave the hospital, a doctor stopped Deborah after noticing that her boot was filled with blood. With dread Deborah rolled up her trouser leg to reveal the skin had been turned red with blood, which was cleaned away, but she still somehow managed to conceal her thigh injury. Determined to see to her own injury, she pocketed 'a silver probe a little curved at the end, a needle, some lint, a bandage and some of the same kind of salve that had been applied to the wound in [her] head' and left to take care of the wound herself.[21]

Back in her tent Deborah took her stolen instruments and removed the musket balls that still remained in her thigh. One ball had penetrated the skin by 2 inches and so it took three attempts to extract it. Another was too deep to reach and so she was forced to leave it in the wound. Using the wine for pain relief, she cleaned the wound and applied the salve. When the bleeding had finally stopped, Deborah lay down on her bunk to rest. After an hour, she was woken by the doctor who had come to check on his patient. He noticed the tear in her breeches where she had performed her operation and questioned her about it, to which Deborah replied it had probably been caused by a nail from the saddle and fell back asleep. Whether or not he believed her explanation, the doctor did not question her further and she was left alone to recover. It is possible that the wound was serious enough to warrant a discharge had it been received by a male soldier who had allowed it to be treated, as Deborah's leg was never to fully recover from the injury and she suffered pain all the rest of her life. Having concealed the wound, however, she soon found herself back on the front lines.

At the time Deborah was performing her heroic solo surgery, back in her home town her 'unchristian like behaviour' in the 'Timothy Thayer' matter was being discussed at the Third Baptist Church and she was being expelled. It is interesting to ponder if the congregation that was at that time condemning her would have approved more, or less, of her conduct as Robert Shurtleff as it did of the actions of Timothy Thayer.

After her recovery and subsequent return to duty, Deborah was sent as part of a large detachment of Continental soldiers to the north to quell Indian incursions that were occurring there. Deborah marched with her detachment along the North River from West Point to Fort Edward. A blizzard slowed their progress but Deborah and her comrades pushed on. The party came across a group of natives and in the ensuing fire fight fifteen natives were killed and many more wounded. During the battle, Deborah found herself in pursuit of one man who had fled into the forest, but once captured she discovered that he was in fact not a native but had been 'a child of white parents'.[22] The troops then returned to the rest of the unit, where the full extent of the devastation soon became apparent. A family home, apparently that of Deborah's captive, had been completely destroyed by fire. In the ashes, the man's wife lay dead while his two children were hung by their heels from a nearby tree. Another girl was found injured but alive having hidden under some straw during the attack. She had a wound on her shoulder from a tomahawk and was blue with cold. This was a scene of such horror that Deborah would never forget it and she would later describe it to crowds who would come to hear the 'woman warrior' speak. Deborah returned with her company to Fort Edward and eventually to the New Winsor Cantonment camp.

Mutiny in the Ranks

On 17 June 1783, officers from the Philadelphia line of the Confederate Army contacted the Congress of the Confederation and threatened munity unless missing back wages and retirement pay were paid in full. Congress funds were depleted by the length and expense of the war, but the troops felt their labour had been 'stolen from them by Continental officials unable or unwilling to pay them'. When they failed to get a satisfactory answer, eighty soldiers left their post at Lancaster, Pennsylvania, to march on the State House in protest. When they arrived, they were joined by soldiers from eleven regiments under the command of General Anthony

Wayne, making a mob of approximately 500 men. These men presented a real threat as they also had control of the weapons and ammunition from their barracks in New Jersey. Officers who attempted to stop the mutineers were attacked, shot and bayoneted by their own troops. The soldiers then descended on the State House, blocking the delegates from leaving, as they made their demands. General George Washington sent 500 troops under the command of General Howe to suppress the insurrection. Howe was able to subdue the mutineers and arrest the ringleaders in a predawn attack, and two sergeants were subsequently sentenced to death. Deborah and four of her comrades had initially requested permission to join Howe's detachment but by the time they arrived in Pennsylvania, just a day later, the rebellion had already been quashed.

The Fever Breaks

Although she missed the insurrection, Deborah's stay in Pennsylvania would prove to be a major turning point in her life and the end of her military career. Shortly after her arrival she was struck down by the 'malignant fever' that would eventually lead to her hospitalisation and the subsequent discovery that she was a woman. Deborah's symptoms from the infection were so severe that while she unconscious, in the confusion of the overcrowded hospital, she was mistaken for one of the deceased and almost taken for burial before she was rescued by Dr Binney, who was so impressed by her courage and patriotism that he not only kept her secret but took the vulnerable soldier into his home to prevent anyone else making the same discovery. Binney even kept Deborah's secret from his own family, referring to her always as Shurtleff.

The Battle of Schellenberg in 1704, where Kit Cavenaugh was wounded. (Rijksmuseum)

The Battle of Ramillies in 1706, where Kit Cavenaugh was wounded again. During her treatment it was discovered that she was a woman. (Rijksmuseum)

Left: Mary Read. Her time as a poacher turned gamekeeper — serving on an anti-pirate privateering expediton — didn't last long: she was apparently one of the most persuasive voices on board in urging the crew to mutiny and take up (or return to) piracy. (© National Maritime Museum, Greenwich, London)

Left: Mary Read runs a man through.

Below: The infamous Ann Bonny and Mary Read. It is a fascinating footnote to the endless nature/ nurture debate that both were brought up as boys. (© National Maritime Museum, Greenwich, London)

Above: The pension card for 'Albert D. J. Cashier', Jennie Hodgers. (National Archives and Records Administration)

Right: Another famous woman who fought in the US Civil War, Frances Clayton. She disguised herself as a man to fight in the Union Army alongside her husband, leaving after his death in the Battle of Stones River. (Library of Congress)

Vue et Representation de la Bataille de Mons ou de Malplaquet, donnée le 11 Septembre 1709

1 Le Prince Eugenee de Savoye 2 Bois du Sart 3 Ataque des Imperiaux et des Anglois 4 Retranchements du Centre 5 Bois de Senfart 6 Ataque des Hollandois par le Prince D'orange 7 Village de Malplaquet 8 Village de Belangé 9 Marche de Cavallerie au travers du Bois 10 Retraitte des François

Above: The Battle of Malplaquet, where Hannah Snell's husband died. (Rijksmuseum)

Left: A stipple engraving of Hannah Snell. (Wellcome Library, London)

HANNAH SNELL,

(Born at Worcester 1723.)

THE
Gentleman's Magazine,
For JULY 1750.

Some account of HANNAH SNELL, the Female SOLDIER.

 ANNAH SNELL, was born in Fryer-street, Worcester, April 1723. Her father was a hosier and dyer, and son to lieut. Snell who was at the taking of Namur, in the reign of K. William, and afterwards served in Q. Anne's wars.

When her father and mother, who by their industry brought up 3 sons and 6 daughters, died, Hannah set out for London, where she arrived on Christmas day, 1740, and resided some time with her sister, who had married one Gray, a carpenter, and lived in Wapping. Here she became acquainted with James Summs, a Dutch sailor, to whom she, was married in 1743; but he treated her with great inhumanity, and left her when seven months with child, which dying at six months old, she decently buried it. She put on a suit of her brother-in-law's apparel, on Nov. 23, 1745. left her sister without communicating her design, and went to Coventry, where she enlisted herself in Guise's regiment of foot, and march'd with it to Carlisle. Here her serjeant, whose name was Davis, having

Above: Ripley Castle, where Trooper Jane kept watch over Oliver Cromwell after the Battle of Marston Moor in 1644. (Wikimedia commons)

Left: Musket ball scars found on the gatehouse wall of Ripley Castle where Oliver Cromwell executed Royalist prisoners after the battle of Marston Moor. (Courtesy Denise Kidger at Born2Be Studios)

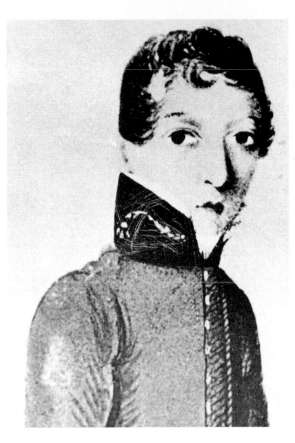

Portraits of 'Dr James Miranda Barry', Margaret Bulkley. (Right and bottom right courtesy Army Medical Services Museum.) Below, the *Cape Times* Christmas Annual 1904 mocks, fairly gently, 'The amazing woman "Dr James Barry" in uniform.'

THE AMAZING WOMAN, "DR JAMES BARRY," IN UNIFORM—"HIS" PONY NETTED AND HIS NEGRO VALET AND HIS DOG IN ATTENDANCE.

Reproductions by Courtesy of the "Cape Times," from its Christmas Annual dated December, 1904.

Not the most flattering of portraits. A hangdog Margaret Bulkley with a hangdog cat, Corfu 1852. (Courtesy Army Medical Services Museum)

The gravestone of Margaret Bulkley. (Courtesy Army Medical Services Museum)

DEBORAH SAMPSON.

Right: Deborah Sampson Gannett. (Library of Congress)

Below: Deborah Sampson Gannett delivers a note to General Patterson, at the same time revealing her gender. (Library of Congress)

Left: Dorothy Lawrence, aka Private Denis Smith.

Below: A trench at the Somme. Dorothy worked on the tunnels at Albert, not far from the Somme front. (Library of Congress)

THE WOOD CALLED DES FERMES IN THE SOMME   4172

The Siege of Valenciennes, where Mary Anne Talbot served as a drummer boy. (Rijksmuseum)

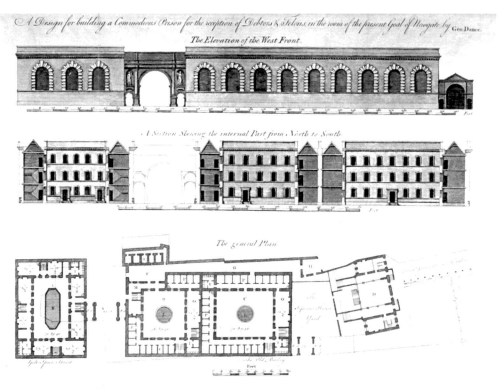

Newgate, where Talbot was placed in debtors' prison.

HOW WIVES MAY MAKE THEIR HUSBANDS ENLIST.
LADY—" *Either you or I, sir.*"

Above: A cartoon riffing on Loreta Janeta Velázquez's service in the US Civil War.

Below: The Battle of Ball's Bluff, where Velázquez served. (Library of Congress)

Above: The Battle of Shiloh. Having previously had her secret discovered, Velázquez re-enlisted and served here. (Library of Congress)

Right: Frontispiece of Velázquez's memoirs.

THE WOMAN IN BATTLE:

A NARRATIVE OF THE

Exploits, Adventures, and Travels

OF

MADAME LORETA JANETA VELAZQUEZ,

OTHERWISE KNOWN AS

LIEUTENANT HARRY T. BUFORD,

CONFEDERATE STATES ARMY.

IN WHICH IS GIVEN

Full Descriptions of the numerous Battles in which she participated as a Confederate
Officer; of her Perilous Performances as a Spy, as a Bearer of Despatches, as
a Secret-Service Agent, and as a Blockade-Runner; of her Adventures
Behind the Scenes at Washington, including the Bond Swindle;
of her Career as a Bounty and Substitute Broker in New York;
of her Travels in Europe and South America; her Mining
Adventures on the Pacific Slope; her Residence
among the Mormons; her Love Affairs,
Courtships, Marriages, &c., &c.

EDITED BY

C. J. WORTHINGTON,

LATE OF THE UNITED STATES NAVY.

Command the trumpets of the war to sound!
This stillness doth perplex and harass me:
An inward impulse drives me from repose,
It still impels me to achieve my work.
SCHILLER — *The Maid of Orleans.*

PROFUSELY ILLUSTRATED.

HARTFORD:

T. BELKNAP.

1876.

The Confederate general Jubal Early, who refused to accept Velázquez's memoirs as fact. (Library of Congress)

Above: Molly Pitcher, the nickname given to a woman who supposedly fought at the Battle of Monmouth in the American Revolutionary War. She was said to have taken over her husband's duties swabbing and loading the gun after he was carried from the field. (Library of Congress)

Right: The gravestone of Phoebe Hessel, who fought at the Battle of Fontenoy in 1745. She is buried at the Church of St Nicholas, Brighton.

Left: The Canadian-born Sarah Emma Edmonds, who served in the US Civil War on the side of the Union. (Library of Congress)

Below: By the time of the Second World War, there was no problem among the Soviets about putting women into combat. Pictured are two incredibly well-fed and healthy-looking Ukrainian Soviet partisans, probably in 1943. If this wasn't a propaganda shot, it should have been.

In September 1783, the Treaty of Paris was signed and the war officially came to an end and with it, so did Deborah's military service. She and the rest of her regiment were called to the fort at West Point, where the regiment was to be disbanded. At this point she produced a letter written by Dr Binney to West Point commander General Patterson, which proclaimed her true identity and the story of her wartime service. Patterson at first refused to believe the tale but was reportedly convinced once he saw Deborah dressed in women's clothes. Deborah received an honourable discharge in October and was given sufficient money to allow her to return home.

After her return to civilian life, Deborah found employment as a farmhand and she later sold her story to the *New York Gazette* where it was printed anonymously, at her request. Deborah married farmer Benjamin Gannett on 7 April 1785 in Sharon, Massachusetts; they had three children and later adopted a fourth child. Encouraged by her husband, Deborah Sampson-Gannett caused controversy when in 1791 she applied for back pay for her service during the war. It was initially refused but she appealed against the decision and in January 1792 she was granted $34 back pay for her service by a Massachusetts court. With her story now having been made public, Sampson-Gannett was then approached by writer Herman Mann who offered to write her story, which was published as *A Female Review*. Deborah herself did not rate the publication highly. In 1802, she decided to take her story to the public herself and became the first woman in America to be paid for a lecture tour during which she would stay in the homes of her former officers, who were very supportive when they discovered her secret. She performed in venues such as the Federal Street Theatre in Boston, where she would be dressed in her uniform and discuss her experiences during the war, before performing rifle drill and singing songs for the audience. In direct contrast to this display of her military prowess, Deborah gave the audience a profuse apology for her actions in which she lamented her actions as '[a swerve] from the accustomed flowery path of female delicacy, to walk upon the heroic precipice of feminine perdition'.²³ Her humble demeanour only served to endear her further to the public.

Unfortunately, as with many ex-servicemen and women warriors before her, it was not long before Deborah began to experience financial difficulty. After her paid lecture tours failed to develop into a theatrical career she began her campaign to be granted a military pension, as had been granted to the male former members of her regiment.

Knowing she would face some opposition to her claim, Deborah enlisted the help of some influential figures. The poet Philip Freneau wrote an ode in Sampson-Gannett's honour and Paul Revere, who was a neighbour of hers, wrote a letter in support of her:

Sir

Mrs. Deborah Gannett of Sharon informs me, that she has inclosed [*sic*] to your care a petition to Congress in favour of her. My works for manufacturing of copper, being at Canton, being but a short distance from the neighbourhood where she lives, I have been induced to enquire her situation, and character, since she quit the male habit and soldier's uniform, for the most decent apparel of her own sex; and obliges me to say that every person with whom I have conversed about her, and it is not a few, speak of her as a woman with handsome talents, good morals, a dutiful wife, and an affectionate parent.[24]

Although a character reference from an American revolutionary hero was surely of benefit, it should not have been necessary for her claim as her service had already been verified and acknowledged by the military when she was granted an honourable discharge, and by the government when she was paid her back pay. In March 1805, Deborah's claim was successful and she was placed on the Massachusetts Invalid Pension Roll and awarded $4 per month. She was the first woman in America to be granted a military pension in this manner and only one of three women to be officially recognised by Congress for their service in the Revolutionary War. In granting her pension, the American Government was not only acknowledging her service but also her right to be compensated on the same level as male soldiers. Deborah's pension was later increased to $96 a year, by the Pension Act of 1818, which she received until her death on 29 April 1827, at which point her husband was then made eligible for death benefits. Unfortunately, Benjamin Gannett passed away in January 1937, before he was able to receive his claim. On 4 July 1838, a Special Act of Congress was passed to pay $466.66 to Deborah Gannett's heirs, an amount that was equivalent to a full pension of $80 per year from the day of Mr Gannett's petition until his death.

The legacy of Deborah Sampson-Gannett is one that is still felt throughout the United States of America today, where she continues to be honoured by her countrymen. In 1944, the Second World War liberty ship the *Deborah Gannett* was launched, while her home town of Sharon, Massachusetts, erected a statue in her honour in 1982, which still stands to this day. Rather than rejecting Deborah for crossing the boundaries of gender in warfare, the people of America have embraced her as a heroine and a symbol of patriotism.

Notes

1. Young, Alfred F., *Masquerade: The Life and Times of Deborah Sampson, Continental Soldier* (New York, Random House, 2004), p. 4
2. ibid, p. 29
3. Evans, Elizabeth, *Weathering the Storm: Women of the American Revolution* (New York, Paragon House, 1989) p. 304
4. ibid, p. 304
5. Allison, Robert, J., *The American Revolution – A Concise History* (Oxford: Oxford University Press, 2011), p. 11
6. Young, p. 41
7. ibid
8. Graydon, Alexander, *Recruitment during the American Revolution*, in Ed. Albert Bushnell Hart, *American History Told by Contemporaries, Vol. II: Building of the Republic* (New York, MacMillan, 1899), p. 481-2
9. Wheelwright, Julie, *Amazons and Military Maids – Women Who Dressed as Men in Pursuit of Life, Liberty and Happiness* (London: Pandora Press, 1989), p. 133
10. Evans, p. 309
11. ibid, p. 306
12. Young, p. 77
13. Evans, p. 306

14. Young, p. 103

15. ibid, p. 43

16. ibid, p. 100

17. ibid, p. 97

18. Wheelwright, p. 52

19. Evans p. 308

20. ibid

21. ibid

22. ibid, p. 310

23. Gannet, Deborah, *An Address Delivered with Applause at the Federal Street Theatre, Boston, Four Successive Nights of the Different Plays Beginning March 22, 1802, by Mrs Deborah Gannet, The American Heroine, Who Served Three Years with Reputation (undiscovered as a Female) in the Late American Army* (Minerva Office: H. Mann, 1802)

24. Evans, p. 330

8

DOROTHY LAWRENCE
AKA PRIVATE DENIS SMITH –
JOURNALIST AND FEMALE TOMMY

I'll see what an ordinary English girl, without credentials or
money can accomplish.[1]

In the summer of 1914, the world exploded into the 'Great
War'. On 28 June 1914, two pistol shots fired at the Archduke
Franz Ferdinand of Austria and his wife Sophie by Bosnian
Serb Gavrilo Princip led to a bloody and gruesome war that
would involve 65 million soldiers worldwide. The hope for a
short war 'over by Christmas' was not to be and soldiers found
themselves in dirty, disease-ridden trenches, sometimes only
100 yards from the enemy. Almost nine million soldiers would
lose their lives, and more than 23 million would be injured.

In 1915, in the British trenches near the French town of
Albert, the 179th Tunnelling Company of the 51st Division of
the Royal Engineers were employed to tunnel under the German
trenches and lay explosives. This was a very dangerous job
undertaken by specialist Sappers (military engineers) and civilian

'clay kicker' miners, who had been drafted into the Royal Engineers specifically for their skills in mining. Among their number was 'Sapper Denis Smith' who had only been with the regiment for ten days when he was approached by two military policemen who arrested the new recruit. Earlier that day, Smith's sergeant had reported to his superiors his discovery that 'he' was actually a woman in disguise. Her hidden passport declared her to be nineteen-year-old Dorothy Lawrence from England but British authorities were reluctant to take this identity at face value so arrested her on suspicion of being a German spy. In fact, Dorothy was a British journalist who had deliberately infiltrated the regiment in the hope of getting the greatest scoop of the war, a first-hand account of life in the trenches. After ten days of enduring the terrible conditions, handling dangerous explosives and under fire from trench mortars, Dorothy had revealed her true identity to her sergeant, under the mistaken assumption he would keep her secret. Dorothy had already received help from several British soldiers and military policemen to get this far. However, this time she was disappointed and reportedly screamed at her betrayer 'you are the biggest blackguard I ever met'[2] as she was unceremoniously marched to the British Army headquarters, where she was declared a prisoner of war until her story could be confirmed or denied.

Eventually, Dorothy was able to prove her identity to the satisfaction of her captors but her confession that rather than being a spy she was in fact a journalist hoping to write a story on the war at the front lines did not endear her to the British authorities. Instead, her deception and infiltration of the front lines meant she was a danger to military security, and at the same time had challenged the very fabric of masculinity and society's gender roles.

Born in 1876, Dorothy had a typical middle-class British upbringing. Her father was a drainage contractor, who saw she was well educated, and she grew up to be a strong, independent individual. However, her early life was not without tragedy and, in her later years, she would reveal she had suffered sexual abuse as a young girl at the hands of a church warden. The details of the attack were never released to the public but were recorded by doctors who treated Dorothy for mental illness as an elderly woman. Perhaps this experience contributed to the somewhat hardened exterior she often presented to the world.

At the age of eighteen Dorothy was living in Paris, where she was pursuing her career in journalism. In the late nineteenth and early twentieth centuries, journalism was a very male-dominated occupation and Dorothy found she was not taken seriously by any of the major newspapers. At the outbreak of war, Dorothy was witness to the influx of 160,000 members of the British Expeditionary Force, sent into France to join the considerably larger French forces. It soon became obvious this would be a war on a scale that had never before been seen, and for the single-minded Dorothy it represented the ultimate story. As a war correspondent, she would be perfectly placed to provide first-hand accounts of the war in France and its effect on the French people. However, Dorothy came up against the brick wall of the attitudes of the editors of newspapers in London, who flatly refused to accept a female war correspondent's work. They openly mocked the idea that a woman would be able to secure a story where their own male reporters had failed, but these rejections only made Dorothy more determined:

> If war correspondents cannot get out there, I'll see whether I cannot go one better than those big men with their cars, credentials and money. I'll see what I can manage as a war-correspondent.[3]

In the summer of 1915, after her unsuccessful trip to London to sell her story, Dorothy returned to France via the Channel steamer, determined to get as close to the front as possible. Her chosen mode of transport was a 'ramshackle cycle' that she purchased in London for £2 and paid a further £3 to have shipped to Paris. The city of Paris had already suffered greatly from artillery fire, and bombardment by German aircraft. On 30 August 1914 one such bombing campaign resulted in the destruction of buildings on three streets, with one death and three other casualties, but Dorothy wanted to get even closer to the fighting to witness it first-hand. To do this, Dorothy cycled 67 kilometres to the French base camp in the town of Creil. In the often poetic language of Dorothy's autobiography, she described the visible effects of the conflict on the landscape in an area that had so recently been 'at the very foot of the war':

> In the summer air dull booms rolled both day and night. Other war notes punctuated these regular boomings; *mitrailleuses* at work and maxims that kept them company; R-ap! R-ap! Rap! Rap R-a-rr-p! *Mitrailleuses* crackled far away; it sounded like impatient knocks at a wooden door by human knuckles. Another sound followed. Boom! B-o-om![4]

Although the homes in the towns she passed had seen action in the past, it soon became obvious to Dorothy that she would have great difficulty in passing through the military lines to the forefront of the fighting. She decided that a daring plan was required. The first step was to procure an effective disguise and Dorothy was not above using her womanly charms to accomplish this. She befriended two English soldiers in a Parisian café who, in return for a few hours in her company as a tour guide around the city, agreed to obtain a uniform for her. The two Tommies smuggled the required garments out, a little at a time, by disguising the bundles as dirty laundry. By degrees, Dorothy was able to obtain khaki trousers, braces, a shirt, a jacket, a cap, and leggings known as puttees, which wrapped in a spiral around the lower legs, and a pair of military boots. Dorothy then used similar methods as previous women in disguise, such Christian Davies and Hannah Snell, to disguise her figure by wrapping her chest with bandages and padding her back with cotton wool and sacking. Her long brown hair was cut into a short military style by a Scottish military policeman Dorothy had charmed into helping her. She stained her pale, feminine face with a furniture stain, Condy's fluid, to give herself a dirty, bronzed complexion. Dorothy seemed to enjoy her transformation, describing it as 'a lark' and her description of getting dressed is comical:

I was left alone to struggle with unknown buttons, braces, and the division sum of how to make a big body go into small size of trousers! Eventually I got in by a series of jumps, jerks, and general tightening up![5]

Now disguised, she moved on to acquiring the documentation that would allow her to pass through checkpoints to the frontlines. This was a difficulty not faced by many of her predecessors, who were often assisted by the disorder and lack of unity in the military; the British Army Dorothy was attempting to infiltrate was very different from the disjointed militia under separate commanders of Kit Cavenaugh's time, or the predatory recruitment processes of the Royal Navy that Hannah Snell joined. In 1915, the British Army was a highly organised, professional body and would therefore be more difficult to infiltrate. One of Dorothy's 'khaki friends' obtained for her a brown leather identity disc which read 'D. Smith, No. 175331, 1st Leicestershire Regt. R.C.' and a blank pass, which they told her how to complete.

> Pass
> Private Denis Smith has leave to be absent from his quarters
> from August 16th till August 23rd on special business.
> Signed------, Commanding Officer,
> 1st Leicestershire Regiment[6]

She signed a fake name in the commanding officer's space and forged a headquarters stamp by using a disc purchased from a cycle shop. It was a huge risk to forge these military documents. The crime of fraudulent enlistment was a court martial offence, punishable by imprisonment; although Dorothy was infiltrating the ranks rather than actually enlisting, she risked prosecution for espionage. Indeed, her blasé attitude to her actions and the risks taken by others on her behalf continues throughout her account, and she makes no claim of patriotism or a wish to fight alongside her countrymen found in many other tales of women warriors. Instead, her pursuit of the story is all.

Dorothy was not the only soldier to lie her way into the trenches at this time. In the 251st Tunnelling Company, two recruits provided false information on their enlistment papers. Sapper Richard John Rolling claimed to be nineteen years old when he enlisted in April 1915, when he was actually only sixteen years old. Rolling would never reach his eighteenth birthday, he died in March 1916. Similarly, Sapper Edward Uren enlisted at seventeen against both the military rules and his mother's wishes. Uren's mother attempted to have the War Office send her son home by providing them with proof of his underage status. Unfortunately for her, Uren was permitted to serve.[7] While these 'boys' were accepted to fight a man's war, the British authorities refused to allow a woman the same privilege.

However, Dorothy was not attempting to go through the enlistment process to temporarily present herself as a soldier. Armed with false papers and the required components of her disguise, Dorothy announced to all that she was returning to England and would make her way to the English coast. Instead, she set off on her bicycle, with the minimum of supplies, 2s 6d and her uniform hidden in brown paper packages for her journey to the front lines. She boarded a train to Amiens, from where she intended to cycle to the British trenches in Béthune. Dorothy was heading into territory that no respectable young lady was permitted to enter. She risked not only injury from enemy shells but also arrest as a spy or being dubbed a prostitute. During her journey, her short hair and stained face drew unwanted attention when at Amiens

Cathedral she encountered a French paramilitary policeman and was almost arrested after it was discovered she now no longer resembled her passport photograph.

As she drew closer to the fighting, Dorothy began to see the scars of war on the beautiful landscape and the displaced families who found themselves refugees in their own country, including a woman whose home was now in the possession of the Germans and had fled 'with only one article of underclothing to her back, and a tiny child who clung tightly to the bedraggled skirt'.[8] On the road Dorothy discovered other poignant scenes, such as the lone grave of a British soldier buried in a corn field. Although moved by these signs of war, Dorothy was not put off her quest and she continued on her journey. However, she soon discovered that poor directions had led her not to her destination of Béthune but to the town of Albert on the River Somme, which a year later would see one of the bloodiest battles of the entire War. Between 1 July and 18 November 1916, the Battle of the Somme would produce 420,000 British casualties, with nearly 60,000 on the first day alone, in an attempt to cross the average 800 yards between the two lines of trenches.[9]

At the time of Dorothy's arrival, the town of Albert had already experienced the ravages of war. The Allied armies consisted of British, French and Belgian troops, who faced the army of the German Empire. Both sides pushed their armies northwards to the French/Belgium coastline, in an attempt to control the industrial region of France and outflank their opponents. This series of battles became known as the 'Race to the Sea', during which the citizens of Albert saw four days of conflict between 25 and 29 September 1914. When Dorothy arrived in the town in the summer of 1915, she was shocked by the seemingly peaceful scene before her that was so different from the image she had in mind. The soldiers were relaxing beside lorries, smoking and joking. She was surprised at their apparent ability to rise above adversity.

> Of course I do not describe the state of the front as experienced during the great push. In the daily life of ordinary days the front means deadly monotony to our English soldiers; and thus ennui gets periodically punctuated by intense excitement, together with horrible bloodshed.[10]

Over the next ten days she would see this 'intense excitement' and 'horrible bloodshed' for herself. She was certainly getting her story, but would it prove to be worth the considerable risk?

At the time of her arrival, the town of Albert was so far into the war zone that even nurses and war correspondents were forbidden to enter, so the sight of a single Englishwoman was met with shock and suspicion. Dorothy had already partly effected her transformation in a field just outside Amiens where she removed her dress, and with no petticoat or corset, Dorothy proceeded on her journey wearing only a green blanket coat, old boots and a white cricket cap. She was stopped by French sentinels just outside Albert and escorted to the headquarters of the Third Army for an interview. Here she found herself surrounded by the 'splendid' soldiers from the Scottish regiments, the Black Watch, Seaforths and the Argyll and Sutherland, whom she would later reflect were 'mostly all dead men today'.[11] She presented her forged papers to officers who showed great surprise at her appearance but accepted her story of becoming lost on the way to Béthune. They allowed her to rest in the town overnight before she 'continued her journey'. Of course, Dorothy had no intention of going anywhere. It may not have been her original destination, but she had reached the frontlines, just as she had set out to do.

Dorothy spent the night in a room above a tavern, which was frequented by the local troops. That night she began to see the darker side of the seemingly peaceful town as she listened to the nightly bombardment of German artillery fire, nicknamed 'enemy hate' by the Allied troops, and saw the evidence of its destructive power in the shell-battered buildings and monuments. In the morning, she planned to join up with the troops and was lucky enough to find another sympathetic Tommy willing to help her in her endeavour. Sapper Thomas Dunn first spotted Dorothy on the morning after her arrival. No doubt the sight of a young girl on a bicycle so far forward from the safe areas was unusual and prompted a lot of notice from passing troops and, unfortunately for Dorothy, assumptions about the kind of girl she was. So far, Dorothy had experienced mainly kindness from the various military personnel she had encountered; however, that morning she was approached by one individual who 'broke the rules of British chivalry'.[12] In the resulting affray, Dorothy was forced to hit the man and kick his shins to break away from him. Sapper Dunn saw this unpleasant encounter and decided to follow the young lady to ensure she reached her destination safely. Dorothy quickly realised this was a man she could trust and she decided to reveal her plans to him. At first, Dunn was appalled by Dorothy's plans and tried to talk her into leaving for the safety of home;

however, he soon realised this was futile. Dunn agreed to assist Dorothy, but only after he was convinced she was not simply a prostitute attempting to solicit business among the soldiers. He told her, 'Now I see thoroughly the sort of girl yer are, I'll help yer. Yer no bad 'un. You're a lady.'[13] However, the naïve Dorothy did not completely grasp Tom's meaning, as she admitted she had mistaken the term 'camp follower' as referring to the wagons that carried provisions. She was aware, however, of the precarious position she was placing herself in as a lone woman in a trench full of men. But although she carried with her a large concealed knife, she never had any cause to use it.

The first step was to find shelter where Dorothy could both shield herself and effect her transformation into her male alias. A row of abandoned one-room cottages became her refuge. She began to make her 'barracks' as comfortable as she could despite the flies, creepy crawlies and the nightly bombardment of 'enemy hate'. A sodden mattress, a rusty jam cauldron, and some string stretched from the door to the wall as a clothesline, were among the few comforts she managed to procure. The row of cottages also had a cold water tap on one wall that, at first, Dorothy delighted in, but she would soon discover the water was contaminated and, as a result of drinking it, she contracted septic poisoning. But for the time being, she had a base camp that shielded her from detection from passing troops.

Dorothy was entirely dependent at this point on the actions of Sapper Dunn, who could have easily reported her or even abandoned her to her fate. Instead he returned with a 'Tommy cooker' filled with stew, a large biscuit and bread, and Dorothy was pleasantly surprised by their quality.

The Role of the Mining Engineers

A plan was formulated by the two co-conspirators that Dorothy would remain hidden until nightfall and then, dressed in her stolen uniform, she would 'fall in' with Dunn and the troops of the Royal Engineers. Then she would accompany them on their nightshift, laying mines under the German trenches. Dorothy found herself working just 400 yards from the front lines, alongside members of the 179th Tunnelling Company, 51st Division of the Royal Engineers. Mining engineers played an important role in the war of attrition that was developing. This war would not be fought on the open battlefield but in the trenches and so new tactics were required. Lieutenant General Sir Henry Rawlinson, Commanding Officer of the 4th Division, had served with distinction in the Second Boer War in South Africa fifteen years before, so had experience in the difficult nature of trench warfare. The Boers had used the lethal combination of trenches and artillery to great effect against the more traditional tactics of the British Army. However, the dry conditions of the South African veld required very different equipment and training than did the sodden fields of France.

In December 1914, Rawlinson requested a special battalion of sappers to be sent to the Western Front to counter the mine attacks of the German forces. The mines were a powerful weapon, not simply for their destructive force but also for their 'demoralising psychological effect' on the enemy troops.[14] A fact that demonstrates this is that on 20 December 1914, Germany blew ten mines under the British trenches at Festubert, near the Franco-Belgian border. With 750 lbs of explosives, the Germans had captured nineteen officers and 815 fighting men. Specialists known as 'clay kickers' were drafted in to assist the Royal Engineers due to their experience in conditions similar to those on the Western Front. Field Marshal Sir John French called for the War Office to acknowledge the contribution of these specialist engineers in his report in November 1915:

> I desire to call your Lordship's attention to the splendid work carried out by the Tunnelling Companies. These Companies, officered largely by mining engineers, and manned by professional miners, have devoted themselves whole-heartedly to the dangerous work of offensive and defensive mining, a task ever accompanied by great and unseen dangers.[15]

It was not only the enemy's mines that proved dangerous, the laying of mines itself was a treacherous task, often undertaken in terrible conditions. Lieutenant J. French of the 254th Tunnelling Company described his experiences of working 12-hour shifts: 'In wet sap again working past the knees in water and water coming down your back like a shower bath. After about three hours air so bad that we had to come out – candles would not burn.'[16] It was in conditions such as these that Dorothy would find herself for the next ten days, during which time she worked side by side with Dunn and learnt a great deal about the techniques of mine-laying, although in practice Dorothy was restricted to preparing the fuse while Dunn sunk the mine himself. This was partly because she was untrained and inexperienced and, as Dorothy herself states, an unplanned explosion 'would [leave] few remains to identify'.[17] However, Dorothy is also quick to point out that at no time did she light the fuse and so could not be accused of 'murder'. This refusal to kill shows Dorothy really did not see herself as a soldier, she was an undercover journalist. Her refusal to break the combat taboo was completely in line with the British government policy at the time, which allowed women to create weapons but not to wield them.

In 1915, the Minister for Munitions, Lloyd George, began to utilise the large female workforce for the war effort by employing them in the production of munitions. These mainly working-class women, nicknamed 'munitionettes', were employed to make shells, hand grenades and cartridges, filling them with highly dangerous explosives. Munitions work offered workers regular hours and pay, but also came with the risks of illness such as headaches and seizures from the ether in the cordite. Miss G.M. West, a munitionette from South Wales, described both the conditions and the girls as 'rough':

> If the worker has the least tendency to epilepsy, even if she has never shown it before, the ether will bring it out. There are 14 or 20 girls who get these epileptic fits. On a heavy windless day we sometimes have 30 girls overcome by the fumes in one way or another.[18]

Those who worked directly with TNT fell victim to toxic jaundice, which turned their skin a shade of yellow and their hair orange, leading to them to be known as 'canaries'. As well as the potential damage to their health, munitions workers also face the more immediate threat of industrial accidents. On 19 January 1917, an explosion in the Brunner, Mond & Company's chemical factory in Silvertown, East London, was seen and heard throughout the city, reportedly killing sixty-nine people and injuring 400 others.[19] But despite the inherent dangers of their profession and the lethal nature of their product, these women were still kept distanced from the deaths their munitions would eventually cause. Even those women who served in the newly created Women's Army Auxiliary Corps after 1917 were given a uniform, a rank and an official military role, but were still kept firmly away from the fighting. Their lack of weapons led to the nickname the 'ladies of the frying pan'. Despite the importance of their service, women's status in the military machine remained inferior and as historian Ian Beckett states 'the military as a whole never quite came to terms with the concept of women in uniform'.[20] This was particularly true of those men already employed in support roles such as cooks, clerks, drivers and storemen; jobs the WAAC took over in order to free up men for service on the front lines. Some of these men felt it devalued their role when they were replaced by women. Some women faced direct hostility similar to that Dorothy faced from the London newspaper editors. When Dr Elsie Inglis of the Scottish Women's Hospital in Serbia proposed to the War Office the formation of a women's ambulance unit, the response she received was, 'My good lady, go home and sit still.'[21]

In direct contrast to the British attitude to women's roles during the First World War, Russia had recruited 5,000–6,000 women for active combat roles by the end of 1917. Two all-female infantry regiments were created in the form of the 1st Petrograd Women's Battalion and the 2nd Moscow Women's Battalion of Death, which consisted of between 1,000 and 1,400 members each.

Another woman who found herself legitimately fighting on the front lines was Englishwoman Flora Sandes. The thirty-eight-year-old rector's daughter from Poppleton, Yorkshire, originally enlisted as a St John Ambulance nurse and had 'no more idea of going as a soldier than any other lady'.[22] She set out for her unit in Serbia on 12 August 1914; she served for a few months at the First Reserve Hospital alongside six other English nurses. These seven were the only women in a hospital full of male Serbian doctors and orderlies. The conditions Flora and her fellow nurses endured there were harsh, with limited amenities and the sights she saw were often gruesome. Flora's diary entry for 1 March 1915 reads 'cut off a man's toes with a pair of scissors this afternoon'.[23] However, during these few months, Flora found that she drifted away from nursing and towards soldiering, something she was actively encouraged in by the Serbian soldiers around her. Her ability to ride and shoot, as well as speaking English, were all seen as assets and when the Second Infantry Regiment, to which Flora was attached, withdrew, she officially transferred to a combat role. In doing so, Flora Sandes became the only Englishwoman to officially serve in a combat role during the First World War.

Although Dorothy was neither a fighting soldier like Flora, nor on the front lines in any official capacity, she did manage to remain in the trenches of Albert for ten days. During this time, Dorothy would work her shifts alongside Sapper Dunn, digging holes and preparing the fuses for the mines. She would then retreat to the privacy of her 'barracks' in her one-room cottage. During her brief time at the front, Dorothy developed painful joints and chills from standing in the cold, stagnant water all day, and began to feel the symptoms of the septic poisoning she had unwittingly contracted from the contaminated water tap. At the ten-day mark, she decided to reveal her true identity to her sergeant who greeted the news in an apparently 'affable' manner. However, if Dorothy believed this meant he would keep her secret she was sorely disappointed. The sergeant immediately followed the proper procedure and reported Dorothy's presence to his superiors.

Dorothy was forcibly removed her from her cottage barracks by military policemen, who placed her under arrest on suspicion of being a German spy. Furious at what she considered a betrayal by her sergeant she screamed at him in protest 'If I *were* really a man I'd knock you down here and now.'[24] Dorothy was taken to the regimental headquarters where she was subjected to rigorous questioning by twenty officers of the regiment, one of whom reportedly met the news of the female interloper with the words 'Oh-O-O-! it is a woman. Certainly we shall never get even with a woman, if she wishes to deceive us.'[25] Suspicions about Dorothy's motives focussed on her being a spy or a prostitute. Nobody was able to quite grasp the truth of her motivation, wanting to get a story. Dorothy's actions were certainly a serious security breach and the members of the regiment were embarrassed she had been able to infiltrate their ranks for so long. Dorothy was finally able to persuade the military authorities that her true intentions, although less than noble, were not treasonous. In fact, she was very open about her journalistic ambitions and made no pretention of having patriotic notions of fighting for her country or the romantic aim of following a lover to battle as many cross-dressing soldiers had done before her. Her honesty did little to endear her to her interrogators and although it was decided she would not face charges for her conduct, Dorothy was not immediately released. Instead, she was held in the strict Couvent du Bon-Pasteur for two weeks before being escorted back to England under guard.

Dorothy claimed in her autobiography that her illness precipitated her revealing her true identity but she claimed she did not anticipate she would be arrested. Perhaps Dorothy did not expect such rough treatment from military authorities but, despite her protests to the contrary, it is hard to imagine she did not anticipate that revealing her identity to the sergeant would result in anything other than her abrupt removal from the trenches. Indeed, there seemed no other motivation for her to do so as she was in no apparent immediate danger of discovery. Perhaps Dorothy had everything she needed from her escapade – she had experienced the cold, damp conditions the troops lived in, the horror of the artillery shells of the enemy and witnessed the camaraderie of the British troops even in such an appalling situation. Dorothy had her story but rather than quietly slipping away, it could be argued that in going through official channels Dorothy gave herself maximum exposure and ensured she had corroboration of the fact she was actually present at the front lines.

Dorothy had achieved her seemingly impossible aim and had returned to England safe and sound with all the information she needed to write the perfect first-hand story. However, the War Office had forbidden Dorothy from publishing her story under the Defence of the Realm Act, perhaps because they were afraid she would unwittingly reveal too many military secrets. She had undergone a gruelling undercover campaign, all to no avail; her story would not be told. Dorothy was further disappointed after she encountered suffragette campaigner Emmeline Pankhurst during her journey home to England. Dorothy told her the story of her experiences in Albert, and Pankhurst was so fascinated that she invited Dorothy to speak about her experiences at an upcoming meeting. Regrettably for Dorothy, the ban prevented such a lecture from taking place. It was not until four years later, after the end of the war, that Dorothy was permitted to publish *Sapper Dorothy*, a heavily censored version of her memoirs.

Sapper Dorothy was published in Britain, America and Australia, but it was not as successful as Dorothy had hoped. Memories of the war were still raw and many people wished to move forward rather than look back, while other sectors of society wished to curb the new-found power and freedom many women had experienced during the war and stories such as Dorothy's were seen as a potentially challenging to traditional gender roles. As gender historian Julie Wheelwright states, 'her frank admission that a by-line and a potential furthering of her career' motivated her actions meant the public did not find her as endearing as female marine Hannah Snell or American Civil War heroine Jennie Hodgers.[26] As a result, Dorothy's story is often not treated with the same sympathy as other female warrior stories.

Dorothy did, however, maintain one fervent supporter in her 'chum' Tom Dunn. After her discovery, the co-conspirators exchanged letters and Dorothy even visited Dunn in hospital when he was wounded. Dunn's letters contain no animosity towards Dorothy – instead his tone is friendly and almost flirtatious in nature:

Well, for the moment I did not recognise you as you came down the ward the other day. You looked so different dressed as a girl from the Royal Engineer comrade-in-arms which at Albert in September 1915 you happened to be ... It seems so short time ago since you, looking so fine as a khaki soldier.[27]

Death and Legacy

As limited as the success of her book was, it proved to be the height of Dorothy's journalistic career and by 1925 she found herself out of work, out of money and with increasingly failing mental health. In March that year, at 49, Dorothy was committed to the London County Mental Hospital at Hanwell. She was later moved to the Colney Hatch Lunatic Asylum in Friern Barnet Road, north London (renamed the Friern Hospital) where she passed away in 1964. Upon her death, Dorothy had no money and no family, and so was buried in a pauper's grave in New Southgate Cemetery. No headstone marks this remarkable woman's final resting place but that does not mean that she is not remembered. Recently historians have become fascinated by Dorothy's tale as we anticipate the first female infantry soldiers in the British Army. Dorothy was featured in a recent exhibition at the Imperial War Museum, celebrating women in war.

On the surface, Dorothy's story appears very different from many women warrior's tales. But Dorothy's strong ambition to make it in the world of journalism is no different from Dr James Barry's ambition to be a doctor, or Kit Cavenaugh's mercenary desire for war booty. These women wished to be independent, to earn their own living and forge careers – on their own terms. What does set Dorothy apart from the others in this study is that she does not identify herself as a soldier. Instead, she very deliberately holds herself apart from the military world she is observing. Dorothy refers to her uniform as 'my little khaki outfit',[28] showing she considers her time as Sapper Denis Smith to be little more than playacting and that her cross-dressing was only ever going to be temporary and to achieve a definite goal. She also demonstrates her beliefs by her refusal to light the fuse on the mines, because as a civilian she considered such an action would be 'murder' on her part, yet she shows no such moral objection to the actions of her 'comrades'. As soldiers, they had the right to kill; Dorothy was a civilian, so she did not.

Notes

1. Lawrence, Dorothy, *Sapper Dorothy: The Only English Woman Soldier in the Royal Engineers 51st Division, 179th Tunnelling Co. During the First World War* (Leonaur, 2010), p. 41-2
2. ibid p. 66
3. ibid, p. 41–2
4. ibid, p. 13
5. ibid, p. 32
6. ibid, p. 37–38
7. Johns, Robert K., *Battle Beneath the Trenches: The Cornish Miners of 251 Tunnelling Company RE* (Croydon, Pen & Sword, 2015), ebook p. 60
8. Lawrence p. 39
9. Tucker, Spencer, C., *The Great War 1914–18* (London: University College London, 1998), p. 107

10. Lawrence, p. 41

11. ibid, p. 42

12. ibid, p. 48

13. ibid, p. 50

14. Field Marshal Sir John French, *The Times* November 1915, as found in Johns, ebook p. 211

15. Johns, ebook p. 82

16. ibid, ebook p. 123

17. Lawrence, p. 64

18. Adie, Kate, *Corsets to Camouflage – Women and War* (London: Hodder and Stoughton, 2003), p. 96–7

19. Woollacott, Angela, *On Her Their Lives Depend: Munitions Workers in the Great War* (California: University of California Press, 1994), p. 85

20. Beckett, Ian F.W., *The Great War 1914-1918* (Essex: Pearson, 2001), p. 325

21. ibid, p. 324

22. Wheelwright, Julie, *Amazons and Military Maids – Women who dressed as men in pursuit of Life, Liberty and Happiness* (London: Pandora Press, 1989), p. 35

23. ibid, p. 38

24. Lawrence, p. 66

25. ibid

26. Wheelwright, p. 44

27. Lawrence, p. 11

28. ibid, p. 81

9

MARY ANNE TALBOT
AKA JOHN TAYLOR – THE LADY TAR

I was born to experience a large portion of the disagreeable
circumstances incident to human nature

Mary Anne Talbot[1]

Nineteenth-century Newgate Prison was an appalling place,
housing inmates awaiting trial at the local courthouse,
awaiting execution on the gallows and those in the debtors'
ward. Unlike the criminal prisoners, incarceration in the
debtors' ward was for an indeterminate time and release
was only possible once the sums owed were either satisfied
or prisoners were released from their debts by their
creditors. The harsh reality for those who found themselves
in the debtors' ward was that the very act of imprisonment
often increased the amount they owed, making it incredibly
difficult to ever find a way out. On admission inmates were
charged a standard fee, which was added to the sum they
owed, then they were expected to pay rent for their cell, and
to buy food, clothing, bedding, and any other comforts they

could afford. With little means of earning money and with most inmates relying on the charity of friends and family, debts could accumulate to the point where release was no longer a realistic prospect; they needed a miracle to release them from their ever-spiralling debts.

At the close of the 18th century, one inmate of the debtors' ward was a former actress and apparently also a female sailor, Mary Anne Talbot, who found herself incarcerated after she was unable to pay her landlady Mrs Nicklin the £11 3s 6d rent she owed. After her arrest, Mary Anne was initially remanded in a lock-up house in Carey Street, Lincoln's Inn Fields, for a week, before her transfer to Newgate Prison. Mary Anne was not alone in her cell, she was joined by her devoted female friend, who kept the two women fed and clothed during their residence with money earned from her needlework. After their living expenses were taken into account, the pennies that were saved would never be enough to make a dent in the debt that was owed, and release seemed hopeless. Then a story appeared in *The Times* on 4 November 1799. This exciting tale of a young girl smuggled on board a Navy ship to serve as a common sailor thrilled readers and grabbed the particular attention of publisher Robert S. Kirby, who immediately sought out the protagonist of this tale. When Kirby discovered Mary Anne's situation he not only paid her debts but offered her a position as a domestic servant in his home. In return, Mary Anne recounted her tale to Kirby, who published *The Life and Surprising Adventures of Mary Anne Talbot in the Name of John Taylor* in 1804. The story proved so popular that an extended version was published in 1809. However, the dramatic and tragic tale of Mary Anne's origins, which gripped readers of Kirby's *Mary Anne Talbot,* differs greatly from the version detailed in *The Times* article five years previously. That story had described a young woman who fell in love with a handsome naval officer against her family's wishes and willingly followed him to sea as opposed to the harrowing tale of betrayal and kidnap of a young girl portrayed in Kirby's account. Even before the contradictions in Kirby's publication became apparent, the *The Times* reporter seemed to have had doubts about Mary Anne's story when he describes her as 'a young and delicate female who calls herself Miss T---lb---ot', suggesting he doubts it is her true identity.[3] Was Mary Anne Talbot really a female soldier and sailor, a fraud, or was she the victim of an unscrupulous publisher?

The Life and Surprising Adventures of Mary Anne Talbot begins with the story of Mary Anne's birth in Lincoln's Inn Fields, London, on 2 February 1778. She was her mother's sixteenth child, but Mary Anne would never know either of her parents, or all but one of her siblings. Her mother died in childbirth and so, as a child, Mary Anne was raised by a nurse in the village of Worthen near Shrewsbury, where she lived until she was five years old. She was then removed from the only home she had known to attend a boarding school in Chester, where she was reportedly given a 'liberal' education under a Mrs Tapperly. Until she was nine years old, the only contact with family Mary Anne had was with a lady named Mrs Wilson of Trevalyn, County Denbigh, whom she would occasionally visit. Over the years Mary Anne began to believe Mrs Wilson might be her mother, despite her claims that she was her older sister. The truth was only revealed to the young Mary Anne when she found a picture among her older sister's belongings of 'a female of small size and very delicate appearance'.⁴ It was then that her sister told her the 'true' story of her origins. She revealed that their mother had been the daughter of a high-ranking family (which family was never revealed), who had been the mistress of 'Lord William Talbot, Baron of Hensol, steward of his Majesty's household and Colonel of Glamorganshire militia' and that all sixteen siblings were his illegitimate children. This claim has vanishingly small credibility. Records show there never was a William Talbot who held such a rank. In fact, historian Suzanne Stark suggests that all evidence of who Mary Anne really was, gleaned from her later theatrical years, points to an uneducated, working-class woman. This suggestion is supported by the fact that Mary Anne did not write her own story as the educated Kit Cavenaugh did, but left the telling in the hands of a publisher, as did the illiterate female marine Hannah Snell. By elevating Mary Anne into the aristocracy, Kirby made her a heroine more in the literary tradition of the day.

The tragic tale continues when, at thirteen, Mary Anne lost the mother figure in her life through the death of Mrs Wilson. Kirby claimed that her sister left Mary Anne the substantial sum of £30,000 as well as an annuity of £1,500. In comparison, a surgeon or medical officer in 1797 earned the equivalent of £174.95 per year while a general labourer earned £25.09 per year.⁵ This inheritance, if it existed, would have been more than enough to keep the young teenager comfortably and serve as a dowry to attract a suitable society husband. The money was placed in the hands of Mary Anne's newly appointed guardian, Mr Sucker. Who he was remains a mystery; perhaps he was a friend of her sister's, her deceased mother's or even appointed by her absent father? However, whoever he might have been, his position as the 'villain of the piece' in Kirby's retelling is made clear in the cruel, mercenary treatment of the young girl in his care.

Sucker immediately removed his young charge from her school and took her to live with him at his home in Newport, three months after her sister's death. During her residence, Kirby claims that Sucker began to receive a regular visitor to his home, Captain Essex Bowen of the 82nd Regiment, who took great interest in the thirteen-year-old resident. As her guardian and trustee of her fortune, it would be deemed perfectly appropriate, even at Mary Anne's young age, for Sucker to begin to seek a suitable match for his charge. At first Bowen's frequent visits and Mary Anne's claim that the officer appeared to be 'well acquainted with the particulars of [her] birth' would seem to support that this was the case.[6] However, Kirby's tale takes a more sinister twist as it soon became apparent that it was not marriage to Mary Anne that Captain Bowen and Mr Sucker were discussing. Mary Anne was informed soon after her acquaintance with the Captain that she was to be released into the care of this near stranger and that she would accompany him to a new ladies' school in London. She was instructed by the stern, severe Sucker to pay her new guardian every attention and follow his every instruction. Perhaps Mary Anne was relieved to leave Newport, which had been neither a comfortable nor hospitable experience. During her time there, she had reportedly been confined to her room, only being permitted to leave at mealtimes. Her guardian's general demeanour was one designed 'to inspire [her] with a dread of his person, and consequently to avoid as much as possible any conversation'.[7] So it was perhaps with excitement that Mary Anne left with Captain Bowen in hope of starting a new life in the capital. But it was not to school and society that their journey would take her but to a life of hardship and servitude at sea: unbeknownst to Mary Anne, Sucker had taken control of her inheritance and 'sold' the young girl to the villainous Captain Bowen.

A New Life and Identity

During their journey to London, Mary Anne was still unaware of the danger she was in and the crimes that already been committed against her. She was glad to leave the confines of Sucker's home, which had been little better than a prison, and still believing she was on her way to a finishing school, she was looking forward to enjoying the delights of the capital. Captain Bowen continued to play the part of the solicitous guardian during their journey; however, the reality of her situation became apparent when they reached the city and he dropped the pretence. The frightened Mary Anne began to realise the hopelessness of her situation as her companion became 'a determined ruffian'. She was completely under the control of Captain Bowen, she had no money and no friends to assist her and so she did the only thing she could think of to survive; she entered into a sexual relationship with Bowen and 'became everything he could desire'.[8] At this time Mary Anne Talbot was just fourteen years old.

After their arrival in London in January 1792, Captain Bowen was ordered to report to his post in St Domingo, on the Caribbean island of Hispaniola, in modern-day Haiti. In the late 18th century, St Domingo was a French colony that produced about forty per cent of all the sugar and sixty per cent of all the coffee consumed in Europe, far more than all of the British West Indies combined.⁹ In 1791 the Haitian Revolution saw the island slaves revolt against French control, supported by both Spain and Britain. As a result, many British soldiers and sailors found themselves sailing towards the West Indies at this time. Kirby claims Bowen was determined his mistress would accompany him on his trip so the soldier bought a suit of male clothes to disguise Mary Anne as a young boy and reported to his ship for deployment with his new 'foot-boy', John Taylor, in tow. On 20 March 1792, the two travellers set sail for the West Indies with no one any the wiser that young John was Mary Anne in disguise.

On board ship Mary Anne found the conditions difficult to bear. While Captain Bowen was quartered with the officers in the small cabins, she was forced to live below deck with the ordinary seamen in the typically 'low, cavernous space dominated by rows of guns'.¹⁰ Mary Anne would sleep in hammocks just a few inches from sailors in similar conditions to those faced by Hannah Snell, who found herself aboard ship more than four decades earlier. Kirby's account would have us believe that Mary Anne found the tough circumstances and rough company intolerable because she was a born a gentlewoman. However, even if Mary Anne was actually a working-class woman, as Stark suggests, this still does not mean that the hard physical labour, lack of proper food and accommodation, and the harsh discipline on board ship would have been anything but horrible for her. Many men found they could not tolerate the conditions and between 1795 and 1805, more men were court-martialled for desertion than for any other crimes including drunkenness or theft, despite the threat of 200 to 300 hundred lashes that was the standard punishment. Sailor Richard Hall, who served on board the HMS *Zealand* at the turn of the nineteenth century, described conditions on board as worse than a prison '[which] if I had known it was so bad I would not have entered'.[11] Mary Anne and the crew's circumstances became increasingly treacherous when a severe storm hit the ship. The main topgallant mast broke and four men were lost to the sea. The crew, including Mary Anne, had to use the pumps and had thrown many supplies overboard to prevent the ship from sinking, including casks of water, bags of biscuits and some of the guns. As a result, the crew were placed on a short allowance of one biscuit per day and had to drink the rainwater they collected in their watch coats. Mary Anne said, 'I have gladly flown to any little settlement of water on the deck, and eagerly applied my lips to the boards to allay the parching thirst which I experienced.'[12]

The ship was then forced to dock on the Mosquito Shore Islands for repairs and to replace the supplies lost in the storm. While the ship was docked, Mary Anne accompanied five other crew members ashore to forage for food. The expedition was not without incident as the party shot and killed a bear for meat, and encountered a band of natives, one of whom the party killed in the ensuing gun battle:

On coming up to the dead man, we found that he was naked, except a wisp around his body, like a hay-band; his hair was long, black, and strong as that of a horse. He was about six feet in height, and proportionally lusty; armed with a tomahawk, or scalping hatchet with which each of his companions that fled were furnished.[13]

Mary Anne had experienced her first taste of battle and it was not something that she cared for. While some female sailors such as Hannah Snell found freedom and excitement in their new roles, Mary Anne learnt to despise her situation. This was possibly because unlike Hannah Snell, Mary Anne did not choose her fate but was either lured or forced depending upon which version of her story we believe. Despite this, Mary Anne continued to maintain her disguise and did not choose to reveal her true identity to the crew, perhaps for fear of her treatment should her true sex be known. Mary Anne was still a young teenager who had probably witnessed the harsh punishments, such as flogging, meted out to those who broke the rules. Had Mary Anne been aware that other women had also stood in her place and that there was a possibility she would have been treated with sympathy, perhaps she would have been tempted to seek help.

Mary Anne finally arrived at Port-au-Prince, St Domingo, in June 1792 but her stay was short and the ship was ordered to turn around and head for the Continent to join the Duke of York's Regiment. Soon after they arrived on the coast of Flanders, Bowen received his orders to join his new unit. Mary Anne had seen little of him during the long voyage, but he informed Mary Anne she would be accompanying him on his assignment. Bowen procured for her a new uniform and enlisted her in the Duke of York's Regiment as a drummer boy. Bowen even arranged for Mary Anne to have instruction in drumming from a Major Rickardson. With Bowen's introduction, there was no difficulty in arranging her enlistment and those who had accompanied the two of them on the voyage already knew Mary Anne as the foot-boy 'John Taylor'. In addition to her drummer duties, 'John Taylor' was placed directly under the command of Captain Bowen as his 'drudge and foot-boy' and, although it is not stated, it is implied that their relationship continued to be sexual, otherwise why would Bowen have insisted on her presence? Mary Anne's attitude towards Bowen at this point of her tale is curiously ambiguous. She expresses genuine fear of his threat to sell her into slavery should she disobey him, yet Mary Anne also describes him as her 'abandoned betrayer', a phrase that seems to show she was angry at their lack of contact during the voyage. This would support the more romantic, if still dysfunctional and immoral, relationship described in *The Times* over Kirby's later version of events.

War Is Hell

The uprising of the French people and subsequent abolition of the French monarchy led to far-reaching consequences across Europe. Fears that revolution would spread to their own nations led the British to join forces with the Dutch and the Holy Roman Empire to attempt to quash the French First Republic that had taken power. Between 6 November 1792 and 7 June 1795, the theatres of this campaign were the fields of Flanders, and it was here that Mary Anne's army service would be short but bloody. Kirby describes her presence at several skirmishes with the French troops, the most noteworthy of which was the siege of Valenciennes, on 13 June 1793. On this day, the Duke of York led his men, with 14,000 Austrian troops, to the battlements of the French garrison at Valenciennes, under the command of Jean Henri Becays Ferrand. The siege was the bloodiest battle that Mary Anne had witnessed so far, with hundreds of deaths occurring around her. Among the British troops were the 11th Dragoons whose hand-to-hand combat, armed with broad swords, was particularly gruesome to watch,

> I was shocked to see many a brave fellow at first but slightly wounded, meet his death by the trampling of horses, spurred on by the contending antagonists.[14]

In her role of drummer boy, Mary Anne was required to keep a continual roll on the regimental drum throughout the battle. The drum served the dual purpose of drowning out cries of wounded troops and conveying orders through selected drum rhythms. The coalition prevailed on 28 July and there are some scholars who suggest that the nursery rhyme *The Grand Old Duke of York* was coined at this time.

Mary Anne allegedly received two wounds during this siege; a musket ball to the chest and a stab wound from an Austrian broad sword, which was accidentally inflicted in the small of her back. As with other woman warriors Hannah Snell and Kit Cavenaugh before her, Mary Anne describes a situation in which she was forced to treat her wounds alone to prevent discovery. She did this using basilicon ointment (perhaps having some effect on beestings and splinters, not so great for musket balls), lint and the extract oil of turpentine known as 'Dutch drops'.[15] Her treatment was successful but she recovered slowly. Captain Bowen was not as lucky as he was one of three men killed by an enemy shell during the battle. As his personal foot-boy it was Mary Anne's duty to locate the body and deal with his personal belongings. While performing this duty, Mary Anne found letters from her guardian Mr Sucker. These letters apparently proved to her that money had changed hands for possession of her and she finally realised that she had been bought and sold. Despite the cruel treatment she claimed to have received from him, Mary Anne cried for Captain Bowen. Had she begun to feel close to her captor, or is her reaction evidence that the original romantic version of their relationship was closer to the truth?

The siege was just one of the many harrowing events that Kirby claims Mary Anne witnessed during her short army service. One scene of horror was the execution of a deserter from the 14th Light Dragoons. All troops were forced to witness his hanging from a tree as a deterrent against any others who considered desertion. Yet despite this, Mary Anne, who had so far hated her experience in the military, decided that with Bowen gone she would rather risk execution than continue to fight. The fifteen-year-old Mary Anne, still nursing her as yet unhealed wounds, stole from the camp with the naïve plan of walking home through a war-torn region. She had chosen to maintain her male disguise for protection, but her uniform identified her to all as British and therefore she endeavoured to avoid French troops who would attack her, and British patrols, who would arrest her for desertion. Sleeping in trees and under haystacks, she managed to make her way as far as Luxembourg. But on 17 September 1793, Mary Ann found herself walking into enemy territory. Her British Army uniform was no longer a protection but a danger so she required an alternative identity to continue her journey home to England. Kirby claims that at this point Mary Anne managed to gain employment on board a French merchant ship in the hopes of sailing home. However, she was unaware that the Captain, Le Sage, was in fact a privateer who planned to attack and rob any British merchant ship he encountered.

It was not long before the crew came across the British fleet under the command of Admiral Lord Howe, at which point Mary Anne realised the precariousness of her situation.

> I was concealed among the ballast, to which I had contrived to gain access through the cabin, for fear of being obliged to act against my country; and finding that I persisted in an obstinate refusal to come on deck, [the captain] beat me on the back and sides with a rope in a most inhuman manner.[16]

Le Sage's ship was eventually captured by the British and the crew were taken prisoner. Mary Anne was, of course, treated by her British captors as a traitor to her country and was brought before Admiral Howe on board the *Queen Charlotte* for interrogation. Mary Anne was still in disguise as John Taylor at this time so Lord Howe saw before him a frightened orphan boy, alone in the world. While it is understandable that Mary Anne withheld the truth of her desertion from the Duke of York's Regiment, it is curious that even faced with the sympathetic Lord Howe she continued to keep her gender a secret. Such a disclosure may have garnered her assistance back to England. It is also not clear how she explained her appearance in the uniform of a British foot-boy. However, the obvious hostility between Mary Anne and Le Sage, and his description of her refusing to fight against her countrymen, earned her a place in the Admiral's crew as his cabin boy. Mary Anne was again back in the Navy that she had so detested previously, although this time she appeared to have far more enthusiasm for it and was especially pleased to be back serving with her own countrymen.

Mary Anne Talbot continues with our heroine's transfer to the crew of the HMS *Brunswick*, where Kirby claims she served as a powder-monkey under Captain John Harvey. The powder-monkey, like the army drummer boy role, was considered a non-combat role and was primarily filled by young boys; however, there was still the very real danger of being caught in crossfire. Their primary duty was to hand cartridges to the gunmen during conflict. Mary Anne was placed on duty at the second gun on the quarterdeck of the *Brunswick*. Kirby then claims that she came to the notice of Captain Harvey because of her better hygiene and manners than that generally observed among her crewmates. Harvey judged this to be evidence that his new powder-monkey was an educated 'boy' who had run away from school, rather than suspecting that 'he' was, in fact, a she, and took the young Mary Anne under his wing and made her his cabin boy. On the 'Glorious First of June' 1794, the *Brunswick*, the *Queen Charlotte* and the *Ramillies* were involved in the largest sea battle of the French Revolutionary wars, against the French ships the *Vengeur* and the *Achille*. During the battle, Kirby claims Mary Anne was again wounded. However, this is one of the many scenarios in which his version of events contradicts those previously described by Mary Anne. *The Times* article of 1799 describes a completely different scene, in which Mary Anne claims to have received the same wounds:

On board Earl St Vincent's ship on the glorious 14 February [the Battle of Cape St Vincent, 1797], and again bled in the cause of her country in the engagement off Camperdown [11 October 1797].[17]

After the battle, the British ships returned to England and berthed at Spithead, Hampshire, on 12 June, where Mary Anne supposedly recovered from her wounds at the Haslar Hospital, Gosport, although there are no records to support such a stay. And while official records of the *Brunswick* from March to April 1794 do show a fourteen-year-old crew member named John Taylor was on board, there is no record of him ever being wounded in battle.[18] What is probable is that Kirby, like his literary hack counterpart Robert Walker who was responsible for Hannah Snell's biography, distorted the facts to attempt to place Mary Anne at a heroic victory to increase the drama and appeal of her story. These embellishments continue with Mary Anne's transfer to the *Vesuvius,* in which Kirby describes how the crew sailed around the French coast in search of French merchant ships. This was a tactic often used by both the French and British Navy. As a result of this expedition, Kirby describes Mary Anne's arrest by the French authorities and subsequent imprisonment for eighteen months at the prison of St Clare. Fellow soldier-in-disguise Kit Cavenaugh, also known as Mother Ross, was also taken prisoner by French troops, but she remained in custody for only nine days and was able to maintain the secret of her gender over that short time. It is difficult to believe that Mary Anne would be able to maintain such a deception for the full eighteen months in such close quarters with other prisoners. This seems to be yet another of Kirby's attempts to add drama to Mary Anne's story.

The Long Journey Home

At this point in Mary Anne's life she was without money, friends, far from home and, Kirby would have us believe, just

out of prison. But she still had her alias John Taylor as a means
of protection and employment. In August 1796, Mary Anne
found a place on the crew of the merchant ship *Ariel,* which
was bound for New York with a cargo of French lace and
bale goods. This time Mary Anne found her responsibilities
more to her liking as she was charged with keeping the ship's
books, paying wages, and detailing the inventory of the ship's
cargo. Her relationship with her new captain, John Field, was
such that she asked to accompany him to his family home in
Rhode Island, where she 'was treated rather as a friend and
companion'. During her stay in the Field household, Mary
Anne became acquainted with Captain Field's niece who
developed an affection for the young sailor. Although Mary
Anne expresses regret at her attraction, she did agree to pose
for a miniature, for which she paid the not inconsequential
sum of $18, and presented it to the young lady as a present
on her departure. Perhaps Mary Anne was not as indifferent
as she appeared to be and this may have been the point when
Mary Anne began to realise her own attraction to women.

After a two-week stay in America the *Ariel* sailed for England
and the crew landed in the port town of Wapping, London, on
20 November 1796. After a few days in port, during which the
crew delivered their cargo and took on new members, Mary Anne
and her American crewmate John Jones were walking ashore
seeking recreation. The two merchant seamen were dressed in
plain seaman's dress when they were seized by members of a
naval press gang, attempting to fill the crews of the Royal Navy
ships. Mary Anne strongly resisted the violent confrontation
'taking up one of the scullers of the boat, with which I struck
one or two who attempted to secure me'.[19] She suffered a head

injury from a cutlass and, as a result of the attack, was taken on board the recruiting ship (the name of which is not disclosed) and detained for three days and nights. Her companion had managed to avoid this by presenting his warrant showing his status as an American naval officer. Mary Anne, however, had neglected to have her paperwork about her person and her English accent gave her away as a target. Violent encounters such as these were not uncommon for young men in the coastal towns of England throughout the seventeenth and eighteenth centuries. Pressgangs would often use unscrupulous methods such as plying men with drink until they were unconscious or simply violently knocking them out. When the unfortunate men woke up they were already out to sea and unable to escape. Mary Anne was about to be shipped back into a situation she had detested. Unlike the relatively comfortable position of responsibility with a captain who respected her abilities, Mary Anne had only nightmarish memories of her time with the Royal Navy and the British Army alike. For the first time, she resolved to remove her disguise, which had served as protection for so long.

> I accosted the inspecting officers and told them I was unfit to serve His Majesty in the way of my fellow-sufferers, being a female. On this assertion they both appeared greatly surprised, and at first thought I had fabricated a story to be discharged, and sent me to the surgeon whom I soon convinced of the truth of my assertion.[20]

After three days of detention she was released from service and her naval career ended at just nineteen years old. The young Mary Anne only expressed one regret about her disclosure, which was that she had to admit her deception to Captain Field who, when confronted with his crew member's real identity, not only paid her every shilling she was due but made her 'a very handsome present' as well.[21]

Return and Revenge

The money she had received from Captain Field was enough for a short while but Mary Anne knew she would soon require more. She made several trips to the Navy pay office in Somerset House to claim pay owed to her for her service on the *Brunswick* and the *Vesuvius*. At first Mary Anne's assertions that she had indeed served aboard several merchant and Navy ships were disbelieved but after several lengthy interviews and production of necessary documents she was granted the sum of 12s per week for her service. While Mary Anne had begun to again dress as a woman in her private life, she would still on occasion dress in her old seaman's attire and take a trip to a tavern where she would drink, smoke and socialise with her old messmates. She may have detested the Navy but there were elements of being John Taylor that she was not yet ready to give up.

There was one other occasion when her male disguise proved invaluable. After her return to England Mary Anne decided to seek out and confront the man she believed was the orchestrator of her misery, Mr Sucker. When she arrived on his doorstep in her male attire, Sucker did not recognise his young charge and granted her entry to his home. Mary Anne then questioned him as to the whereabouts of Miss Talbot, to which he replied that his unfortunate charge had sadly died at sea in 1793. Mary Anne then reportedly drew her sword and announced that she was in fact Miss Talbot and demanded the return of her stolen inheritance, to which he admitted that the whole amount had already been squandered. Mary Anne did not receive any recompense for her financial losses but she did succeed in frightening her betrayer, which must have brought some satisfaction after the pain and misery his actions had caused her. Three days after this surprise visit, Sucker, who had always enjoyed good health, apparently died from the shock brought on by his confrontation with Mary Ann.

The main focus of Mary Anne's life at this time was obtaining enough money to live, and she would change addresses several times over the next few years in search of cheap accommodation. At the turn of the century, Mary Anne took to the stage at London's Tottenham Court Road Thespian Society and the Drury Lane Theatre, where she played both male and female roles. She also secured for herself the patronage of several members of the aristocracy to supplement her income. She received a small pension from the Duke of York and some suitable female clothes from the Duchess, which may have been a nod of disapproval to Mary Anne's continued habit of wearing her sailor's uniform. Mary Anne also received charitable contributions from the Duke of Norfolk and Lord Spencer, first Lord of the British Admiralty. Her health at this point was deteriorating rapidly and her leg wounds caused her constant pain, for which she was treated in several hospitals including St Bartholomew's, St George's and Middlesex Hospital at various times. Despite assistance from her benefactors, her mounting debts became beyond her control and eventually Mary Anne was thrown into Newgate debtors' prison, where she was joined by her devoted female friend and possible lover.

It was not uncommon for dependants such as spouses and children to join a debtor in their imprisonment and the fact that this unnamed female friend voluntarily accompanied Mary Ann suggests the relationship was intense, and possibly sexual. As historian Julie Wheelwright states, her companion 'displayed all the virtues of a faithful wife'.[22] Lesbianism was a concept still not fully understood in the early nineteenth century. Not only was the word 'lesbian' not commonly used but laws against homosexual activity did not include any mention of sexual acts between women. Sexual love between two women was 'not condoned, but it was ignored or denied'.[23]

After Kirby's rescue of Mary Anne from Newgate, and the subsequent publishing of her story, charitable donations were solicited from readers and admirers and sent to her at Kirby's address. She was forced to retire from domestic service three years later due to ill health caused by her war injuries. Mary Anne Talbot died on 4 February 1808, in poverty and dependent on charity, aged just thirty.

Fact or Fable?

The story of Mary Anne Talbot has endured for over 200 years and until recently the main source of information came from Robert Kirby's biography *The Life and Surprising Adventures of Mary Anne Talbot in the Name of John Taylor*. There are several elements of Kirby's account that do not hold up under scrutiny, such as Kirby's claim that Mary Anne was descended from the aristocracy. Once the reality of Mary Anne's social status is taken into account, several other elements of Kirby's story fall apart – such as the existence of her inheritance, and her relationship with Mr Sucker and Captain Bowen. There are no records of the villainous Captain Bowen to be found in the military between 1791 and 1796,[24] and the 82nd Regiment, with which Kirby claimed she served in was not yet in existence in 1792. Furthermore, the *Crown*, on which Kirby has Mary Anne and Bowen sail, was not sent to the West Indies until three years after the events of his tale took place.[25] But this does not mean we should dismiss Mary Anne Talbot as a fraud. In fact, Mary Anne's story suffers from the same problems as those found in the biography of fellow female sailor Hannah Snell, in that an unscrupulous publisher has added embellishments of famous ships and battles to increase the drama and appeal of her story. If we remove the elements of an aristocratic birth and the drama of the various battles, we are left with the story of a young working-class girl who was possibly reduced to prostitution, who was either forced or willingly entered into military service in the guise of a male. Perhaps Mary Anne's seagoing adventures were limited to merchant voyages, and maybe the injuries were down to the dangers found on board any ship rather than more 'heroic' adventures. The reality not as appealing to the readership Kirby hoped to attract with his embellished version, but it is still a tale worthy of telling and it is a shame that the truth has been lost due to one man's greed.

Notes

1. *The Life and Adventures of Mary Anne Talbot*. London: R.S. Kirby, 1809 as reprinted in *The Lady Tars: The Autobiographies of Hannah Snell, Mary Lacy and Mary Anne Talbot*: Fireship Press 2008, p. 147

2. Quoted in Stark, Suzanne J. *Female Tars – Women Aboard Ship in the Age of Sail* (London: Pimlico, 1998), p. 108

3. Kirby, p. 148

4. Williamson, J.G, '*The Structure of Pay in Britain, 1710-1911*', *Research in Economic History*, 7 (1982)

5. Kirby, p. 149

6. ibid

7. ibid, p. 150

8. http://www.globalresearch.ca/france-and-the-history-of-haiti/17130 accessed 1 June 2017

9. Cordingly, David, *Women Sailors and Sailor's Women – An untold Maritime History* (New York: Random House, 2001), p. 61

10. Cordingly, p. 45

11. Kirby, p. 151

12. ibid, p. 152

13. ibid, p. 154

14. ibid

15. ibid, p. 156

16. Cordingly, p. 78

17. Kirby, p. 163

18. Ibid, p. 166

19. Ibid p. 167

20. Ibid, p. 167

21. Wheelwright, p. 57

22. Stark, p. 114

23. Records of Regimental Headquarters, Queen's Lancashire Regiment as found in Stark, p. 190, note 57

24. Stark, p. 109

LORETA JANETA VELÁZQUEZ
AKA LIEUTENANT HARRY T. BUFORD – CONFEDERATE OFFICER OR CON ARTIST?

God hath given you one face, and you make yourself another.[1]

So many persons have assured me that my story is full
of romance, and that it cannot fail to interest readers both
South and North.[2]

On the morning of 21 July 1861, at the Bull Run Creek
near Manassas Junction, Virginia, the Confederate forces
commanded by Brigadier General P.G.T. Beauregard stood
ready to face the Union Army in the first major battle of the
American Civil War. Both sides had a relatively equal number
of poorly trained troops at their command. The hilly terrain
could have been used as an advantage had the officers of
either army been more experienced; instead, the landscape
hindered the movement of troops and concealed the soldiers
from each other until they almost ran into the enemy through

'choking dust and smoke [and] close range cannon fire'.[3] The lack of unity was exacerbated by the fact that uniforms were not yet standard; some Confederates, who usually wore grey, were wearing blue, while some Union soldiers instead of wearing navy blue sported grey uniforms, making the identification of the enemy even more difficult. The resultant battle was a bloodbath of confusion and disorder. Union troops were unable to position themselves before Confederate reinforcements arrived to outflank them. The battle was a Confederate victory, but it had also exposed the weakness of both sides and made it clear to all that this would be a long and bloody war.

Among the Confederates was a young officer known as Lieutenant Harry T. Buford, an independent officer, unattached to any particular regiment who had provided his own uniform and supplies. Buford had served as courier to General Barnard Bee but was now eager to distinguish himself in his first major battle. 'Buford' would later declare that 'the supreme moment of my life had arrived, and all the glorious aspirations of my romantic girlhood were on the point of realisation', for unbeknown to his fellow officers and troops, under the false beard and moustache and altered uniform was a woman the world would come to know as Loreta Janeta Velazquez; a woman soldier in disguise and a Confederate spy.[4]

In 1876 the memoirs of the purported Confederate Officer Lieutenant Harry T Buford, *The Woman in Battle: A Narrative of the Exploits, Adventures and Travels of Madame Loreta Janeta Velazquez,* were published. It was received with both fascination and scepticism as it told the tale of Cuban-born Loreta and her journey from a wealthy childhood in

Mexico to her eventual involvement with the Confederate campaign against the Union forces. Loreta claimed to have served as a fighting soldier under her assumed male identity of Harry T. Buford, to have raised her own troops from small Southern towns and to have faced dangerous missions as a Confederate spy under various female pseudonyms. There are many elements of Loreta's story that differ greatly from those of other women who disguised themselves to serve as soldiers and some elements seem too far-fetched to be believable, however, as we have discussed regarding women warrior's tales such as those of Hannah Snell and Mary Anne Talbot, the presence of embellishments and inaccuracies does not necessarily mean Loreta should be dismissed as a complete fraud.

The Woman in Battle begins with the Loreta's origins as the youngest of six children born to her Spanish diplomat father and a half-American, half-French mother. Loreta's parents met while her father served as attaché to the Spanish embassy in Paris and were soon married. They returned to Madrid at the end of his tenure in Paris, then relocated to Havana, Cuba, in 1840, where Loreta was born on 26 June 1842. The family again relocated when Loreta was two years old, this time to a cattle ranch in Texas, which was still part of the Republic of Mexico at the time. Velazquez resigned from his diplomatic career and settled down with his family for a prosperous new life as a rancher, but just twelve months later tensions between Mexico and the United States over the disputed borders of Texas came to a head, which destroyed their peaceful life. Loreta claimed her father sought a commission in the Mexican Army to drive out the invading Americans, while she was sent to safety in the British West Indian province of Saint Lucia with her mother and siblings. The Mexican-American war was a disaster for both the Mexican nation and the Velazquez family. A large portion of Northern Mexico territory was lost to America, including Velazquez's land. They moved to a new property in Puerto de Palmas where Mr Velazquez began a very successful trade in sugar, tobacco and coffee.

The picture that Loreta paints of herself in *The Woman in Battle* is of a high-class lady, with a good family pedigree, raised with every luxury. She claimed Don Diego Velazquez, the conqueror and first governor of Cuba, whose expeditions discovered Mexico, as one of her direct ascendants, which, she said, explained her fiery, headstrong temper. Highly educated, she reportedly had an English governess, was sent to an aunt in New Orleans to perfect her English and later to the Catholic Sisters of Charity to learn the 'ornamental branches' that were necessary to complete a lady's education. Loreta was a studious and ambitious young woman, with a love of history. She claimed to be particularly inspired by tales of women warriors such as Molly Pitcher, who took up her husband's weapon and his post after his death at the Battle of Monmouth, and Catalina de Eranso known as 'the nun lieutenant'. The Spanish De Eranso left her convent in the early seventeenth century to join an expedition to the New World. She was known as a skilful and daring soldier but, perhaps most importantly to Loreta, she dressed in male attire and after her military career ended, she obtained permission from Pope Urban VIII to continue to dress as a man for the rest of her life. Loreta pays tribute to both of these women in her memoir, published at the end of the Civil War. But she reserves her greatest admiration for the French heroine Joan of Arc. Loreta saw in the Maid of Orleans a woman who fought for her beliefs and, as a result, achieved greatness and fame. Loreta's love of these tales of heroic women, coupled with her American education and friendships, began to grow into a strong dislike for her conservative, Catholic upbringing. She proclaims that the life before her as a woman was restrictive and confining and that she would often wish she had been born a man, 'such a man as Columbus or Captain Cook'.[5] It was at this time that she claimed to have begun to experiment with cross-dressing for the first time.

> It was frequently my habit, after all in the house had retired to bed at night, to dress myself in my cousin's clothes, and to promenade by the hour before the mirror, practising the gait of a man, and admiring the figure I had made in masculine raiment. I wished that I could only change places with my brother Josea. If I could have done so I would never have been a doctor, but would have marked out for myself a military career, and have disported myself in the gay uniform of an officer.[6]

So far Loreta's rebellion had occurred privately but she was soon to openly resist her parents' wishes. A betrothal was arranged for her to a young Spaniard named Raphael and although Loreta originally agreed to the marriage, her experiences in America had made her impulsive and rebellious. Loreta had set her sights on a handsome young American army officer named William. The fact that William was the lover of her very close friend was not an obstacle to Loreta, who contrived to meet him alone one day and confessed her feelings to him in a note left in his pocketbook. They began an affair, which they conducted through secret notes and clandestine meetings at the home of friends, all the while maintaining an indifference towards each other in public. Eventually, Loreta claimed, their love was discovered due to the observations of his jealous betrothed. Loreta was threatened with banishment either to Cuba or to a convent. Faced with these threats, she determined to take control of her own life. William wrote to her father, at Loreta's urging, to formally ask for her hand; when this was refused, they married against her family's wishes on 5 April 1856. As a result, she was disowned and disinherited. However, despite the romance of their elopement Loreta claimed to regret going against her family's wishes and for the great 'crime' of marrying a Protestant. After the birth of her first child, Loreta decided it was time to reconcile with her family. To this end she approached her brother, who had shown her the most understanding and forgiveness after her departure. With his help, she was able to persuade her mother to accompany her brother to visit her grandchild in their new home in St Louis. Although her father superficially forgave her indiscretion, they were never able to fully reconcile. However, despite saying she regretted her impulsive actions this did not deter Loreta from further future rebellious behaviour.

Over the next few years, Loreta experienced the frequent periods of separation from her husband and the constant changes of residence that come with life as a military wife. The couple were moved from their relatively comfortable home in New Orleans to the remote frontier town of Fort Leavenworth, where the conditions were primitive and especially difficult for a woman supposedly brought up in luxury as Loreta claimed to have been. She was particular critical of the atrocious food, which was not up to the standard she was used to. Then Loreta experienced tragic personal loss – the death of all three of her children in 1860, one in early infancy and her two other children due to fever in October of the same year. Despite this, Loreta claimed to have loved the challenges this life presented her with and, in particular, that her experiences had made her loyal to her new nation. She was especially enamoured with military life and studied military tactics in the hope that she could one day follow her husband into battle.

In the spring of 1860, while Loreta and her husband were quartered in Fort Arbuckle, the relations between the North and South were almost at breaking point. As a Texan, William was feeling pressure from his father to resign his commission and join the Southern forces. Loreta was a strong supporter of the cause and used her influence to convince him to resign despite his reservations about the conflict. While her husband hoped for a diplomatic resolution, Loreta claimed she was praying for war to come. 'I was dreadfully afraid that there would be no war, and my spirits rose and sank as the prospects of a conflict brightened or faded.'[7]

The Birth of Lieutenant Harry T. Buford

On the day of Loreta and William's fifth wedding anniversary, after a quiet celebration at the old Commercial Hotel, in Memphis, Tennessee, Loreta assisted her husband to pack his trunks for his departure to his new regiment in the Confederate Army. It was at this point that Loreta told her husband of her desire to disguise herself and join him to fight for the South. This shocked William, who attempted to dissuade her from such an audacious course of action. Interestingly, his appeal to her did not stress the dangers of combat, or even the distress caused by taking a life that inevitably comes with warfare; instead, William attempted to discourage her by showing her the coarse behaviour of men when they were without the refining company of women. Loreta claimed that with her husband's help, she dressed in a suit of his clothes, and used a wig and a false moustache to change her appearance, then she walked with a masculine gait, and they took a trip to local bars, saloons and gambling establishments to experience the 'loud-talking, hard-drinking, and blaspheming' company she would be exposed to if she joined the Confederate Army to fight against the North.[8] Instead of being deterred by the crudity of the men's conversation, Loreta found the experience liberating and she saw the men as patriots. She smoked cigars, drank cider and discussed the upcoming conflict with enthusiasm. This experience strengthened her resolve to throw off the constraints of her gender and to go to fight. When William left for his new regiment in Richmond on 8 April the 'obstinate' Loreta was even more determined to follow him.

Again dressed in her husband's clothes, Loreta set out to perfect her disguise. She entered a local tailor's shop and, claiming to be a twenty-two-year-old graduate of West Point, requested two uniforms to be made at the impressive cost of $85 each. Although she said she was measured for the uniforms, Loreta claimed the tailor did not realise her true gender, which is just one of the many unlikely elements in Loreta's story. To further the disguise, she padded the coat to hide her feminine frame, but after she found this too uncomfortable to wear, she commissioned a series of fine wire net shields, which she wore under her uniform to alter her shape. She also cut her hair. With her disguise packed away in her new trunk with the name Lieutenant H.T. Buford C.S.A emblazoned on the front, Loreta was almost set to carry out her plan but she realised she would need help to put it into action. She called upon a close friend of her husband's, but said she did not name him to protect his identity, and that he assisted her to make the change and introduce Lt Buford into society. They began the introduction at a barber's shop, at which she managed to convince the proprietor that her lack of beard was due to her youth. The friend then took her on her second trip to saloons but this time, rather than attempting to persuade her against her plan, the purpose was to teach Loreta the skills that would help her pass as a man – when to buy drinks, how to play billiards, and how, in general, to act like a gentleman. It was this friend whom Loreta claimed thought of the idea to complete her look with a false moustache, which she glued on with a solution strong enough to keep it in place while eating and drinking without danger of it falling off and giving her away.

Recruiting

Loreta's plan was not to join the regular army but to raise and equip her own battalion, which she planned to finance herself and present to her husband for him to command and in this way avoid the complexities of fooling a recruitment officer.

I pictured to myself again and again the look of astonishment he would put on when he recognised his wife as the leader of a gallant band who had pledged to fight to the death for the cause of Southern independence, and flattered myself with the idea that, so far from being inclined to censure me for my obstinate persistence in carrying out my idea of becoming a soldier, He would be disposed to praise without reservation, and so far from being ashamed of my action, he would be proud of it.[9]

To accomplish this, Loreta travelled, as Buford, to the town of Hurlburt where she began to recruit in earnest. Hurlburt was a small town with just a school, a store and a sawmill and would have been a perfect spot for recruitment as the young men had few prospects beyond the local industry, were used to hard labour, and looking for adventure. Loreta announced herself to the locals as an officer of the Army of Virginia, who had been granted permission to raise a battalion to be trained to fight for the South when, in fact, Loreta had only a copy of army regulations with which to school herself late at night. Loreta found accommodation with a local family named Giles whose eldest son she decided would be the perfect first recruit and so immediately began to persuade him to enlist. The family were immediately taken with their dashing and knowledgeable guest. Buford particularly struck a chord with the sixteen-year-old daughter of the family, whom Loreta claimed was particularly enamoured with the 'gallant young officer, in a gay uniform'.[10] This would not be the last woman to fall for Lt Buford's charms, who would find 'himself' accosted by giggling girls and brazen women. Loreta admits to flirting with these women and telling them lies to impress them, and even more lies to discourage them.

After a very successful trip, Loreta claimed to have been able to recruit a total of 236 men in four days, whom she then marched to Pensacola, Florida, and presented to her husband for him to lead into battle. He, apparently, at first did not recognise his wife in her disguise. Despite his previous objections to her involvement in the war effort, Loreta's husband reportedly accepted the troops and sent her back to New Orleans for supplies. William was killed during a weapons demonstration before she was able to return. Despondent over her husband's death, she handed over command of her troops to another, a Lieutenant De Caulp, and left the camp. This is one of the many difficulties with Loreta's tale. Not only is no evidence to be found of the battalion she claims to have recruited, but with no actual affiliation to the military, no official paperwork or resources it is nearly impossible to believe that she would have been able to persuade so many men to join her and so this part of her story can probably be dismissed as a fabrication.

So far, the heroine of *The Woman in Battle* had yet to take part in any actual fighting but this was soon to change. After the loss of her husband Loreta attempted to obtain a commission in a different regiment and approached several. Despite offering $500 she was refused by several until she approached Brigadier General Bontham whose company was holding position at Mitchell's Ford and she was invited to join his men. This was not the only purchase Loreta made as she also obtained an eighteen-year-old Negro slave named Bob who was to accompany her to her first sight of battle at Blackburn's Ford. The Union Army attacked at 12:30 on 18 July and Bontham's men, including Loreta, jumped to its defence. Standing facing the enemy in the flesh for the first time, Loreta picked up the rifle of a dead soldier and fired. The fight was but a skirmish; however, it was the first time Loreta had fired a weapon for the South. Alongside her servant Bob, who was apparently unaware of her true identity, Loreta helped to dig the trenches in which the bodies of her fallen comrades were buried.

Just a week afterwards, Loreta found herself in the midst of a real battle at Bull Run Creek. Despite the many casualties and general disorder of the battle, it was a Confederate victory and so it was with pride that Lt Buford arrived in the nearby town of Lynchburg and registered at the Piedmont House Hotel. After 'Lt Buford' signed the hotel register, he chose to take a walk through the city where his 'gay and dashing appearance' caused the local press to speculate that 'he was one of the chief dignitaries of the military world'.[11] But it would only be a matter of days before Loreta's deception was discovered and she was arrested. This would only be the first of many arrests of the intrepid Southern patriot. A later visit to the War Department to request a passport and rail transportation raised more eyebrows, when Lt Burford appeared to curtsy rather than salute the clerk. His behaviour was reported to the Provost Marshal General John H. Winder, who ordered the arrest. Loreta gave her name to the authorities as Mrs Mary Ann Keith. But after her interrogation by Judah Benjamin, the Confederate Secretary of War, Loreta was released without charge. She was arrested again after she attempted to obtain two separate passes in two different names, one in her disguise as Harry T. Buford and another while dressed as a woman under the name 'Martha Keith'. A few days after her arrest, the Lynchburg police were again ordered to release her. It would seem that Loreta had some friends in high places.

She had been recruited to spy for the Confederate government and her frequent trips across enemy lines in both male and female dress were part of her assignments. In between these trips, Loreta would return to the front lines to fight as Lt Buford.

Those who disbelieve Loreta's story, such as historian William Davis, cite her trip to Lynchburg as the actual first appearance of Lt Buford. Davis suggests Loreta's disguise was purposefully bad, 'a thin veneer', which she intended to be seen through, perhaps as a means of establishing her character for a later confidence trick. However, if Loreta was not working as a spy how did she escape from her frequent arrests?

In October 1861 Loreta, again in the disguise of Lt Buford, was attached to the troops of the 8th Virginia Infantry Regiment. At Ball's Bluff on the Potomac River in Virginia, Union soldiers found themselves in an untenable situation when reports of an unguarded Confederate camp proved to be false and their attack, under the command of Brigadier General Charles Pomeroy Stone, was quickly rebuffed. The Confederate soldiers took aim from their elevated position at the Union soldiers, who were cut down while they attempted to clamber on board one or two boats, which were too small to take all of them to safety. Many were slaughtered and many others drowned in their attempts to escape. During the attack, Loreta took command of a company whose First Lieutenant was captured by the enemy. But she was quickly relieved after his return. Loreta was not convinced by the officer's story that he had escaped custody, instead believing that he had run for cover when shots began to fly. Loreta was not quite as enamoured of her experiences as she had been at Bull Run. She declared it 'a horrible spectacle' and a 'ruthless slaughter':

All the woman in me revolted at the fiendish delight which some of our soldiers displayed at the sight of the terrible agony endured by those who had, but a short time before, been contesting the field with them so valiantly.[12]

The second real battle of the war saw losses on both sides with 49 killed, 158 wounded, and 714 captured for the Union and 33 killed and 115 wounded for the Confederates.[13] But perhaps the most horrific experience for Loreta was that it was here that she first took the life of an enemy soldier.

I fired my revolver at another officer, a major, I believe, who was in the act of jumping into the river. I saw him spring into the air, and fall: and then turned my head away, shuddering at what I had done.[14]

After her experiences at Ball's Bluff, Loreta lost her enthusiasm for soldiering but was still an enthusiastic Confederate and therefore decided to find another way to contribute to the war effort. She obtained female clothing from a Negro woman and made her way to Washington D.C. where she tried to ingratiate herself into the company of federal officials and even claimed to have met President Lincoln himself. She was at this time still working alone and had no official appointment but she hoped that she could hone her spying skills and impress enough to obtain an appointment with the Confederate detective corps. In the meantime, Loreta had to return to her duties as Lt Buford. She returned to uniform and set out to Columbus,

Tennessee. After a short employment as a military conductor on the Nashville Railroad, she found herself involved in the siege at Fort Donelson.

Loreta arrived at Fort Donelson, on the Cumberland River, Tennessee, on 12 February 1862 with her servant Bob back at her side. It was an important strategic point for the Confederacy on the Tennessee-Kentucky border and so its loss after three days of siege was a blow to the South and one of the first major victories of the war for the Union, ensuring that Kentucky would remain within the Union. At this point Loreta's disillusionment with military life was at its height. She struggled with the physical aspects of the role, such the wintry climate and the digging of entrenchments. At the end of the three-day ordeal, Loreta was sick from exposure and admitted herself to be 'greatly depressed in spirits'.[15] This time Loreta was determined to make her mark 'as a detective rather than a soldier'.[16] She made her way to Nashville, where she approached General Albert Sidney Johnson to request assignment to the detective corps. To her horror her disguise, which was much dishevelled, saw her looked upon with suspicion and she was arrested by the Provost Marshall on suspicion of being a Union spy. She was released for lack of evidence but was quickly rearrested, this time for being a woman. Loreta was fined and sentenced to ten days imprisonment and forced to return to women's clothing.

It would seem that Lt Buford's days were numbered but Loreta was not one to give up so easily. Taking advantage of the disjointed nature of the Confederate Army and the lack of communication between regiments, she re-enlisted in Captain Moses's company, the 21st Louisiana Regiment. This was Lt Buford's first official enlistment but the confines of the enlisted soldier did not suit her and so she made several transfers between regiments until she found herself under the command of Captain Thomas DeCaulp, an old friend of 'Lt Buford', who gladly accepted him into his company. On 6 April, Loreta stood alongside her friend as the Confederates launched a surprise attack on General Ulysses S. Grant's Union forces at Shiloh, southwest Tennessee. The initial success of the first day of battle was lost by what Loreta considered to be the bad leadership of the Confederate officers – a total of 23,000 soldiers were killed in the battle and the heavy losses shocked North and South alike. While Loreta had survived the battle unscathed, she was hit by a shell burst while helping to bury the dead. She was severely wounded by shrapnel from the blast in her right arm. Loreta was evacuated on horseback. In camp she was treated by a surgeon who found her shoulder to be dislocated. Loreta feared the surgeon had suspected her true sex while examining her and so she confessed the truth for the second time. Rather than reporting his find, the doctor obtained travel papers for Loreta to allow her to leave for Grenada, against his own recommendation that she remain where she was in order to heal.

In April of 1862, Loreta found herself in New Orleans, still not yet fully healed. Her shoulder and arm had become inflamed, and she had become feverish on her journey, forcing her to seek help from a widow and her daughter who had taken her in and nursed her back to health. As a result, when the Union Army proceeded to take the city, Loreta knew she was in no condition to fight and so again took on a female identity. She resolved that if she could not fight, then she could 'detect' and so proceeded to ingratiate herself among the soldiers of the 31st Massachusetts Infantry, Union Army. This time she appeared before the Union officers in a dress, calling herself Ann Williams. She charmed and 'deceived' the officers despite their polite and considerate attitude towards her, much to her regret, in order to smuggle dispatches and medical supplies across enemy lines. She continued her missions for the next few months, alternating between female and male identity depending on the situation. On 30 October 1862, Loreta was charged under the alias Ann Williams with the theft of a gold watch and chain, for which she was sentenced to six months in prison. But yet again Loreta found herself out of prison after only 10 days. An officer who recognised the recently convicted woman out on the streets was told that after a trip to the hospital for treatment, 'Ann' had been given a pass by a hospital surgeon. However, 'Ann' never did return to prison and was still free a month later when she was arrested again, for selling liquor to Union soldiers. Had the government powers again arranged for her release and were these crimes in fact a cover for spy missions for the Confederate Army? After two more arrests Loreta was declared a 'registered enemy' of the Union on 17 May 1863.

Heroine or Hoax?

At the end of the war Loreta's resources were severely limited and so she wrote and sold her biography *The Woman in Battle* as a means to support herself and her only son. Her story has everything that would appeal to the audience of the day – love and romance, youthful rebellion and a patriotic devotion to her country. She litters her text with the names of well-known, high-ranking officers such as General Robert E. Lee and General Reynolds to attract the reader's eye. But the tale she told is a complicated tapestry of flaws, inconsistencies, numerous aliases and all-out lies. Her continuous flip-flop from male to female dress is difficult to follow and at times is limited on the details of how she managed to achieve these changes. The question is – is there truth also woven in with the fabrications? Although it is admitted by many that Loreta and Lt Buford were one and the same, there is some disagreement as to whether Buford actually fought in any of the conflicts mentioned. William C. Davis claims that it would be improbable, if not impossible, for Loreta to travel from each place in the short time available, in order to be present at each scene, while Loreta herself admits that she was forced to lie while she was Buford 'A good deal of the information I gave them was fictitious, while the rest was made up from telegrams, the newspapers, and conversations I had overheard,'[17] which raises some doubt about her trustworthiness. While describing her transformation into Lt Buford, unlike most other female warriors, Loreta spends no time discussing how she coped with issues such as personal hygiene, suggesting that she did not spend long in her disguise. It is possible that rather than a fighting soldier, Lt Buford was simply a disguise adopted to allow Loreta to pass through enemy lines.

One of the problems we have in trying to unravel the truth from the fiction is that not only was Lt Harry T. Buford an invention but so, it seems, was Loreta Janeta Velazquez. There are several reasons to believe that the background Loreta describes cannot be the truth of her origins. One of these is the details of her highly educated background, which is belied by the level of literacy found in her correspondence. She frequently misspells common words, such as using 'feild' rather than field, 'eavening' rather than evening, and 'presedent' instead of president, which William C. Davis determines 'place[s] her squarely in the lower-middle or working class'.[18] Throughout her life she had used several names including first names Anne, Annie, Mary Ann, Alice, Lauretta as well as the surnames Williams, Roach, Roche, and Clark. She had also claimed to have been born in New York, Louisiana, Arkansas, Mississippi, Texas, Bahamas, and Havana, and the truth is we may never know her true name or her real story, as it is now lost in the myth that she created.

Some of her contemporaries immediately saw the holes in Loreta's story. Southern General Jubal Early was very vocal in his criticism of Loreta's memoirs, which he claimed were full of 'inconsistencies, absurdities and impossibilities'. It was not just the inaccuracies that he objected to, but the 'lack of morality' shown by her breaking of gender taboos and the way the Confederate officers were portrayed as 'drunken marauding brutes'.[19] Early even provided evidence to disprove some elements of her story, including the claim that she took a train from Columbia, South Carolina, to Richmond, Virginia. The gap in the railroad between Gainesboro, North Carolina, and Lynchburg, Virginia, would make such a journey impossible. However, Early's criticism of her was not supported and more than forty members of Congress from the South pledged their support to Loreta. The lady herself even turned up at the general's hotel during his visit to New Orleans to confront him about his criticisms. The interview, however, did nothing to persuade Early that her story was true. It was not only officials who disagreed with Early's assessment but the public too. The story of Deborah Sampson, who had posed as a man to fight in the Revolutionary War, was a well-known and loved tale throughout America. In May 1861 the musical drama *The Female Soldier,* which explored the life of British female-soldier-in-disguise Hannah Snell, had toured American cities. The public was ready to believe that such a brave, unusual, adventurous woman existed.

Even today, historians disagree over the legitimacy of some of Loreta's claims. While it is impossible that she raised an army unit, and it is unlikely that she ever fought on the battlefield, the fact that 'Loreta' was able to constantly escape custody without difficulty seems to prove that she had friends in high places and they had work for her to do. She may not have been a soldier but it would seem that she may have in fact been a spy, and therefore deserves the title of 'woman warrior'.

Notes

1. Shakespeare, William: *Hamlet,* Act 3, Scene 1
2. Velazquez, Loreta Janeta, *The Woman in Battle: A Narrative of the Exploits, Adventures and Travels of Madame Loreta Janeta Velazquez Otherwise Known as Lieutenant Harry T. Buford, Confederate State Army* (New York: Firework Press, 2015), ebook, Loc 588
3. Hall, Richard, *Patriots in Disguise: Women Warriors of the Civil War* (New York, Marlowe & Company, 1994), p. 109
4. Velazquez, Loc 1027
5. ibid, Loc 153
6. ibid, Loc 164

7. ibid, Loc 288

8. ibid, Loc 321

9. ibid, Loc 364

10. ibid, Loc 620

11. Lychburg *Republican,* 26 September, 1861

12. Velazquez, loc 1330

13. www.nps.gov/abpp/battles/va005.htm accessed on 12 June 2017

14. Velazquez, Loc 1360

15. ibid, Loc 2053

16. ibid, Loc 2987

17. ibid, p. Loc 916

18. Davis, William. C, *Inventing Loreta Velasquez – Confederate Soldier Impersonator, Media Celebrity and Con Artist* (Carbondale: Southern Illinois University Press, 2016), p. 7

19. Letter from General Early to W.F. Slemons as found in Wheelwright, Julie, *Amazons and Military Maids – Women who dressed as men in pursuit of life, liberty and happiness* (London: Pandora Press, 1989), p. 139

FURTHER STORIES

These ten courageous women warriors are by no means the only women who have braved the battlefield throughout history. There are examples of hidden women warriors in almost every conflict, throughout the centuries and across continents. The following are just a few of those that you may wish to explore further.

Elizabeth Bowden

Born in Truro, Cornwell, and orphaned at the age of fourteen, Elizabeth Bowden left her home town to seek help from her older sister. When she arrived in Plymouth, she was unable to locate her sister. Alone and destitute, she decided to disguise herself in male clothing in order to volunteer in His Majesty's Service. In February 1807, Bowden was mustered on board Captain Dilke's ship, the *Hazard,* under the name John Bowden, as a boy, third class. Her shipmates discovered her gender after just six weeks on board; after this she was given separate quarters and allowed to continue as part of the crew as an attendant to the officers. She had served for eight months when, in October, she was called as a witness at the trial of Lieutenant William Berry on board HMS *Salvador del Mundo*. Berry was charged on two counts; the first was defined as 'uncleanliness' and the second count was 'performing an unnatural crime with Thomas Gibbs', a young boy with whom Elizabeth had served on board the *Hazard*. When Bowden appeared in court in a long jacket and blue trousers, not only was her state of dress not commented on by the authorities, neither was her military service. Perhaps the sodomy case concerning a young boy was considered too serious for the hearing's purpose to be sidetracked into reproaching her.

William Brown

William Brown is one of the few black female sailors of whom we have record. Believed to be of African descent, she gave her place of birth as Edinburgh to the officers of the *Queen Charlotte*. Brown left her husband and decided to join the British Navy in 1804. She served for eleven years and reached the position of 'Captain of the foretop' – the upper section of the foremast – a position she filled 'highly to the satisfaction of the officers'. She was famous among her peers for her agility and could climb the rigging with ease, and keep her balance above the rolling deck in the fiercest of storms and declared a 'partiality for prize-money and grog'. In 1815 Brown was serving aboard the *Queen Charlotte* when the crew was paid off. Her estranged husband revealed her true identity when he attempted to claim part of her earnings. After her story was printed in a London newspaper in September 1815, her career appeared to be over but she was able to re-join the crew of the

Charlotte in December of that year and in 1816 transferred to the *Bombay*, where records of her end. The Annual Register of 1815 carries a detailed description of her, 'she is a smart, well formed-figure, about five feet four inches in height, possessed of considerable strength and great activity; her features are rather handsome for a black, and she appears to be about twenty-six years of age.' Yet this document fails to record her real name, a fact that to this day has not been discovered.

Mary Lacy aka William Chandler

Mary Lacy was born at Wickham, County Kent, on 12 January 1740. She was educated in a charity school to read, write, knit and sew. At the age of twelve Mary was employed in a series of households as a domestic servant but she found the long hours difficult and hated being cooped up indoors. Mary was a mischievous and fearless child who would sneak out to ride a neighbour's horse without permission. In her later teenage years, she would often leave her employer's home at night to dance and flirt but an unrequited infatuation left her with bitter opinions about romance.

In the spring of 1759, aged nineteen, Mary ran away from home, dressed in a man's frock coat, a pair of breeches, stockings and pumps that she stole from her employer. She enlisted in the Royal Navy under the name William Chandler, and served as a carpenter's assistant. In 1763, she became an apprentice shipwright, a highly skilled trade, and took her examination in 1770, the first female shipwright to qualify. Just a year later she was forced to retire due to rheumatism and so she announced her true identity to the world and she was granted a pension from the Admiralty under her real name, Mary Lacy. She married Josias Sade, a fellow shipwright, on 25 October 1772, with whom she had six children. Her autobiography *The History of the Female Shipwright* was published in 1773 but her book did not bring her the same fame as Hannah Snell or Mary Anne Talbot. Mary Lacy died in 1801 and was buried at St Paul, Deptford, Kent; no portraits or description of her appearance survive.

Further Reading

Lacy, Mary, *The History of the Female Shipwright*

Marianne Rebecca Johnson

Marianne Johnson was very young when her seaman father was killed in action in the Napoleonic wars. Her mother remarried but her stepfather was a cruel and abusive man, who regularly beat both mother and child. During one attack, he struck Marianne on the head with a poker and left her with a permanent scar below her left ear. While she was still young, her mother was forced by her stepfather to enlist aboard a man-of-war, and he pocketed the bounty; she then served for seven years on various different ships. Marianne's mother wrote to her during this time and in her letters she claimed the harsh conditions aboard ship were preferable to those living with her second husband. She was wounded and died during the capture of Copenhagen in 1807.

Three years after he had disposed of her mother, it was Marianne's turn for her stepfather's cruel treatment. He forced her to dress her as a boy and bound her as an apprentice aboard a coal ship; she was threatened with murder if she revealed her true identity to anyone. Marianne served aboard the *Mayflower,* a Sutherland collier ship, for four years without discovery. However, unlike her mother, Marianne found life at sea intolerable. She was once flogged after an illness had prevented her from rising from her bed in time to attend morning call.

She eventually plucked up the courage to desert ship and was found by a bricklayer at Bishops Gate, London, sitting in the rain, weeping about her predicament. Her rescuer brought her before the Lord Mayor of London, who expressed sympathy for her story and assisted her back into a life on shore as a woman.

Phoebe Hessel aka The Stepney Amazon

Depending on the whim of the teller, the legend of Phoebe Hessel is either the sad story of a young child forced into disguise and into military service by her widowed father, struggling to take care of his bereaved daughter, or it is a touching romantic tale reminiscent of the popular ballads of the day. In 1713 Phoebe Smith was born in London's East End borough of Stepney, the daughter of an English military drummer. We do not know which regiment her father served with, but during the early part of the 18th century Britain was involved in several conflicts, including the Great Northern War, the War of the Spanish Succession and the Jacobite Rising of 1715. Therefore, it is likely her father would have been absent for much of Phoebe's childhood. One version of the tale claims Phoebe lived with her mother in the area largely populated by Irish immigrants until her mother's tragic death when Phoebe was still a young child. Her father, who was possibly almost a stranger to her at this time, took full charge of his daughter but was soon called back to his regiment in Flanders. Smith decided to take his daughter with him and, presumably to keep her safe, he disguised the young Phoebe as a boy while she lived with him among the other camp followers. She seemingly took to camp life very well and even took after her father by learning to play the fife, a small wooden instrument similar to a piccolo or flute. This version of her tale has Phoebe eventually enlisting in the 5th Regiment of Foot on her father's insistence, presumably as a means of supporting herself.

An alternative version of this story claims Phoebe's enlistment took place at the age of fifteen after she fell for soldier Samuel Golding, a member of the 2nd Regiment of Foot, a fierce group known as 'Kirk's lambs'. In this version of events, Phoebe made the decision to disguise her gender herself, in order to follow Golding to the West Indies. The two lovers reportedly served side by side for seventeen years in the far away shores of the empire. There are, however, many problems with this version of events. After serving as a soldier for approximately seventeen years, apparently with Golding, Hessel's epitaph claims that she was present at the Battle of Fontenoy, a major conflict of the War of the Austrian Succession on 11 May 1745 when British, Dutch and Hanoverian troops under the command of the Duke of Cumberland clashed with the French troops of Commander Maurice de Saxe. The French were attempting to take control of the Upper Scheldt basin, which would give them access to the Austrian Netherlands in order to place Charles Albert, elector of Bavaria, on the throne of the Holy Roman Empire and supplant Austria as a power in Europe. The conflict was a bloody and decisive victory for the French forces, resulting in more than 5,000 deaths on both sides. It is here that Phoebe reportedly received a bayonet wound to the arm, which saw her taken off the battlefield. Golding was also supposedly wounded but far more seriously, resulting in him being shipped back to England to the military hospital in Plymouth to recover. The romantic version of Hessel's tale claims that she was so distraught by her lover's condition that, despite having successfully maintained her disguise for seventeen years, she chose to reveal her identity to her superiors to obtain a discharge and follow Golding to England. Phoebe claimed her commanding officer supported her when she revealed her deception and she was allowed to leave the military with honour and full pay. Phoebe and Golding were reportedly married and remained together until his death twenty years later.

After her husband's death, Phoebe married William Hessel and they had several children. Her eldest son inherited the family military gene and served in the Royal Navy. Unfortunately, Phoebe was again widowed. She decided to retire to Brighton, where she managed a meagre income selling fruit and gingerbread. Phoebe's adventures caught the attention of the Prince Regent, later George IV, who was so enamoured of her story that he asked how much money she would need for a comfortable existence, to which she replied 'half a guinea a week would make me as happy as a princess'. She was granted her request and became something of a local celebrity. She received parish assistance on three separate occasions in 1792, 1797, and 1806, a situation she deplored. She was able to live independently until she lost the use of both legs, an infirmity that left her bedridden until her death on 12 December 1821. Her tombstone stands in St Nicholas's churchyard, Brighton, with an epitaph that proclaims she reached the impressive age of 108. She is commemorated in Whitechapel, London, where Hessel Street and Amazon Street are named in her honour.

Further Reading

Cannon, Richard, *Historical record of the Fifth Regiment of Foot, or Northumberland Fusiliers containing an account of the formation of the Regiment in the year 1674, and of its subsequent services to 1837* (London, 1838)

Cannon, Richard, *Historical record of the First or Royal Regiment of Foot* (London, William Clowes and Sons, 1836)

The Circulator of Useful Knowledge, Literature, Amusement and General Information, London, March 5, 1825, No X, p. 147

Wheelwright, Julie, *Amazons and Military Maids – Women who dressed as Men in Pursuit of Life, Liberty and Happiness* (London: Pandora Press, 1989)

Dugaw, Dianne, 'Hessel, Phoebe (1713–1821)', *Oxford Dictionary of National Biography*, Oxford University Press, 2004 [http://www.oxforddnb.com/view/article/13132, accessed 31 Jan 2017]

Sarah Emma Edmonds

Born in New Brunswick, Canada, in 1841, the youngest of six children, Sarah Edmonds was raised on her parents' farm.

Disappointed that he had fathered only one son, who was sickly, Sarah's father worked the girls hard and they often dressed in boy's clothes to perform their chores around the farm. Sarah grew up tough, with fine survival skills, including being an excellent shot. When she was thirteen years old a passing peddler, who had spent the night in their home, gave her the gift of a book entitled *Fanny Campbell, the Female Pirate Captain, A Tale of Revolution.* This book strongly influenced Sarah and the decisions she would make. When she was sixteen or seventeen, Sarah ran away from a marriage arranged by her father to an old farmer in the neighbourhood. She disguised herself in men's clothing, cut her long curly hair and assumed her new identity as Franklin Thompson. As Thompson, she was employed for a short while as a bookseller. She returned home a year later in her disguise and had dinner with her family, without being recognised. After dinner, and with her father not present, Sarah revealed who she was to her family. Sarah continued to live under her assumed identity and under her male alias, enlisted in the Flint Union Greys in 1861. She served with her regiment for two years, but a bout of malaria forced her to desert for fear she would give herself away in her fevered state. Sarah returned to female dress but would continue to serve the Union, this time as a nurse. She published her adventures in a biography entitled *Nurse and Spy* in which she also claimed to have served in espionage missions during the war.

Further Reading

Edmonds, Sarah Emma, *Nurse and Spy*
Hall, Richard, *Patriots in Disguise: Women Warriors of the Civil War* (New York, Marlowe & Company, 1994)

BIBLIOGRAPHY

1 *Kit Cavenaugh aka Private Christopher Walsh, aka Mother Ross – 'The Pretty Dragoon'*

Adie, Kate, *Corsets to Camouflage – Women and War* (London: Hodder and Stoughton, 2003)

Almack, Edward, *The History of the Second Dragoon Royal Scots Greys* (1908; reprinted Breinigsville, PA: Kessinger Publishing, 2010)

Broderick, Marian, *Wild Irish Women – Extraordinary Lives from History* (Dublin: The O'Brien Press, 2012)

Defoe, Daniel, *The Life and Adventures of Mrs Christian Davies, Commonly called Mother Ross on Campaign with the Duke of Marlborough* (reprinted by Leonaur, 2011)

Holland, Anne, *The Secret of Kit Cavenaugh – A Remarkable Irishwoman and Soldier* (Cork: The Collins Press, 2013)

Holmes, Richard, *Redcoat – The British Soldier in the Age of Horse and Musket* (London: HarperCollins, 2001)

Lloyd, G. R., *Mother Ross – An Irish Amazon* (Author House, 2012)

Salmondson, Jessica Amanda, *The Encyclopedia of Amazons – Women Warriors from Antiquity to the Modern Era* (New York: Paragon House, 1991)

Scott, Joan Wallach, *Gender and the Politics of History.* (New York: Columbia University Press, 1989)

The Soldiers Companion or Martial Recorder, Consisting of Biography, Anecdotes, Poetry, and Miscellaneous Information Vol I (London: Edward Cock, 1824)

Wheelwright, Julie, *Amazons and Military Maids – Women who dressed as men in pursuit of Life, Liberty and Happiness* (London: Pandora Press, 1989)

2 Mary Read aka Mark Read – Female Pirate of the Caribbean

Cordingly, David, *Spanish Gold: Captain Woodes Rogers and the True Story of the Pirates of the Caribbean* (London: Bloomsbury Publishing, 2011)

Cordingly, David, *Women Sailors and Sailors' Women: An Untold Maritime History 2001* (New York: Random House, 2001)

Cordingly, David, *Under the Black Flag: The Romance and the Reality of Life Among the Pirates* (New York: Random House, 2006)

Ed. Creighton, Margaret, and Lisa Norling, *Iron Men, Wooden Women: Gender and Seafaring in the Atlantic World 1700 – 1920 Gender Relations in the American Experience* (Baltimore: John Hopkins University Press, 1996)

Druett, Joan, *She Captains: Heroines and Hellions of the Sea* (New York: Simon and Schuster, 2000)

History's famous Women Pirates – Grace O'Malley, Anne Bonny and Mary Read (Charles River Editors, 2012)

Eastman, Tamara and Constance Bond, *The Pirate Trial of Anne Bonney and Mary Read* (Cambria Pines, CA: Fern Canyon Press, 2000)

Johnson, Captain Charles, *A General History of the Pyrates, From Their First Rise and Settlement in the Island of Providence, to the Present Time* (London: 1724). The identity of Captain Charles Johnson has been much disputed and his work is often attributed to Daniel Defoe.

Pugh, Cherie, *Mary Read – Sailor, Soldier, Pirate*

Salmonson, Jessica Amanda, *The Encyclopedia of Amazons – Women Warriors from Antiquity to the Modern Era* (New York: Paragon House, 1991)

Sanders, Richard, *If a Pirate I Must Be: The True Story of Bartholomew Roberts, King of the Caribbean* (New York: Skyhorse Publishing, 2007)

Stark, Suzanne J., *Female Tars: Women Aboard Ship in the Age of Sail* (London, Pimlico, 1996)

Turley, Hans, *Rum, Sodomy, and the Lash: Piracy, Sexuality, and Masculine Identity* (New York: NYU Press, 2001)

3 Jennie Hodgers aka Albert D. J. Cashier – 'The Smallest Soldier in the US Civil War'

Blanton, DeAnne and Lauren Cook Wike, *They Fought Like Demons: Women Soldiers in the American Civil War* (Barton Rouge: Louisiana State University Press, 2002)

Dawson, Lon, *Also Known as Albert D. J. Cashier: The Jennie Hodgers Story, or How One Young Irish Girl Joined the Union Army During the Civil War* (Chicago: Compass Rose, 2005)

Durrant, Lynda, *My Last Skirt: The Story of Jennie Hodgers, Union Soldier* (New York, Clarion Books, 2006)

Hall, Richard, *Patriots in Disguise: Women Warriors of the Civil War* (New York, Marlowe & Company, 1994)

Heimerman, Cheryl A., Lt Col, USAF, *Women of Valor in the American Civil War* (Pickle Publishing, 2014)

McPherson, Marcus, *Women Soldiers in the Civil War: 26 True Stories of Female Soldiers who fought in the Bloodiest American War* (2015)

Tsui, Bonnie, *She Went to the Field: Women Soldiers of the Civil War* (Connecticut: Globe Pequot Press, 2006)

Wood, Wales W., *A History of the Ninety-Five Regiment Illinois Infantry Volunteers From Its Organisation in the Fall of 1862, until its Final Discharge from the United States Service in 1865* (Chicago: Tribune Company's Book and Job Printed Office, 1865)

Blaton, DeAnne, 'Women Soldiers of the Civil War', *Prologue Magazine*, Spring 1993, Vol. 25, No. 1

The Hartford Republican, 6 June 1913

The Leveanworth Times, 20 January 1916

Davis, Rodney O., 'Private Albert Cashier As Regarded by His/Her Comrades', *Illinois Historical Journal*, Vol. LXXXII/Number 2/ Summer 1989

4 Hannah Snell aka Private James Grey – Female Marine

Adie, Kate, *Corsets to Camouflage – Women and War* (London: Hodder and Stoughton, 2003)

Broderick, Marian, *Wild Irish Women –Extraordinary Lives from History* (Dublin: O'Brien Press, 2012)

Bryant, G. J, *The Emergence of British Power in India 1600–1784: A Grand Strategic Interpretation* (Suffolk: Boydell Press, 2013)

Cannon, John, *The Oxford Companion to British History* (Oxford University Press, 2002)

Cordingly, David, *Women Sailors and Sailors' Women – An Untold Maitine History* (New York: Random House, 2001)

Creighton, Charles, *A History of Epidemics in Britain from the Extinction of the Plague to the Present Time Vol 2* (Cambridge: Cambridge Press, 1894)

Dugaw, Dianne, 'Female Sailors Bold – Transvestite Heroines and the markers of Gender and Class' in *Iron Men, Wooden Women: Gender and Seafaring in the Atlantic World 1700–1920*

Druett, Joan, *She Captains: Heroines and Hellions of the Sea* (New York: Simon & Schuster, 2000)

Harvey, Robert Clive, *The Life and Death of a British Emperor* (Hodder and Stoughton, 1998)

Holmes, Richard, *Redcoat – The British Soldier in the Age of Horse and Musket* (London: HarperCollins, 2001)

Salmonson, Jessica Amanda, *The Encyclopedia of Amazons – Women Warriors From Antiquity to the Modern Era* (New York: Paragon House, 1991)

Scott, Joan Wallach, *Gender and the Politics of History* (New York: Columbia University Press)

Stark, Suzanne J., *Female Tars – Women Aboard Ship in the Age of Sail* (London: Pimlico, 1998)

Stephens, Matthew, *Hannah Snell:The Secret Life of Female Marine, 1723–1792* (London: Ship Street Press, 2014)

Wheelwright, Julie, *Amazons and Military Maids – Women who dressed as Men in Pursuit of Life, Liberty and Happiness* (London: Pandora Press, 1989)

The Lady Tars: The Autobiographies of Hannah Snell, Mary Lacy and Mary Anne Talbot (Fireship Press, 2008)

The National Museum and HMS Victory – information *sheet 078*

5 Lady Jane Ingleby – Trooper Jane

Ackroyd, Peter, *The History of England Volume III, Civil War* (London: Pan Books, 2014)

Dugaw, Dianne, *Warrior Women and Popular Balladry, 1650–1850* (Cambridge: The University of Chicago, 1996)

Fraser, Lady Antonia, *The Weaker Vessel – Woman's Lot in Seventeenth-century England* (London: Phoenix Press, 1984)

Hughes, Ann, *Gender and the English Revolution* (Oxford: Routledge, 2012)

Lewis-Stempel, John, *The Autobiography of the British Soldier from Agincourt to Basra, in His Own Words* (London: Headline Review, 2007)

Plowden, Alison, *Women All On Fire – The Women of the English Civil War* (Gloucestershire: Sutton Publishing, 2004)

Purkiss, Diane, *The English Civil War: A People's History* (London: Harper Perrennials, 2007)

Wheelwright, Julie, *Amazons and Military Maids – Women who dressed as Men in Pursuit of Life, Liberty and Happiness* (London: Pandora Press, 1989)

Yvette Huddleston and Walter Swan, http://www.yorkshirepost.co.uk/news/analysis/family-home-is-our-castle-1-2330173

www.royalarmouries.org

www.ingilbyhistory.ripleycastle.co.uk

6 Margaret Bulkley aka Doctor James Miranda Barry – Surgeon and Soldier

Bynum, William, *The History of Medicine: A Very Short Introduction* (Oxford: Oxford University Press, 2008)

Du Preez, Michael & Jeremy Dronfield, *Dr James Barry – A Woman Ahead of Her Time* (London: Oneworld Publications, 2016)

Dunne, Charles, *The Chirurgical Candidate or, Reflections on Education: Indispensable to Complete Naval, Military, and Other Surgeons* (London: Samuel Highley, 1808)

Gleig, George Robert (ed.), *The Veterans of Chelsea Hospital*, vol. 3 (London: Richard Bentley, 1819)

Golding, Benjamin, *An Historical Account of St Thomas's Hospital, Southwark* (London: Longman, 1819)

Holmes, Rachel, *Scanty Particulars: The Mysterious, Astonishing and Remarkable Life of Victorian Surgeon James Barry* (London: Viking, 2002)

McCowan, R. T., 'The Late Dr Barry', *The Whitehaven News*, 24 August 1865

Simonton, Deborah, 'Women and Education' in *Women's History: Britain, 1700-1850*, eds Hannah Barker and Elaine Chalus, pp. 35–56 (Abingdon: Routledge, 2005)

Surgeon James Barry (London, Penguin Books, 2003)

Rae, Isabel, *The Strange Story of Dr James Barry* (Aberdeen: The University Press, 1958)

Rooney, Anne, *The Story of Medicine: From Early Healing to the Miracles of Modern Medicine* (London: Arcturus Publishing, 2009)

Rose, June, *The Perfect Gentleman* (London: Hutchinson, 1977)

McLoughlin, Tim (ed.), *The Correspondence of James Barry*, online archive, www.texte.ie/barryimages

7 *Deborah Sampson Gannett aka Robert Shurtliff – Heroine of the Revolutionary War*

Allison, Robert, J., *The American Revolution – A Concise History* (Oxford: Oxford University Press, 2011)

Cogliano, Francis D., *Revolutionary America 1763–1815 – A Political History* (Oxford: Routledge, 2009)

Cross, Robin and Rosalind Miles, *Warrior Women – 3000 Years of Courage and Heroism* (London: Quercus, 2011)

Diamant Lincoln, *Revolutionary Women in the War for American Independence – A One Volume Revised Edition of Elizabeth Ellets 2848 Landmark Series* (London: Praeger, 1998)

Dorwart, Jeffery M., *Invasion and Insurrection: Security, Defence, and War in the Delaware Valley 1621–1815* (Newark: University of Delaware Press, 2008)

Evans, Elizabeth, *Weathering the Storm: Women of the American Revolution* (New York: Paragon House, 1989)

Gannet, Deborah, *An Address Delivered with Applause at the Federal Street Theatre, Boston, Four Successive Nights of the Different Plays Beginning March 22, 1802, by Mrs Deborah Gannet, The American Heroine, Who Served Three Years with Reputation (undiscovered as a Female) in the Late American Army* (Minerva Office: H. Mann, 1802)

Graydon, Alexander, *Recruitment during the American Revolution*, in Albert Bushnell Hart (ed.), *American History Told by Contemporaries, Vol. II: Building of the Republic* (New York: MacMillan, 1899) pp. 481–483

Komechak, Marilyn Gilbert, *Deborah Sampson: The Girl Who Went to War* (self-published, 2012)

Mann, H., *The Female Review: Life of Deborah Sampson, The Female Soldier* (1797) revised by Revd J. A. Venton in *The Magazine of History No 47* (Tarrytown, New York: 1806)

Neimeyer, Charles Patrick, *America Goes to War: A Social History of the Continental Army* (New York: New York University Press, 1996)

Salmonson, Jessica Amanda, *The Encyclopaedia of Amazons: Women Warriors from Antiquity to the Modern Era* (New York: Paragon House, 1991)

Wheelwright, Julie, *Amazons and Military Maids – Women who Dressed as Men in Pursuit of Life, Liberty and Happiness* (London: Pandora Press, 1989)

Young, Alfred. F., *Masquerade: The Life and Times of Deborah Sampson, Continental Soldier* (New York: Random House, 2004)

www.history.com/topics/american-revolution/american-revolution-history

8 Dorothy Lawrence aka Private Denis Smith – Journalist and Tommy

Adie, Kate, *Corsets to Camouflage – Women and War* (London: Hodder and Stoughton, 2003)

Asselin, Kristine Carlso, *Women in World War I* (Minnosota: Abdo Publishing, 2016)

Beckett, Ian F. W., *The Great War 1914-1918* (Essex: Pearson, 2001)

Cook, Bernard (ed.), *Women and War: A Historical Encyclopedia from Antiquity to the Present, Volume 1* (Oxford: ABC Clio, 2006)

Cross, Robin and Rosalind Miles, *Warrior Women – 3000 Years of Courage and Heroism* (London: Quercus, 2011)

DeGroot, Gerard J. and Corinna Peniston-Bird (eds), *A Soldier and a Woman – Sexual Intergration in the Military*

Johns, Robert K., *Battle Beneath the Trenches – The Cornish Miners of 251 Tunnelling Company RE* (Croydon: Pen & Sword, 2015)

Lawrence, Dorothy, *Sapper Dorothy: The Only English Woman Soldier in the Royal Engineers 51st Division, 179th Tunnelling Co. During the First World War* (Leonaur, 2010)

Terry, Roy, *Women in Khaki – The Story of the British Woman Soldier* (London: Columbus Books, 1988)

Tucker, Spencer C., *The Great War 1914–18* (London: University College London, 1998)

Wheelwright, Julie, *Amazons and Military Maids – Women who dressed as Men in Pursuit of Life, Liberty and Happiness* (London: Pandora Press, 1989)

Woollacott, Angela, *On Her Their Lives Depend: Munitions Workers in the Great War* (California: University of California Press, 1994)

9 Mary Anne Talbot aka John Taylor – The Lady Tar

Cordingly, David, *Women Sailors and Sailor's Women – An untold Maritime History* (New York: Random House, 2001)

Dugaw, Dianne,'Female Sailors Bold – Transvestite Heroines and the markers of Gender and Class' in *Iron Men, Wooden Women: Gender and Seafaring in the Atlantic World 1700–1920*

Druett, Joan, *She Captains: Heroines and Hellions of the Sea* (New York: Simon & Schuster, 2000)

The Life and Adventures of Mary Anne Talbot (London: R. S. Kirby, 1809), reprinted in *The Lady Tars: The Autobiographies of Hannah Snell, Mary Lacy and Mary Anne Talbot* (Fireship Press, 2008)

Fortescue, Sir John, *British Campaigns in Flanders 1690–1794: Extracts from Volume 4 of A History of the British Army* (London: Macmillan, 1918)

Howard, John, *The State of the Prisons in England And Wales with Preliminary Observations and an Account of Some Foreign Prisons* (Warrington, 1777)

Salmonson, Jessica Amanda, *The Encyclopedia of Amazons – Women Warriors from Antiquity to the Modern Era* (New York: Paragon House, 1991)

Stark, Suzanne J., *Female Tars – Women Aboard Ship in the Age of Sail* (London: Pimlico, 1998) Wheelwright, Julie, *Amazons and Military Maids – Women who Dressed as Men in Pursuit of Life, Liberty and Happiness* (London: Pandora Press, 1989)

Williamson, J. G., *The Structure of Pay in Britain, 1710-1911*

www.britishonlinearchives.co.uk

10 *Loreta Janeta Velázquez aka Lieutenant Harry T. Buford – Confederate Officer or Con Artist?*

Blanton, DeAnne and Lauren Cook Wike, *They Fought Like Demons: Women Soldiers in the American Civil War*

Cordell, M. R, *Courageous Women of the Civil War – Soldiers, Spies, Medics and More* (Chicago: Chicago Review Press, 2016)

Davis, William C., *Inventing Loreta Velasquez – Confederate Soldier Impersonator, Media Celebrity and Con Artist* (Carbondale: Southern Illinois University Press, 2016)

Hall, Richard, *Patriots in Disguise: Women Warriors of the Civil War* (New York, Marlowe & Company, 1994)

Lychburg Republic, 26 September 1861

McPherson, Marcus, *Women Soldiers in the Civil War: 26 True Stories of Female Soldiers who fought in the Bloodiest American War* (2015)

Perkins, Norma Jean, 'The Soldier: Loreta Janeta Velazquez alias Lt. Harry T Buford' in *Confederate Women*, Muriel Phillips Joslyn (ed.), pp. 63–76 (Gretna, LA: Pelican, 2004)

Teoney, Matthew, 'Unmasking the Gentleman Soldier in the Memoirs of Two Cross-dressing Female U.S Civil War Soldiers', in *War, Literature and the Arts* 20 (November, 2008), pp. 74–93

Tsui, Bonnie, *She Went to the Field – Women Soldiers of the Civil War* (Connecticut: Pequot Press, 2006)

Bibliography

Valerie Arkell-Smith, 'My Amazing Masquerade', *Empire News and Sunday Chronicle*, 19 February 1956

Velazquez, Loreta Janeta, *The Woman in Battle: A narrative of the Exploits, Adventures and Travels of Madame Loreta Janeta Velazquez Otherwise Known as Lieutenant Harry T. Buford, Confederate State Army* (New York: Firework Press, 2015)

Wheelwright, Julie, *Amazons and Military Maids – Women who dressed as men in pursuit of life, liberty and happiness* (London: Pandora Press, 1989)

Young, Elizabeth, 'Confederate Counterfeit: The Case of the Cross-Dressed Civil War Soldier' in *Passing and the Fictions of Identity*, Elaine K. Ginsberg (ed.), pp. 181–218 (Durham, NC: Duke University Press, 1998)

www.civilwar.org/education/history/biographies/loreta-janeta-velazquez.html

www.historynet.com/madame-loreta-janeta-velazquez-heroine-or-hoaxer by Sylvia D. Hoffert

www.nps.gov/abpp/battles/va005.htm

INDEX

284

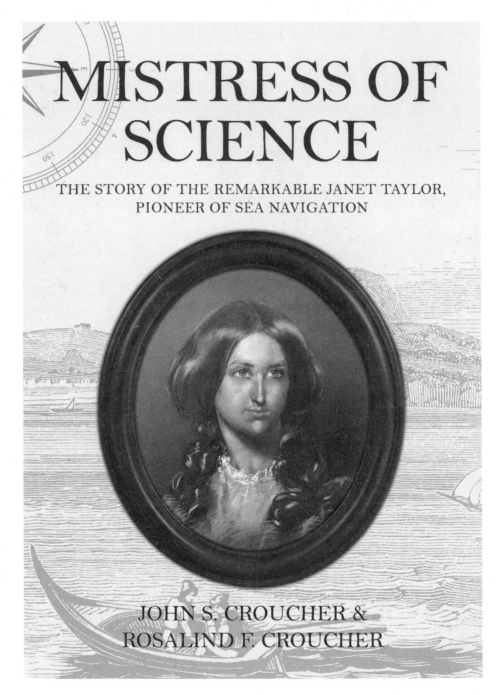

MISTRESS OF SCIENCE

THE STORY OF THE REMARKABLE JANET TAYLOR, PIONEER OF SEA NAVIGATION

JOHN S. CROUCHER & ROSALIND F. CROUCHER